R.G. Wright.
November 2015
Dunvegan,
Skye.

To Veronica.
With my very best wishes –
Ian Bell.
12/11/2000.

NO PLACE TO HIDE

Ian Bell

MINERVA PRESS

LONDON
ATLANTA MONTREUX SYDNEY

NO PLACE TO HIDE
Copyright © Ian Bell 1998

ISBN 0 75410 281 5

First Published 1998 by
MINERVA PRESS
195 Knightsbridge
London SW7 1RE

Printed in Great Britain for Minerva Press

NO PLACE TO HIDE

Author's Note

This story is based on fact. However, owing to the nature of
the author's work at the time, it was not prudent to keep a
log. The period of the story runs from 1946 to 1947, and
apart from the identifiable characters, the other names are
fictitious. Any similarity between them and actual persons,
living or dead, is entirely coincidental.

Preface

The fact that I had been juggled into a position of being an official investigator of war crimes, seconded to the Judge Advocate General's Department of the British Armed Forces in the Central Mediterranean Area, intrigued me a great deal. Having the responsibility to hunt down and bring to justice the pitiless men who perpetrated many heinous crimes against Allied prisoners of war made me feel determined to carry out my task with the utmost vigour and urgency.

Even though I had been a victim of much evil brutality from my captors, the SS and the Gestapo, as described in my first book *And Strength Was Given*, I knew that if justice were to be done, then I must exercise utmost restraint and impartiality right up until the moment the criminal received the court's verdict.

After my unforgettable experiences during my three years of captivity between 1942 and 1945, I had the good fortune to be nursed back to normal health and strength of mind at one of the Army Officers' Nursing Centres. It was the gracious home of the Earl and Countess of Harewood. One wing of Harewood House near Leeds was turned into the Nursing Centre, whilst the rest of the house was out of bounds, for the Earl and the Princess Royal were in residence.

On taking up my duties with JAG, beginning at Klagenfurt, Austria in 1946, my service life took on a very different meaning. Promotion to Staff Captain was great but the greater bonus was the team and its replacements from time to time, which the story reveals.

After years of army rations and then POW starvation, we entered a new gastronomic world, for the Austrians were recovering from their Nazi domination and were quick to show off their resilience to hardships by flooding their restaurants and cafés with pastries of such delicious varieties, never before seen by ourselves. Our greediness perhaps could be excused, as our jeep's accommodation, coupled with the long arduous journeys kept up our youthful hunger for the 'perks' of the task.

Chapter One

The small dining room at the Moser Verdino Hotel at Klagenfurt Austria smelt fresh from a recent application of polish to the woodwork, and from the disinfectant that had been used in the water when the terrazzo floors had been mopped. Wood panelling covered the bottom part of the walls up to about five feet, and above that the walls had long since seen a fresh coat of cream coloured distemper.

Here and there was a dirty outline showing where a picture had once hung. Along the outer wall was a window which looked out on to the main street leading into the town. Wooden shutters were partially blocking out the daylight. Set into the end wall was another window which also had shutters partly open. I could see very little else inside from the doorway, as I waited for Lieutenant Jan van Halstaar of the Dutch Army. We had met in the hotel bar the previous evening and struck up a friendship, arranging to meet today for lunch.

Arriving on time, Jan – pronounced 'Yan', which I assumed was Dutch for John – led me into the dining room and picked a table fairly near to the door. The waiter, who had been standing behind a desk, went over to the windows and opened the shutters wide. We could now see who the other diners were and to my surprise, saw that there were three Russian army officers at a table in the far corner of the room. Their uniforms were a strange colour of yellowish khaki, not like the field green of our army. They looked to be in their fifties. On the left breast of their jackets were rows of multi-coloured ribbons, and gold braid adorned their epaulettes and cuffs, so we assumed that they were well up in the echelons of rank.

The waiter fussed around his desk and the wooden dumbwaiter alongside and found a serviette, which he draped over his arm as he approached our table. Jan and the waiter both happened to speak at the same time, causing a little nervous chuckle, Jan ordering two beers whilst the waiter told him what was on the menu.

There was *Holstein Schnitzel*, which was veal steak dipped in flour, egg and crumbs and deep-fried, plus a fried egg on top of the meat and crossed over with strips of anchovies. Jan did the interpreting. Very quickly, the waiter returned with two tankards of beer and as he did so, we noticed that he was slightly disabled in his right leg and his hand had been badly scarred. He appeared very nervous when attending to the Russian party, so we thought that perhaps he had been wounded on the Russian front, resulting in his nervous aversion.

Whilst Jan was studying the Russians, I was eyeing Jan and wondering what a Dutch officer was doing in Klagenfurt, for no Dutch troops were away from their borders any more. He carried no service ribbons nor unit insignia, only his badge of rank on his epaulettes and cuffs. He seemed to be an extremely pleasant fellow. He told me that before he was called up into the army, he was a college student at The Hague, studying to become a member of the Consular Service. I imagined he would have quite a story to tell as to how he survived during the Nazi occupation of Holland. One could see that he had come from a well educated family, and this was borne out the deeper I delved into his family background.

Although to trust anyone under strange conditions and surroundings was taboo, I could not help but warm to the friendship which he was offering. So as he too enquired into my background, I told him where I lived, which was a seaside village called Hoylake, situated between the River Dee estuary and the River Mersey, on the west coast of England. By this time our lunch had arrived. We carried on chatting but each trying to avoid asking what was the reason we were at Klagenfurt. Every now and again, we both glanced over to the table of the Russians out of sheer curiosity, for they were the first Russian military either of us had seen. They might also have been wondering why we were occupying 'their' hotel. As we sipped our last drops of coffee, I told Jan that probably sometime that day I would have to go along to Headquarters, and Jan said that he too had to go out on a mission. Just then, a car arrived at the front door and a Dutch soldier leaped out and entered the hall, flinging a salute in our direction. Jan said that he would not be back for dinner but would meet me for breakfast if I was still around. With that, the two Dutchmen boarded the car and swiftly drove off.

Shortly after Jan left, I was up in my room when I was called and told that I was wanted downstairs. Waiting for me was a sergeant who had come to take me to Headquarters in the town, as the Adjutant wanted to see me in his office. The fact that a sergeant had come for me was unusual, and I suppose he saw my reaction, as he immediately put me at my ease by saying that there was only good news for me at the office.

By jeep, it was a quick ride to Headquarters and I was dropped off at the main entrance. A corporal met me in the hall and took me to the Adjutant's office. Quietly and efficiently, the door opened, and once I was inside the room, the door closed behind me.

There was a young man in civilian clothes sitting in a chair at the desk and a corporal clerk at a desk near the window. The Adjutant was a Captain, and I gave him a salute as I entered. He acknowledged the salute and offered me his hand in welcome, bidding me to sit down in the spare chair.

From a file open on his desk, he took hold of a sheet of paper and read out the contents.

Lieut. Bell
War Crimes Investigator

The position at the moment is that your attachment to this unit has been authorised by GHQ CMF A-9. This means that you are attached to this unit pending absorption within War Establishment as a Staff Captain War Crimes Investigator. At the moment there is no vacancy on the WE but it is expected that there will be one within the very near future, as the release of a Captain Investigator is anticipated very shortly.

Signed, Captain
Admin Officer
30th October '46.   D.J.A.G. GHQ CMF

The Adjutant offered his congratulations and then introduced me to the civilian who was sitting on my left. He was introduced as Mr Gustav Pless, a Czechoslovakian from the town of Zvolen. We shook hands in greeting. The Adjutant went on to say that Mr Pless had been interned in Italy during the War and had escaped after the Allied invasion in the south and courageously found his way through enemy lines to join our forces at Anzio. I was informed that Mr Pless was to be my official interpreter, as he was fluent in German, French, Italian and Polish, and had some knowledge of Russian.

His background seemed all right to me and, appreciating his firm handshake, I felt that we were going to get along splendidly.

The Adjutant then picked up a sheet of paper with an ornate heading and said that we were lucky to get our first job so quickly. The Americans, he told me, had asked GHQ for our assistance to track down the whereabouts of an escapee from their Military Police custody at Salzburg. Their Intelligence Field Units could not cope with tracking down people as they were too conspicuous and without training in this type of work in Europe. Our man to find was an ex-SS Lieutenant Hans Vogle. He was one of the élite from the Hermann Goering Division.

He is wanted by the Americans for war crimes committed in a huge prisoner of war concentration camp at Moosberg. I wondered if it was the same one that I had been in when in transit from Italy to several camps in Germany. Moosberg, I could well remember, was one of the most dreadful camps, with thousands of multinational prisoners.

'Apparently', continued the Adjutant, 'it is rumoured that Vogle was known to have been in the area of St Johann, about 155 miles away. According to the report, he is ruthless, cunning and may have an alias, which is not surprising,' he added.

I could hear a soft tapping noise behind me as the Adjutant was speaking, and as I had a chance, I looked over my shoulder and saw an office clerk using a stenographic machine to record every word of the conversations. The Adjutant retrieved a little bright red booklet from the file and gave it to me. It was a very special Identification booklet and carried strict instructions to anyone of whom assistance was required in four languages: English, French, German and Italian. It was a sort of Pass Book, enabling me to approach the highest Command without prejudice or hindrance.

Phew, what a document, I thought to myself. I was asked to read it there and then I saw a space for a photo and was immediately told to go to a photographer in the town and get a photo taken. Austrian money and petrol coupons were then given to me and a notebook. I was advised to begin as soon as I was able and to meet the third member of my team, which Gustav would now arrange by taking me over to the transport garages.

When the Adjutant asked us if we had any questions, I asked if there was any time limit, and were we to arrest the man if we were to find him. Our instructions were to find Hans Vogle, make the arrest, take the 'bastard' to Salzburg, and leave him in the hands of the American judiciary.

The meeting was closed and Gustav and I left the building. He showed me the way to the garages, and there was the same sergeant who had picked me up at the hotel. Now he introduced himself as Nobby Morgan of the RAOC, with a broad grin on his face and a firm handshake. He said that he had already been briefed as to his duties and would be my driver for as long as I would be needing him. He then showed me his pride and joy. It was an American jeep with an estate-type body custom-made to fit on top. It was painted green and had special spotlights fitted, as well as twin wind-tone horns fitted on to brackets in front of the radiator. As I looked around the vehicle, noting all the extras, Nobby said that the engine had been 'hotted up' and went like a bomb!

We had the best opportunity to try the vehicle out as I had to go into the town to get my photo taken. I also wanted to buy some civilian clothes, for I left the UK without an item of outer wear. Guss and Nobby were well established with their civvies, so it was only I who needed the alternatives to the uniform.

As we went to a proper photographer, my photo came out very well and for once looked a likeness. Then the three of us had a bit of fun choosing for me trousers and a jacket, then a couple of shirts. I also bought a waterproof three-quarter length coat, rather after the style of a poacher's jacket but without such voluminous pockets. Shoes I had, but I did buy a couple of pairs of socks as an afterthought. With the shopping completed, we went to the Moser Hotel for me to dump my shopping in my room and then to have some tea and some delicious Austrian pastries.

While we were comfortably settled in the lounge, Nobby went out to the jeep and retrieved his road map. As we were alone, we were free to formulate a plan of action for our mission. The tea and cakes had arrived, so there was no one now who could overhear our conversation.

Hans Vogle might have an alias. He was ex-SS and a lieutenant, Hermann Goering Division. They were all known to be crack troops, and ruthless. Vogle's last known whereabouts: St Johann. Nobby asked, 'Why there, of all places, as it is reputed that he comes from the Württemberg region?'

'How do you know that?' I asked, because the Adjutant hadn't mentioned it.

Nobby explained that he had heard the GIs talking about this SS lieutenant who had escaped from their custody at Salzburg and were furious because he was a right bastard and the Yanks wanted him caught. They said that his home town was Ravensberg and usually, Germans from that area had a distinct accent, very pronounced. Nobby heard this chatter when he went to Villach for the CO, as a special messenger. He said that one of the GIs there had a brother who had been a prisoner at that concentration camp after he had been taken prisoner during the battles with General Patton's army.

'Okay,' I said, so we have a German, speaking with a marked Württemberg accent, five feet eleven inches tall and well built. He is forty-two years old. Now to go back to the point as to why the rumour has it that he may be in the St Johann district—'

Guss spoke up and said that St Johann was a great ski centre and if his guess was right, most troops from the Hermann Goering Division were good skiers.

'Right,' I replied. 'Now, Nobby, how far is St Johann away from here?

Nobby began his calculations, running his finger along the route which Guss and I could see threaded its way through mountainous country to Winklern and Mittersill, via the Gross Glockner Pass. I said it might not be a bad idea if we stopped at those places and enquired a little about Vogle. Perhaps we could get some good clues, who knows.

Guss remarked that we should be going through Kitzbühel if we took that road, and began to tell us that it was a very famous ski resort before the War, and should be again now. His eyes lit up at the thought of seeing one of his old haunts for his family's skiing holidays before the War. They loved it as much as Davos and St Moritz, and even though they had splendid resorts of their own in Czechoslovakia, none could match the Swiss or Austrian resorts.

Nobby said that it was about 155 miles to St Johann. If we left at 8.30, we would be more or less at St Johann in time for some grub, unless we stopped somewhere on the way. This last utterance was made with half his mouth chewing at the flaky pastry of an *Ischler Torte*. Guss was tucking into his second cake.

'What do you think about uniforms,' I asked the guzzling pair, and unanimously they opted for civvies. I think Nobby said this because he was curious as to what I would look like in my new outfit! However, I decided to take along my battledress top and trousers, with my cap and certainly my revolver, just in case it was necessary to put on a little 'show'.

It was now dark outside as the two lads made their way back to barracks, eager to begin their adventure in the morning. It was decided that we would meet at the hotel at 0830 hours.

That evening, the bar was beginning to fill up with some townsfolk who lived nearby and some Americans with their girlfriends, in company with some of our troopers from Villach, and their female companions. It was a change to hear a babble of voices and see the activity it brought to the hotel. I sidled my way to the bar counter and ordered a lager. I was on my second refill when I felt a tap on my shoulder and turned to see Jan, all spruced up.

Jan urged me to hurry into the dining room for a quick meal as he had two tickets for us to go to see the operetta *Die Fledermaus*. It was an amateur company but it was at the State Theatre in the town. I jumped at the opportunity and in response, I treated Jan to some Muscat Ottonel wine with our meal. We asked each other how we had fared and Jan showed me a small blue book. On the cover was imprinted a coat of arms in gold leaf, something like our passports. It was the strangest coincidence, for his book contained pages almost identical to the pages in my little red booklet. He did not have a photo like mine. After I read his and smiled at the strange coincidence, I showed him my booklet. He said that he had been successful that day and as he was so pleased with his success, that he bought two tickets for the operetta, and thought of my company. Now we knew what we were both doing and the realisation that our work had brought us both to Austria, especially to Klagenfurt, was amazing.

We hurried with our meal and Jan took me in his car to the Stadtheater. It was a very good performance and the atmosphere in that old theatre was great. One could imagine the glamour that had been attributed to the operas in the glorious days before the War. Thank goodness the Opera House had not been destroyed.

Back at the hotel, the bar was still being patronised but Jan and I found a corner in the lounge and had a nightcap while we continued our chatting. Jan told me that he was going off in the morning to Italy. That was like a bomb shell being dropped, yet one was used to sudden flashes of friendship breaking up. I asked him if he would be coming back, but the answer was no. I thought that I would never see him again and felt sorry, for he was a very friendly person.

In the morning, I had my big grip of clothes packed and my overnight bag both ready in the hall. I was hoping to see Jan again but I was informed by the receptionist that Lieutenant Jan van Halstaar had left.

Punctually at eight thirty, the lads appeared and I got some light-hearted teasing when they saw me in my civvies. Nobby informed me that all was well with the jeep and brought a message from the Adjutant to say, Good hunting. The grips packed in very neatly behind the bench seat to the rear of the two front bucket seats, which incidentally, were part of the 'extras' and were very comfortable.

We passed the Wörthersee and the lovely village of Maria Wörth and seemed to reach Villach in no time at all. Journeys before to Villach in other jeeps seemed to have taken much longer. Now we were beginning to climb up the valley towards the mountains. The scenery was fantastic, with the chalets adorned with brilliant coloured flowers in their window boxes, outlining the sills to their windows and balconies. The rich greenery of the fields was backed by graceful pine forests and this was all dominated by the massive Alps.

The road surface was beginning to be potholed the further we motored and soon we left the tarmacadamed surface behind. We had clocked fifty-nine miles when we came across the little town of Winklern. We spotted a coffee bar and slowly pulled up so that we would not create any dust. Two empty tables stood outside on the pavement so we sat down at one and Guss ordered three *Kapuziners* from the attentive waiter. Both Nobby and I asked Guss at the same time, what on earth was a *Kapuziner*. Guss brashly said just to wait and see.

With eager expectation, we waited and in a few minutes, the *Kapuziners* arrived. Each cup was bigger than our normal teacups back home and filled with delightfully smelling coffee, topped with an enormous heap of whipped cream. We had to spoon it out but it was absolutely delicious. To the waiter, Guss asked if he had heard of any rumours about some German soldiers being on the loose up in the High Alps. The waiter hesitated, gave us a quizzical stare and shook his head in the negative, but did say that some months ago, there had been staying in the area a German who turned out to be a very unsavoury character, and had been obliged to move out by the townsfolk.

'Did you know his name or can you tell us anything else about him? Where he lived, or what was he kicked out for? asked Guss.

Unfortunately, the waiter didn't know anything else, so we paid our bill and left. We wondered if this man could possibly be Hans Vogle but as Nobby remarked, that would be far too early to get on his track and too much in our favour. However, it was a thought and inwardly, we felt we were beginning to scent our quarry.

Crossing from one side of a river to the other, the road became steeper and steeper as we passed through Döllach up to the summit of the Gross Glockner Pass. We were lucky to have such a fine day, giving us stupendous views of the snow-capped mountains and the lush green valleys below. The steep inclines were no bother to the jeep. There was a covering of snow at the top of the pass but nothing of any significance, and as we began our long descent, it quickly disappeared.

Mittersill had only been a sixty-two mile journey from Winklern but it brought us nevertheless to the time for lunch.

It was a very old town judging by the chalets and the little high street. We had no difficulty in finding a restaurant to the side of the little square. The forecourt next to it contained tables which were shaded by colourful umbrellas. The little area was picketed by tubs of shrubs, enhancing the restaurant. Nobby found a parking place in the middle of the square and also saw a urinal tucked away in one corner. It was a very necessary visit, but because of the stench inside we were glad to get out and away from the place.

We planned to have only a light lunch, saving our stomachs for a bigger meal that evening. The waiter was at the ready to take our order and firstly, served us with three glasses of the best *Apfelsaft*. It was most refreshing as it had come straight from the icebox. During our meal, we began trying our luck in finding out more about Vogle, so Guss did his best to snatch every opportunity to put a question to the waiter, as and when he was free to talk between serving his customers.

The answer to one question was, no, it was only a rumour. There was a tragedy last year however, and come to think of it, no one was caught.

Apparently, a composer called Anton von Webern, who lived here, was lighting a cigar in the night on his balcony when he was shot dead. Guss translated all this to us when the waiter had to go to serve his other clients. Could this incident be a possible connection to our man, we wondered. We learnt also from the waiter that the town was the centre of a very good hunting area. The numerous chalets dotted about the outskirts to the town were frequently used by people keen on hunting chamois.

We thought that this place seemed to be ideal for such a person as our man to conceal himself and pass himself off as a hunter. We could just imagine him with a sporting rifle, for he was used to guns. We thought it might be opportune if we called at the town's police station to get some more tangible information.

Tipping the waiter well, not only for his pleasant service but for his tolerance in answering our questions, he directed us to the police station and left him quite perplexed as to who we were. Nobby stayed in the jeep outside while Guss and I went inside. Courteously but officiously we were approached by a policeman, who showed us to the reception desk, which rather looked like one of our cinema ticket booths but larger. Inside was a more senior policeman reading a newspaper.

As we approached the glass window, he looked up and on seeing us, came outside into the hall to see what we required. I showed him my little red book immediately and it seemed to stun him for a moment. With overreactions, he showed us into an office which was quite adequately furnished, and taking his important seat behind a desk, asked us in what way could he help.

Guss asked him if it was true that a German was involved in the death of Herr Anton von Webern, a year ago. The official appeared very surprised at that question and asked Guss, how did we know about that tragedy. Guss of course quickly asked another question in order to cover the source of information. Was there a renegade group of German soldiers up in the Alps somewhere, as it was rumoured?

The answer to that was a firm yes, although no one could estimate the numbers or anything about them. The police had not solved the mystery killing and as the town often had Germans visiting for the shooting and skiing, it was not easy to accuse anyone in particular.

It was a known fact that numbers of Germans who had escaped capture during the Allied advance into Germany from the south, were ex-military and were roaming from place to place seeking employment wherever they could find it. There was more likelihood of their being able to get a job in Austria than their own country, for the war damage was tremendous, especially in the industrialised areas.

'How would a person tell from where a German came from in his country,' I asked Guss, to interpret for the official.

He replied that it was not very difficult because there were different regional accents, and usually the Germans who came to their part of Austria were from the Württemberg region.

'Why was that,' I asked, and Guss rattled away in his perfect German. The police non-commissioned officer replied that there was more unemployment in that area near to our frontier because of the destruction of the cities and towns and the people spoke German with a very guttural and harsh accent.

The officer had been more than helpful and to a last question, about whether or not he knew of anyone being troublesome over the past year, he paused and went over to his filing cabinet and retrieved a file, plonking it down on his desk.

'Last year,' he said, 'it was reported to us that a Wolf Grüber had been a nuisance to the townsfolk at Winklern. The people had pressed him to move away because it was alleged that he had molested the youngsters. There was no official complaint because no action had been taken by anyone. Apparently, one or two fathers threatened to take their own action if he didn't move away. In this area, we are very short of policemen,' he concluded.

Perhaps that would account for the lack of more details about this Wolf Grüber. We told the police official that we were looking for an ex-SS officer who had a marked Württemberg accent. He said that we should look for a tattoo mark on his left hand in the shape of a skull, if we get near enough to the man we suspect. That was an interesting observation which we should remember.

As time was getting on, we left the police to excitedly contemplate on our visit and to move to our next stage, St Johann.

As we twisted and turned up the steep gradients to the Thurn Pass, we related to Nobby all what we had heard from the police and when we mentioned that little titbit about the skull tattoo mark, Nobby said that it was the mark of those who had served in the élite SS of the Hermann Goering *Totenkopf* Division. They wore the same insignia at the points of their collars to their jackets. It seemed we were narrowing our net the nearer we were getting to St Johann and our excitement was growing every mile we passed.

Uttering many 'oohs' and 'ahs', Guss was ecstatic over the scenery, and memories of this area were coming back to him, although he had not seen it for sixteen years. I must admit that the views from the Thurn Pass were really stupendous. We couldn't make our minds up whether or not we preferred to see the countryside without snow, or with.

According to Guss, Kitzbühel hadn't changed at all and as we drove through the town, Guss even recognised the hotel he used to stay at with his parents before the War.

He remarked how quiet it was, far less bustling than he could remember, and yet to Nobby and me there did seem quite a lot of activity. The shops seemed to be fairly busy. We would have liked to stop but our mission was more important and St Johann was only six and a half miles further on.

Nearly three miles out of Kitzbühel, we saw an attractive *Gasthaus* up a gravel lane and decided unanimously to chance a night's stay. There was no evidence of any other wheeled vehicle having been near, except a narrow wooden cart being pulled by oxen further up the lane. It was a typical Austrian chalet with a balcony running along two sides. The whitewashed walls were freshly painted and the woodwork looked very handsome in its decoration, especially the railings around the balcony. There was a paved forecourt in front of the house and behind, we could see some old barns grouped together. There were several tables on the flagstones, each supporting a colourful umbrella, and near to the front door, was a big man lounging in a canvas folding-type chair.

Nobby had slowed very considerably since leaving the road, as the track was very dusty and stony, so we crawled to a stop near to the Austrian. Guss leaped out and approached, calling a polite introduction which brought the big man to his feet. The welcome was cordial, so Nobby switched the ignition off and we both joined Guss.

Guss introduced us to Herr Bruckner, the owner of the *Gasthaus*, and him to us, without Guss mentioning that I was an officer of the British army. Herr Bruckner asked us to follow him inside as he led the way pushing aside the multicoloured beaded fly curtain. It was our unexpected arrival and noise which brought a very motherly looking woman out from behind a screen which guarded a door to the domestic part of the *Gasthaus*. Immediately, Herr Bruckner introduced us to his wife.

The entrance hall was really a big lounge with a huge fireplace to our left, in front of which were wide floral-patterned easy chairs arranged in a semicircle facing the fireplace. At the opposite end was a double glass door which led into a very attractive dining room. Opposite the front door was the reception counter in front of a wall fixture which boasted eighteen or so pigeonholes, with keys and tabs dangling from brass hooks.

Guss asked Herr Bruckner if we may stay a night or two, and said we would require an evening meal. Moving over to the reception counter, Frau Bruckner turned the register around for us to sign in. Guss then mentioned to me that now was the opportune moment to show the Austrian couple my red book. As they read it, the look of amazement went almost into one of bewilderment until Guss explained further. It was agreed that we didn't sign in, but we were readily accepted as their guests.

Frau Bruckner disappeared and Herr Bruckner came with us to the front door, to show Nobby where he could park the jeep. We got our grips out and I took mine and Nobby's and we dumped them in the lounge, near to a wooden staircase leading to the upper floors.

Although it was now late afternoon, the sun was still very warm and allowed us the joy of sitting outside to have a cool drink. Nobby had joined us, so we ordered three beers. It didn't seem that Herr Bruckner had any staff, for he came with the drinks and then sat down again in his canvas chair, nearby. He looked enormous in his leder-hosen but very handsome in his Austrian jacket. His Tyrolean hat proudly bore a huge brush hackle at the side, but what attracted us most was his pipe. It looked rather like a Turkish chibouk but it was highly decorated with little hunting scenes in colour.

The big man could not contain his curiosity anymore and began his questioning. Guss did nearly all the talking in German with myself asking for my questions to be inter-preted. We said that we were looking for a German supposedly having a Württemberg accent, forty-two years of age and about 1 metre 80 tall. It was no good giving the

Austrian the height of Vogle in feet and inches as he wouldn't know what that would represent.

Puffing away at his newly stocked-up pipe, he stretched his legs out and pondered. We studied him and his very colourful beer tankards and waited for his memory to work in our favour, if possible. You could almost hear the words turning over in his mind as to what he was trying to recall.

'Last year,' he began, 'there was some scandal at Mittersill, some composer bloke who was shot. In these ski resorts, there is always someone who tries to take advantage of the younger set when teaching them to ski.'

'In what way?' Guss interrupted.

Herr Bruckner didn't know, but hinted that perhaps it was sexual interference. 'There are always these wretched types around, on the ski slopes in the winter and in the lidos in the summer,' he said.

'If anyone was caught making a nuisance of themselves, they would be arrested, so perhaps the police would know more about that,' he continued. 'St Johann is what one might call a dormitory for Kitzbühel, and both places take on extra staff for all kinds of jobs, especially in the winter months. The season begins at the beginning of December and lasts until April. Even though the War has just finished, thank God,' he went on to say, 'business in these parts has been booming, considering what we went through during the Nazis' reign. Oh yes, we have had our fair share of troubles. Even my *Gasthaus* had the German soldiers billeted when they were on manoeuvres. At the beginning, we had soldiers with their horses billeted, then came the Panzers and what a mess they made of my place!'

Herr Bruckner excused himself, whilst stretching out of his chair, and said that he would just go and enquire if our rooms are ready.

He was just about to enter the door when Frau Bruckner appeared on the balcony and called down that we could go up now to our rooms. We finished our drinks and went inside. Grabbing our grips, we echoed our footsteps on the polished wooden stairs and met Frau Bruckner at the top on the first floor. She indicated my room and tugging Nobby's arm, led the two lads down the landing to two doors away. My room was spacious, all in pine wood with two windows looking out towards Kitzbühel. An enormous double bed commanded the room on the left and supported an equally enormous pure white down-filled duvet. Between the windows was a washstand, topped with coloured Austrian hunting scenes in ceramic tiles.

A big china bowl and jug stood on the top and alongside it was a dish for soap which was filled with a fresh-scented tablet.

On a rail to the side of the table was a freshly ironed white face towel. Opposite the bed was a low table designed to accommodate luggage, so I plonked my grip down and began to take out the things I needed for the overnight stay.

The next thing which had to be done, was a visit to the loo. Just as I got level with the lads' room, Guss came out in a hurry heading in the same direction, so I let him go first. As the door to their room was open, I saw Nobby taking a few things out of his grip, so I asked him if he thought his room was all right. There were two single beds, each having single duvets, as equally voluminous with feathers as my double one. Guss returned so I was free to go down the passage.

On my way back to my room, I collected the lads and we went out to join Herr Bruckner, who still had his pipe going, resting in his favourite chair.

We continued our enquiries from one to another, learning a little bit more as time went on towards the *Alpen Glühen*. It was always a great sight to see the sunsets, for the flaming red colouring of the sun on to the snow-capped mountains didn't last long, and then night arrived quickly.

About two Austrian beers apiece was quite enough to keep us company during our conversations. It was very strong beer and the tankards held a fair amount.

I remarked to Nobby that I had seen the Death's Head insignia on the collars of the SS troops and officers, as I was trying to remember when he mentioned it. I had seen them when I was a prisoner at their Headquarters at Parma, although I cannot remember seeing the skull tattoo on their hands. Perhaps only the very fanatic of the fanatical would do that, I exclaimed.

Guss was longing to slip into Kitzbühel to have a look round but he would have required the jeep for the short journey and we felt it would be inopportune to exhibit ourselves in any way at all. He didn't want to make anyone suspicious of our presence, so we kept a low profile. Nobby was almost falling asleep through the heat and the beer and kept nodding his head as it fell nearer to the table top. Herr Bruckner, Guss and I watched him every now and again just to make sure he was not going to bang his head.

Frau Bruckner came out and warned us that dinner would be ready in ten minutes. Waking Nobby, we went up to our rooms for a wash and brush-up. Guss had gone down first to the dining room and had found a table near to the window which had a view of the Kitzbühler Horn in the distance. The double doors to the dining room were held open by floor catches, in order to provide more circulation of air to the dining room, and even the windows were open wide. To the left as we entered we passed the little bar which was very nicely made in the corner of the big room.

We had cold smoked trout as an entrée, followed by *Steierisches Brathuhn*, which is roast chicken turned on a spit. It was delicious and all the better for being helped down with Zierfändler white wine. For dessert, we had a soufflé called *Salzburger Nockerl* which only the Austrians can make so well. Obviously, a call had gone out for the staff to come back and help, because the service was first-class as well as the food. We took our coffee outside, as the evening was so humid.

We were able to talk more freely between ourselves on the forecourt. Guss thought it strange that the *Gasthaus* was so empty, but the Austrians were still reeling from the effects of the war. Nobby suggested that we move away in the morning and pay a visit to the police in St Johann. The decision was unanimous. In the far distance, we could catch a glimpse of a thunderstorm with the flashes of lightning seeming to pierce the snow-capped Alps like a skewer penetrating a hulk of beef. It was quite a show and looked like it was going to come our way later.

Suddenly the atmosphere changed and the air became much cooler, so we went inside to the comfort of the lounge chairs. We ordered a nightcap and felt very good with the world. We asked Herr Bruckner if we were going to have a storm as the thunder became louder, but he said that it would pass over towards the Zillertaler Alps. We complimented him on his very good *Gasthaus* and how we enjoyed his cooking. He said that it was not easy to find a chef worthy of his money but he was lucky, as he managed to get one from the Graz area.

As we were not going to see the spectacle of a good thunderstorm, we turned in, and with high hopes for the events of the morrow, bade our hosts goodnight. My room number was one and the lads' was four, so we took our respective keys and asked to be knocked up at 7 a.m.

That morning, we left Herr and Frau Bruckner well pleased with the settlement we had given them to cover all their costs, with gratuities and a little more on account of the information we had received.

Nobby had instructions where to get petrol and Guss was given directions to the police station. We loaded the jeep and bumped down the dust track on to the main road leading into St Johann. We didn't have to go very far before sighting a filling station on our own side of the road, so Nobby pulled in and refuelled. St Johann appeared to be a very attractive town with real old world typical alpine chalets and several good-looking hotels. Near to the petrol station was a rather flashy restaurant, then came some shops, a couple of banks. With the jeep refuelled, we drove off to the police station, finding it near to the post office.

We saw a parking space just near to the front door, between two police cars and Nobby had room to slip into the vacancy with ease. A policeman was just coming out to his car when he saw us and came to us to enquire what we were wanting. Guss asked him if we may see the senior policeman who would be on duty. He asked us to follow him and led Guss and me into the station. Nobby didn't want to come in, he preferred to look after his 'baby'. The policeman escorted us to the reception window and called his sergeant. The man came over and asked what did we require. Guss gave his introductory speech and I showed him my little red booklet. He went over to a phone with my book in hand and must have spoken to his superior.

We had been lucky, for the District Commissioner was visiting several stations in the area that day and could easily have been at another one elsewhere.

It had just gone nine o'clock, so we caught him nice and early. The Sergeant, giving me back my little red booklet, knocked on a door marked *Privat* and heard a soft *'Herein'* in reply. The softness was on account of the thickness of the door as we noticed on entering the office.

A smartly-dressed grey-haired man got up from behind his desk and offered us his hand in welcome. Seats had been positioned for us to sit on, and when he stood up he looked a very imposing figure in his light blue uniform with lots of pieces of gold braid here and there to mark his rank. We acknowledged his gesture for us two to sit down, and I offered him my little red book to read.

He studied it carefully and, looking from the book to me once or twice, must have satisfied himself that the photograph was indeed a good likeness. He remarked to Guss that it was a very important document and asked why was I so young and in possession of such authority? Guss explained that we were interested in a German called Hans Vogle, aged about forty-two, and that this man had a distinct accent from the Württemberg region.

I asked Guss to tell the Commissioner that he was an SS lieutenant and had been in the Hermann Goering Division. Guss mentioned that he was wanted by the Americans for war crimes committed at a Prisoner of War camp at Moosberg, near Munich. The Commissioner asked us if we had a photo of this man but we said, sadly, no.

The officer informed us that there had been a shooting last year and it was suspected that it had been the work of an outsider who had been on a hunting trip. The assassin had never been caught. The incident happened at Mittersill, some forty kilometres away.

'We still have the case on our file,' he said, 'We had a report circulated throughout the area stations, of a person trying to sexually assault youngsters on the ski slopes and in the Ski Schools at Krimml and Mittersill. We even have had it reported here but no one can actually catch the person because for some reason, the alleged victims are too afraid to speak up.'

The Commissioner looked through other notes and came across another important entry. This was a report from the town of Winklern. A German by the name of Wolf Grüber, had been a ski instructor and shortly after being employed, was concerned in reported incidents of child molestation whilst instructing the youngsters on the ski slopes, and also in the swimming pools. The townsfolk soon chased him out.

'Whoever this person is,' he said, 'he is very cunning and escapes without leaving enough evidence for us to act. Here in St Johann, we see quite a few German ski instructors. They don't have to register with us, only with the proprietor of the ski school or hotel.

'It will have to be a process of elimination,' I said to Guss, 'but it seems that we are in the right area; for somehow, I have a feeling that our Hans Vogle, alias Wolf Grüber, are one and the same. According to the notes from GHQ, Hans Vogle was a known sadist and a sex pervert whilst a section commander at the POW Camp at Moosberg. His war crimes warranted his death, apparently.'

The Commissioner listened intently and was ready for Guss to translate what I had just said. The Commissioner summoned the Sergeant into his office by phone, for he had an idea to ask him what he knew about a Wolf Grüber. The Sergeant couldn't remember the details but could remember hearing the name mentioned by his colleague, Constable Welser. He said that he would go and ask him and left the room.

The Commissioner began to express his feelings about the Allied Occupation Forces, and wondered when the Austrians would be left alone to govern their own affairs. He realised that all Western Europe needed that 'God-almighty American dollar' to re-establish democracy. He went on to tell Guss and me about the numbers of Austrians who fled their country to America in 1938 when the Nazis invaded.

He told us about the differences of dialect, habits, politics and culture between the provinces. He said it was only natural that the Austrians hated the Germans, especially those who lived close to the Austrian borders.

This chat piece finished abruptly as the knock on the door signalled the return of the Sergeant. Apparently, Constable Welser had heard that Wolf Grüber had returned to Germany and had got himself an instructor's job at a ski school somewhere up in the Bavarian Alps. Instantaneously, we three got up and went over to the framed wall map behind the Commissioner's head.

He pointed out the area and said that it was on the edge of the Württemberg region. He circled his finger around the Alpine masses and pondered, as if contemplating a particular spot.

His finger stopped, and turning to Guss, said, 'There! Start there – Garmisch-Partenkirchen. It is a well-known resort, as good almost as Kitzbühel. Try your luck there for a start.'

He turned and opened a drawer to his left and pulled out a new pair of handcuffs with two keys. He made the presentation to me and in doing so, told Guss that if we had to use them, always put them on the prisoner with his hands behind him, not in front. In the past, several escapes had been known to occur when the prisoner had his hands fastened in front, and the prisoner had been able to strangle his guard and effect his escape.

We were so pleased with our gift and all the information that had readily been given, and thanked one and all for the co-operation we had received. We left our British-made cigarettes to be distributed as a gesture of goodwill, and judging by their return thanks, the quantity had been sufficient.

On our way out of the building and walking over to the jeep, Guss said that Garmisch was over the Austrian-German border and we would have to go through Innsbruck. Reaching the vehicle, Guss stirred Nobby who had been having a short nap and asked him how far was it to Innsbruck. Nobby jumped down to stretch his legs, grabbing the map as he did so. We opened it out on the snub-nosed bonnet and reckoned it to be about sixty miles. Nobby thought that we might be able to make Innsbruck for lunch, if the roads were good.

With one more wave to our police helpers, who had come out to admire our special jeep, we reversed out of our parking space and drove off through more of the town and out on the road to Innsbruck. Through incredibly beautiful country, we wound our way down towards the River Inn, reaching the little village of Söll, delightfully nestling between the mountains, then running down to Wörgl. We had met some Austrian transport on its way up, probably to service the ski resorts. The dust they created began to cover the jeep and we were beginning to feel the dust in our throats, so we decided to pull in to the first café we saw.

We didn't stop long, just enough time to visit the loo and to drink a good Austrian coffee with their rich cream. We had a further thirty-nine miles to go but as the road was asphalted, we made better time in spite of the hold-ups for road repairs. The heavier military traffic had taken its toll and the workers always allowed the military to pass first. It seemed to be the only road connecting Innsbruck with Salzburg. Many of the American drivers drove right down the middle of the road and often Nobby had to dodge out of the way with only inches to spare. Although Nobby couldn't speak German fluently, he could match anyone with his bad language!

We were delighted to reach Innsbruck safely and more so for the fact of seeing the beautiful town undamaged by war. That was our quick assessment as we drove through to find a restaurant which had a parking space handy. We soon reached a charming little square surrounded by extremely old and beautiful buildings and saw our place for lunch. It was a very old inn called the Goldener Adler.

Whilst we were enjoying a rich lunch of *Lebernodelsuppe*, a sort of meat broth with liver dumplings, then followed by a good helping of Wiener schnitzel, we were finding out some knowledge of the town. Although the waiters are always busy in such a place, they were ready to assist with our enquiries. The inn, for instance, was famous, going back to the sixteenth century, and had hosted many famous people, including Goethe, and Andreas Hofer who fought the French in 1809.

As we had eaten so well for the first two courses, we left the dessert out and just had the coffee, although the Torten trolley looked so tempting with the most delicious pastries on each level. I paid the bill and gave our waiter a reasonable tip, bringing a smile to his face. As we had obtained directions for our way out to Garmisch, we stepped outside into the square and heard the noise of the rushing water of the River Inn. As our road would take us across it, we didn't walk to its banks to see the sight, and in any case, we were anxious to get to Garmisch for our further enquiries about our man.

All around Innsbruck the mountains towered to enormous heights and our road, after crossing over the river, soon began to rise steeply until we reached the Scharnitz Pass. We had already climbed to 3,163 feet through breathtaking scenery and we all remarked on the excellent performance of the jeep. Nobby had taken the precaution to put the vehicle into four-wheel drive at the commencement of our climb which did help our stability, especially on the tight hairpin bends.

As we reached the summit of the pass, the border guards waved us on. I was very grateful, for I was not eager to have a discourse with the Germans. The scenery didn't change at all and yet one had a feeling that the country was not the same. Perhaps this was because we three had a dislike for the Germans after our individual experiences during the years of hostilities. With about twenty-one miles further to reach Garmisch, we changed drivers and I took over.

Chapter Two

Looking for the first ski outfitters and sports shop on our way into Garmisch-Partenkirchen, we saw one near to the bus terminus, so I pulled up outside and switched off the ignition. The peace was rewarding, for the hum of the thick tyre treads on the hard road surfaces, along with the rhythm of the engine, gave the ears a bit of a thumping.

I decided to go in this time and ask for someone who could speak English. Again I was disappointed, for there was no one with whom I could converse, so I had to call Guss in. Guss asked if the business had a ski school in its organisation and if so, were only German Nationals employed as instructors? The young man, in his early twenties perhaps, came forward and acknowledged that he was German and asked why we wished to know. I showed him my ID book which he accepted as my authority to seek information. In fact, he turned out to be very helpful. He said that there were quite a few Germans who worked here for both the summer and winter seasons.

The young man said that only Germans worked at the hotels, restaurants and the sports centres where the ski schools were run by the *Stadtrat*. Then there were the privately-owned ski schools run by rich Austrians who also own restaurants, garages and in some cases, haulage businesses too.

Guss asked him if the name Wolf Grüber meant anything to him but after a long thought, the young man came up with a negative reply. On leaving the shop, at least we felt that we had met one of the better Germans, for he was courteous. Of course we didn't know if his negative reply was genuine or not. Nobby now took the wheel again and we went on into the town. The next sports business we came to was near to the bank so we popped in there. An English-speaking Austrian there was very helpful but still we got no satisfaction, but were given a recommendation to seek out Herr Rudi Schmidt, who owned a good part of Garmisch and usually could be found at his main business near to The Post Hotel.

It didn't take us long to find his place as it was a double-fronted shop, or store to be more precise judging by its size, with *Schmidt's Ski Schule* painted across the front. We parked out front and Guss and I went in. Inside, it was bigger than we had expected with ski outfits to our left and two long fixtures of skis. There was a separate department towards the back which had cupboards full of guns and sporting rifles. There was Archers' equipment, with many types of bow, and arrows with different types of feathers in many colours. On the right were swimsuits, inflatables and canoes and other sports items. Guss went after the ski outfits and the winter clothing stock.

It wasn't long before we were approached by a female shop assistant. I asked her if she spoke English and to my joy she said in very good broken English that she did. What a relief for me to be able to ask the questions directly, instead of always through Guss! I asked her if Herr Schmidt was available, and to that I got a 'no'. I asked if he was in town and she said that she would ring around to find out just where he would be. She then asked who it was that was enquiring.

I gave her my ID booklet and she nearly trembled with fear, thinking that we were from the Secret Police or something, until she read the German translation first and then the appropriate text in English. I told her that there was nothing to be afraid of, but it was urgent that I meet Herr Schmidt. She asked us to follow her and in so doing, gave instructions to an elderly man to look after the store. There were two more assistants, both female, who were now curious as to who we were. The gun department was shut, and I suppose it was only served by Herr Schmidt himself. The youngish woman asked us into an office where I noticed a door ahead marked '*Privat*'.

We sat on the chairs that we were offered and waited whilst the assistant made a phone call. There was no joy there. The woman then rang another number and a conversation developed. The manager of the restaurant knew where Herr Schmidt would be now, and said that he would get hold of him straight away and would get him to come to the office immediately. Now we had to wait, so we chatted to the assistant about business in the town and when do they begin to prepare for the winter season. She said that they were always ready in the town, but their chalets on the outskirts had to be looked at as the summer season changes to the beginning of the winter season.

She said business was picking up quite nicely, but of course it was helped by the extra influx of allied military personnel. They loved their sport and took every advantage of the facilities Garmisch had to offer. Hearing some excitement in the tone of voices by the shop assistants and a good loud German voice proclaiming its authority, we knew that Herr Schmidt had arrived, and with a flurry he entered the office.

Guss and I stood to greet the big man, and in a very jovial gesture of goodwill, he greeted us in English, but with a rather charming accent. For a moment, Guss forgot that Herr Schmidt could speak English and in German, introduced himself and me. After a smile and a firm handshake to us, Herr Schmidt dismissed his assistant and asked us to join him in his inner office. Accommodating ourselves as he indicated, we sat comfortably in leather easy chairs. I showed him my ID booklet, which impressed him and he settled into his leather swivel chair.

I told him that we had information about a certain Wolf Grüber who may be employed in this area as a ski instructor or sports master in other fields of sport. I told him that this man spoke with a marked Württemberg accent. Herr Schmidt said that Württemberg was quite a distance away and covered quite an area.

Schmidt asked us what did we know about him, like his features. We told him that he was about forty-two years of age and about 1.80 metres tall and well built. He is an ex-SS lieutenant of the 'Death's Head' Squad.

'Yes,' remarked Herr Schmidt, 'that was Hermann Goering's collection.'

He reached for his filing cabinet top drawer and pulled it open, revealing a tight wad of files suspended on the rails. Carefully, he picked out one and laid it on his desk. 'I am going through my list of staff who I have taken on as ski instructors and who have shown by their references that they were of managerial potential,' he continued, 'as I wanted a ski instructor – manager for my establishment up at Linderhof and Vils. One man came to us in late spring. We are having people all the time asking for employment and they come from the more destroyed parts of Germany, for there is no money there for the time being.

'Surely, they will need all the manpower they can get to rebuild their Country,' said Guss.

Herr Schmidt indicated to us one by the name of Franz Schiller. His age would be right and he was from Ravensberg. Herr Schmidt appeared to get fidgety and muttered something in his own language, which even Guss couldn't hear, and exhaled loudly.

'So far, I have been very pleased with his work and he has managed the two establishments very well. In fact, I have had a good reference from the skiers, especially the younger set,' Herr Schmidt concluded.

I was now convinced that this Franz Schiller was in fact Hans Vogle, although I knew that I was taking an enormous gamble, I turned to Guss and indicated with my thumb up. Guss nodded his assent. I asked Herr Schmidt where was Franz Schiller now, and he said that he was up at his Linderhof store and ski school but should be coming back in about one and a quarter hours' time.

'How long does it take him to get here from Linderhof,' I asked.

'Oh, it varies, but normally it should take him about forty minutes as it is only twenty-six miles,' said Herr Schmidt.

'Right. Now, I tell you what I would like you to do Herr Schmidt, and I want you to do this right away,' I said. 'Please go up to Linderhof and keep a good eye open for him on your way. If you should see him, stop him. As you said that he will be driving your Volkswagen buggy, which is brightly painted, so you will be able to see him clearly. If you get to Linderhof before he leaves, detain him there somehow until we arrive. Do not give anything away as to what is happening. I want you to know that this man we are after is a beast of a war criminal and is very much wanted by the Americans. My task is to catch him and that I will, but we want your full co-operation now, and no slip-ups.

'You drive a BMW saloon which is faster than our jeep, although our vehicle has a good turn of speed and we will not be too far behind. Now, let's get on the road and please tell your staff here that no one must warn Franz Schiller that we are coming, or else there will be severe trouble,' I concluded.

We realised that the staff had by now suspected that something quite serious was wrong and they were getting very anxious, so Guss quickly told them that for them there was nothing to worry about as long as they didn't communicate with Franz.

If the phone was to ring, they were not to answer it until we were back. Herr Schmidt wasted no time in getting away and roared out of Garmisch on the Oberammergau road. When Nobby saw the BMW start off in a hurry, he had the engine warming ready for our rapid departure, and we piled in quickly and sped off in the same direction as Schmidt's car went. We told Nobby all about what we had heard and how we concluded, on sheer guess work, that a manager of Schmidt's who looks after one of his shops up at Linderhof, the place we were now going to about twenty-six miles away, was our Hans Vogle.

He doesn't know that we are coming, of course, I said, 'but Herr Schmidt has my instructions to stop him on the road if he is on his way to Garmisch. If not, to detain him at the shop or ski school on any pretext until we come.'

Nobby was fairly tearing up the road and in our excitement we passed the turning off to the left for Linderhof and had to do a lengthy reverse. We could see Schmidt's car climbing the hairpin bends on the very steep gradients as well as the long cloud of dust which the car kicked up not very far ahead. Nobby now slipped the jeep into four-wheel drive and we took the gravel bends beautifully, gaining all the time on Herr Schmidt. Guss and I were scanning the road ahead in case we could get sight of the VW buggy. Herr Schmidt told us that it was an ex-German army runabout, but he had it painted yellow top half and the bottom half red and across the bonnet and sides was the name *Schmidt's Ski Schule* in white letters.

Herr Schmidt knew the road well, so he was able to slew round the tight corners on the gravel without slipping into the water duct at the side of the track. It was quite a deep duct, for the amount of rain they have in those parts demanded that the water escape without washing away the track itself.

We had crossed over several bridges which spanned the raging torrent below and we must have been fairly near to Linderhof, and we had just crossed over the last bridge when we saw, on a straight piece of track with tall pine trees bordering either side, two vehicles stopped together on the offside of the road.

'Watch out, lads, for anything,' I said, and I withdrew my revolver from the holster which was just inside my grip. We could recognise Herr Schmidt, and as we had come into sight of the two men, they both looked our way and Nobby drove right up and skidded to a halt, partly trapping Schiller against the bonnet of the VW.

Guss leaped out and Nobby, like a streak of lightning, flung himself from the jeep right into the back of the buggy in one leap, for he saw a hunting rifle across the back bench seat. Schiller had been completely taken by surprise and his first reaction, although it was only for a split second, was to go into a panic – which gave Nobby that opportunity to reach the gun first.

I yelled, 'Vogle, *halt! Oder ich schiess!*'

The moment he heard his real name being called, he went bonkers and tried to grapple the rifle from Nobby. Herr Schmidt ducked out of the way and left us to deal with the madman. Vogle took no notice of my command, so I fired a shot into the air as a warning and at the same time, Nobby brought his foot up into Vogle's groin, making him howl in agony and fall almost in a state of collapse between the two cars.

Guss meanwhile quickly returned to the jeep and grabbed the handcuffs. There was little Vogle could do now as he was in such pain, so it was fairly easy for us to get his hands behind him and snap the handcuffs on. Guss gave Vogle a warning in his own language that we were arresting him for his war crimes and for escaping from American custody at Salzburg. We were now going to take him to Salzburg and hand him over to the Americans, to face trial.

Poor Herr Rudi Schmidt! He was devastated and was shaking like a leaf. Perspiration was streaming down his face and couldn't speak a word for several minutes. Vogle groaned and held his legs together as if to relieve the pain. I slapped Nobby on the back in a congratulatory manner for the quick thinking in grabbing that rifle. He said that what struck him was a glint of the sun on the barrel as we slid to a halt, and he could see clearly that it was a hunting rifle – and he had to get there first.

Making sure that it was unloaded, Nobby handed it over to Herr Schmidt. We told him that we were now going straight to Salzburg and if he had any recourse, to get in touch with the American Military Police Headquarters in Salzburg, and they would do what they could for him, if need be.

We placed Vogle between Guss and myself, making the position rather cramped but it was better that than to have the man try to jump out by bashing himself against the door, which after all, was not all that strong. We felt Vogle would try a suicide, or knock Nobby's arm to alter the steering wheel's direction, if he was in the front.

We again thanked Herr Schmidt for his co-operation, and as the man had regained his composure, he felt relieved that he was rid of possible trouble. His reputation in the area was of the highest, and such a scandal would have ruined him, if events like those at Mittersill or Krimml had occurred at Garmisch.

Now Vogle began to rant and rave in his parochial dialect. Guss told him to shut up. Wasting no more time as the afternoon was rapidly coming to a close, we made a quick turn around and headed back down the valley to Garmisch.

Nobby drove like a cat out of hell and we seemed to arrive at Innsbruck in half the time it took us to get from Innsbruck to Garmisch. We stopped to refuel, and Nobby came to the back of the jeep for the coupons as Guss and I safely guarded our prisoner. We didn't want anyone to know who we had sitting between us and we were ready to stifle any shout from Vogle to cause attention. A little way out of Innsbruck, we stopped and Nobby and I changed places. The change over had to be carefully arranged so that Vogle could not try any tricks. It was also at that point that we each in turn relieved ourselves beside the jeep on the grass verge.

Vogle had the indignity of having to pee with his left hand attached by the handcuffs to Nobby. He moaned in German that his testicles still pained him, but Nobby just shrugged his shoulders and looked away. Feeling nature's comforts once more, we rearranged the handcuffs on Vogle with his hands behind him and boarded the jeep. In the speed of the events up in the mountains, Nobby had forgotten to release the four-wheel drive mechanism and reminded me, so I slipped the lever back and felt the difference to the performance of the car.

We had long since seen the short-lived dusk and we had to use our full driving lights. Thank goodness there was a good moon which showed the road ahead, and the Inn river beside it, quite clearly.

Now and then we hit a pothole, which produced a chorus from Guss and Nobby, who said, 'Think of the car, Skipper!' There was always good humour from the lads. The strain of the past hour and a half had taken its toll on Vogle, for coupled with the drone of the engine and the hum of the tyres on the hard surface, it had made him doze off every now and again, only to be awakened by the jolting of the jeep when a pothole had been aimed at.

We reached Wörgl in good time and, seeing the railway station, I pulled in to the forecourt and stopped outside the main entrance. I instructed the lads to keep a low profile while I went inside to get something for us to eat and drink while we journeyed. I found the 'snack bar' as we would have called it and loaded myself up with *Leberwurst* rolls, sweet buns and some bars of chocolate. I got some small bottles of fruit juice and then went out as quickly as I could.

On my return, the lads reported that they had a little bit of trouble with Vogle. He pretended to be suddenly violently ill and tried to loll forward, and in doing so would swiftly bring his head up and back in the hope of knocking either Nobby or Guss out.

I couldn't blame him for wanting to try to escape, for I would have done the same; but I was not going to allow him to hold us up in any way nor injure either of my good lads. I told Guss to inform Vogle that if he gave us any trouble at all, he would get far more injuries than just a kick in the groin. That threat quietened him down, for he well understood that he was no friend of mine.

I was reluctant to give Vogle a bread roll sandwich, but I just couldn't see the man, semi-trussed and really looking scared, eyeing the food I had brought. Guss and Nobby took it in turns to feed Vogle and to give him a drink of the fruit juice. The respite was welcome and as the last mouthful disappeared, I moved the jeep to the far end of the station forecourt, in order to do a swop around between Guss and me. We took the usual precautions with the handcuffs and always one had my revolver trained on our prisoner to warn him against any escape attempt.

Guss was an excellent driver too but couldn't match the skill of Nobby. He was unique. We had about an hour's drive still to do which should get us into Salzburg, at about nine o'clock. Tucked in once again between two captors, Vogle stared angrily ahead and made every effort to keep awake. Of course, we did the same, for after all, we would soon be in Salzburg at the rate Guss was driving. Thank goodness the other traffic on the road seemed to tail off after dusk became night. Soon, street lights began to appear which marked the outskirts of the ancient city of Salzburg.

It was a well-lit city and was bustling with American army vehicles dashing everywhere. Some streets were very narrow and others were rather like a wide boulevard. Guss spotted an American Army Police Patrol jeep waiting just beside a bus stop. Four men were the crew and one looked to be of sergeant rank. Guss slowed to a halt just alongside the jeep, and before we could speak, one of the patrol told us not to stay alongside but to move over to a wide pavement, pointing to the spot; and, as if attached to us, the jeep followed jeep.

Guss got out and asked the Military Police where was their Headquarters. Three of the men came to our jeep, and looking inside, saw our prisoner and Nobby and myself. One of them asked me what had he been doing, and on seeing us in civilian clothes, demanded to see our credentials. I showed the smart American my red booklet, which brought out an exclamatory whistle and a little more respect. The Sergeant immediately offered to be our escort and said that he would be glad to show us the way and safely inside!

I must say, I was beginning to feel the strain of having such a brute sitting so close. During the journey, I felt that I wanted to vent my anger on him in no uncertain terms, for all the bestial things he had done to others in the past, and who knows what else he had done that we didn't know about. On the other hand, I remembered the times when I was a prisoner between German guards and would readily have killed to effect my escape. At least he was getting better treatment now than I ever had in their hands.

Passing through the big gates of a very imposing building, we pulled up outside the Guardroom, which was manned by Military Police, and one came to the car window. I showed the AMP my ID booklet and a call for 'Sergeant!' was yelled out. Immediately the Sergeant and two MPs rushed out to us, then seeing that there was no panic, the MP took my red booklet in his hands and read it. He asked us to stay where we were for the moment and went inside to the telephone.

Meanwhile, our escort jeep waited too, but had turned around. The Sergeant re-emerged and gave orders to our escort to lead us over to their own General Headquarters, and then if I would return here to meet Colonel C.D. Colacicco of the CIC.

I was only too pleased to comply with the instructions, and Guss turned the jeep around and followed the escort out into the street. We wound our way through the traffic, which was warned of our approach by a siren on the escort jeep. We climbed up a steep hill high above the city and arrived at an ancient fortress. Part of it was used by the Military Police as their temporary Headquarters. It looked a massive structure and was just the place to accommodate our captive.

The barracks itself was at the rear and as our escort stopped beside a door, we stopped too and at last, we had arrived at our destination. I unlocked one of Vogle's hands first, and with the short piece of chain, pulled him out of the jeep. As he struggled, a police guard offered his wrist and I clamped the loose handcuff on to him. Nobby now joined the group and, surrounding Vogle, we almost pushed each other inside the building.

Nobby, Guss and I had seen in a flash the Death's Head tattoo on the arm of Vogle as he stretched it out when pulled by the American, once he was out of the jeep. We nodded to each other in a manner showing great jubilation.

We waited for the Americans to see their prisoner now, safely put inside a cell and to get our handcuffs back. What a relief it was to know that it was all over!

The courtesy shown to us by the American Military Police was very commendable and put us well up in a frame of mind to meet the Colonel, although we were now fairly tired.

Our escort took us back to the American Forces General Army Headquarters and once we were inside the grounds, left us to continue their duties out on patrol.

A soldier asked who it was going to see the Colonel, and I said that it would be the three of us. He looked somewhat surprised, then taking up a sheaf of papers he asked us to follow him. We climbed up some old stone steps which led to a corridor with several rooms leading off to the right. Outside each door, was a marker board bearing the name of the occupant. We passed two and came to the third which was clearly marked, Colonel C.D. Colacicco of the Counter-Intelligence Corps.

The soldier gave a loud knock on the door and immediately, a green light flashed over the portal above our heads. A red light was positioned beside it. He opened the door and ushered us into a very businesslike office. The soldier left as we were now in the hands of the Colonel's personal staff. There were two privates and a corporal in a dress uniform of light khaki shirt and insignia, with the long trousers in a shade of khaki but with the faintest hint of pink in it. It looked a very fresh uniform and seemed very well pressed by the wearer.

Chairs were placed for us to sit on around the Corporal's desk and we responded to the courtesy shown. The Corporal then took down on a form details of our names, ranks, and regiments and the title of our department. A buzzer on the desk sounded and we were asked to follow the Corporal into another room, as the door opened.

Standing before an enormous desk was a tall slim man in his early fifties, his arm outstretched offering a friendly welcome. If I had been in uniform, I would have given him a very smart salute, to match his rank and his congenial approach. By this welcome, we had been put at ease and as indicated, sat down on the three elegantly bound leather easy chairs around a low circular table.

Two private clerical staff swung a fourth easy chair from a corner of the room and placed it with our three. One of the privates then sat down at a small table beside the Colonel's huge, highly polished desk, and prepared to use a stenographic machine. The other private had a desk to himself, with typewriter, telephones and the usual in-out trays. Two filing cabinets dominated part of the wall near his desk. Along the wall behind us was a low wooden cupboard on top of which was an illuminated drinks unit, with glass shelves.

The Colonel offered us drinks and seemed surprised when we asked for some coffee instead of spirits or beer. I explained that, as we had not eaten for hours, we required something substantial in our stomachs before imbibing in alcohol.

'Right!' he said, 'coffee you shall have, and we will get down to your report as to how you found this beast Vogle so quickly – and make your report short, as I would like my Captain to take you to a hotel where you can have a very good meal, and if you like the place, you can stay the night there.'

Each of us provided the Colonel with the details from the moment we suspected the person to his actual arrest, with all his aliases. All the time, the stenographer was almost silently pressing away at the keyboard, recording every word which was spoken in that room, relevant to the report.

The Colonel was magnanimous with his apologies for having a Field Unit not ready to carry out such missions and explained how embarrassed the whole Headquarters was, when Vogle escaped from their Military police escort on the way to the courts. Having had a personal experience of escapes during my prisoner of war captivity, I could agree with the Colonel's extreme embarrassment, but said that it can easily happen if and when an opportunity arose.

This I told to the Colonel, and apparently he had quite a dossier about me and knew all my past military history. I was amazed that they were so interested and that my exploits had been noted, by someone.

The Colonel couldn't thank us enough for what we did for them and he said that if ever again they got 'stuck', they would ask our Command if they could have our services again. We were not used to this informality, especially from such a high-ranking officer, with his 'back-slapping' and praise, but nevertheless we were delighted that we had scored a good point over the Yanks.

Several buttons were pressed by the Colonel on a sort of keyboard on his desk, and after a few minutes a Captain Wally Cartwright came into the office and was so introduced. He was from the 21st Cavalry Regiment. The Colonel, having seen my red ID booklet, asked me if I would show it to the Captain. This was only out of curiosity, not for any proof of my identification, however. He couldn't get over the way in which the booklet had been so cleverly worded and edited and handed back the item, complimenting our Command for its indispensability and originality.

With our stomachs rumbling like a thunderstorm, we were escorted down into the city by the Captain and in no time at all, we had pulled up outside a very old but splendid looking hotel. The Captain leaped out of his car and quickly entered the hotel. Nobby had stopped just behind the car, and Guss and I remained beside the jeep waiting for the return of the Captain. Apparently he had spoken to the receptionist, for he bounced out to us and said that everything had been taken care of and that all expenses would be charged to Headquarters. We didn't have to pay for a single item.

Guss and I grabbed our grips, including Nobby's, and the Captain indicated to Nobby where to go to park the jeep for the night. It was through an arch and behind the hotel. We waited beside the Reception desk for Nobby to come and a page then showed us to our rooms. Mine was on the right of the corridor and the lads' rooms were across the corridor about four doors away.

We made an arrangement that whoever was out first would bang on the doors of the others and we would go down to the dining room together. We didn't expect to see so many people in the room at such a late hour but then we were told that the citizens of Salzburg like eating out late.

As we entered, many eyes swung round in our direction out of curiosity and watched as the *maître d'hôtel* and two of his staff showed us to our table. The two waiters helped us into our chairs, then opened and laid the napkins over our laps. This etiquette amused Nobby, but nevertheless he lapped it all up.

Each table had a lighted candle glowing in a container and with the attractive wall lights, gave a pleasant aura to the room.

We three felt much better after our wash and brush-up, for the dust from the mountain roads seemed to get into everywhere. The service was immaculate and speedy, which pleased us as we were not keen to loiter long because we were fairly shattered from the day's work and travel. We had covered quite a distance that day.

The dinner was sumptuous and was well worth the long wait before we were able to be free of our burden. We now realised the name of the hotel was the Goldener Hirsch on the Getreidegasse. Each course came quickly, but we took our time eating it, for the food was absolutely delicious.

It must have been the effect of the food and the wines which made us begin to yawn and once one started, the other two caught the mode. Over our coffee, we congratulated ourselves on our success, and I couldn't thank Guss and Nobby enough for their endurance and their ability to work so well together. It was a really good team.

We planned our trip for the morrow and agreed to pay Berchtesgaden a visit before going back to Klagenfurt. We also unanimously agreed not to get up too early, but to be away by about 9.30. We would try to meet together for breakfast at about 9 a.m.

My room number was two and the lads had number five and seven. All three were single rooms with bath, and as we had kept our keys, we just lazily climbed the short flight of stairs and vanished into our respective rooms.

Chapter Three

It was about nine o' clock when we gathered at the Reception desk because the lads saw me reading a note which had been left by a messenger from the Americans: 'Thanks a million for all your efforts. Hope accommodation okay. Will inform your Headquarters. Signed: Col. C.D. Colacicco. Salzburg.'

We had nothing but praise for the accommodation, for the rooms were so well equipped. We went into the dining room and luckily, we had the same waiter who served us the previous night. He was a jovial soul, yet meticulous in his duties. We decided to give ourselves a little break and return 'home' via Berchtesgaden and Hitler's mountain retreat – 'The Eagle's Nest' – high above the Königssee.

I gave the *maître d'hôtel* a good tip to be shared between himself and his staff and left a gratuity for the house staff with the lad at the Reception desk. Nobby had brought the jeep to the front and we loaded up. I had now changed to my uniform and Nobby had too. The looks of surprise from many of the staff, including the manager, was interesting. The manager had been out the previous night, that is why we had missed him but this morning, he was on duty and saying his goodbyes to his guests as several were leaving. He came to the front entrance and showed Nobby which route to take to clear us of the city and on the road to Berchtesgaden. He supervised his pages as they were helping Nobby to arrange the grips in the back of the jeep and thanked me for the tip I gave the boys.

Following the clear directions he was given, Nobby soon found the signpost to Berchtesgaden, and looking back we saw the city of Salzburg recede in the distance with the castle remaining still visible. We didn't have a thought for Vogle languishing in his prison cell. Both Nobby and Guss vowed that they would be back one day to see Salzburg properly and to stay in the same hotel if possible. I said that it had stood for eight hundred years, and had been an inn since 1564. I must admit, the antique rustic furniture appealed to me and the arched corridors and the vaulted stairs made the hotel very desirable for a longer stay. Another advantage was that it was situated right in the heart of a good shopping area.

We were over the border into Germany again in no time at all, and arrived at Berschtesgaden, which looked partly war damaged. Driving further up the mountain road, we passed the barracks which had belonged to Hitler's most élite and feared SS troops. It was at these barracks that Himmler planned most of his inhuman acts against Jews, Poles, Czechoslovakians, Russians, Greeks and Austrians, not forgetting the Italians after they signed the Armistice in 1943. Thousands of Italians were taken for forced labour and treated worse than slaves.

American troops were in semi-occupation and had guards at the main entrance. We stopped and I asked if we may have a look round. Everything was okay, so we pulled in through the main gates and parked outside a building which had once been the German administration offices. It was most interesting to see German soldiers dressed in their fatigue uniforms being used by the Americans, well supervised, to clean up the whole area as if the barracks were to be used once more but for the American forces.

An ordinary GI offered to show us around and we started at the admin offices and walked over to the Officer's Mess where Hitler, Goering, Himmler and all his top generals were often entertained. We saw the troop quarters which were luxury to the last word for soldiers. We saw the indoor swimming pools, for there were three altogether. One was for the officers, one for the non-commissioned ranks and one for the troops. The kitchens were vast and the sports section was fit for any top class athlete. There was everything from cinemas to games rooms and even a first-class hospital. It all seemed too good to be true for the comfort of the German soldiery. No wonder they vied to become members of Hitler's élite of the élite troops. Then we saw an appalling spectacle hidden by a copse of tall pine trees: a concentration camp that had held several thousand Jews for slave labour.

Our guide was taking us over to the entrance to the concentration camp, and we passed one of the parade grounds. There in a corner near to the main road, was a peculiar structure formed into a letter X. The guide informed us that it was a whipping post, and walking up to it, we saw the shackles still attached. He told us that the SS used it on their own troops whenever anyone defaulted. This punishment was carried out in front of their colleagues. I declined to be shown the concentration camp as I had seen these before. Nobby and Guss also declined, so we walked back to the jeep and thanked our GI guide, and drove off up the steep mountain road to the entrance of Hitler's retreat. The road had been made entirely with the Jewish slave labour and hundreds had died making it. It was about one and a half miles up extremely steep gradients and as one looked at it, it was almost a shrine to those who perished because it had been made so well. The road ended in a turning circle, bounded by a thick stone wall, 1.5 metres high opposite the sheer rock face of the mountain.

The portico was arched and a tremendously thick bronze door formed the entrance. There was a portable office building to the side which held the American guards and we supposed, the guides. As soon as we stopped, we were approached and I offered my red booklet to the sentry who took it to the Guardroom, such as it was, and I went over to retrieve it. The doors were electrically operated and took time to open as they were so heavy. The GI guard told us that each one weighed one ton. He left us to go our own way.

The tunnel was completely tiled in white and the floor tarred but very smooth. The tar had been painted red. Electric lights were positioned alternatively on either side and were enough to light up the tunnel brilliantly. At the end of the tunnel was a big door to our left and one to our right. The right-hand door led to the lift. We were actually standing in a circular room with a big light in the middle. Both doors were made of heavy brass. We pressed the lift button and after a few moments, the doors opened and we stepped in. It was a very strange feeling. It took us about half a minute before the doors opened automatically and we stepped out into a corridor.

Opposite the lift doors was an arched entrance leading into a reception room, to the left were two doors marked 'Herren' and 'Damen'. At the other end was a rectangular sliding door, almost the width of the room. We slid it back and entered a huge room with several big windows, showing the thickness of the outer walls, at the far end. The ceiling was of the finest wood and ornate chandeliers had once hung down. The room was enormous but completely devoid of any furniture as it had long since been pillaged by the French troops, who got to the Eagle's Nest before the Americans. They of course had their fair share of the souvenirs as soon as they got to the place. The marble fireplace was of the finest red Italian marble, given to Hitler by Mussolini.

The view from the windows was tremendous. As far as the eyes could see, right into Germany and the surrounding mountains, there was an unobstructed view.

We could see how easy it was for Hitler to be carried away, claiming that the world was his. As we wondered on the construction of the house right on the pinnacle of the mountain, we thought of the poor souls who had been forced into building it. Martin Bormann was the brain behind it all. We saw Eva Braun's bedroom, the SS Guards' quarters and the machine rooms. It was a shame to see the damage done by the many souvenir hunters. We had to go back and have another look through the windows of the big lounge. The view was so fantastic. As it was a fine day, the atmosphere made the scene more beautiful.

We could just imagine Hitler proclaiming to his cohorts that he would soon be 'Master of the World'! Guss said that he wouldn't like to be the window cleaner.

There were quite a few American servicemen also looking round the strangely shaped building. Sometimes we didn't know if the Americans were more interested in us than the building. Nearly all of them had a camera and flashbulbs were popping continuously. However, everyone was enjoying the exceptional experience of actually standing where Hitler, Ribbentrop, Mussolini, Himmler, Goering, Goebbels, Speer and Prince Philipp of Hessen once stood. As we gazed at the ornate fireplace, we met two GIs also having a look around. They flung a salute as they approached and I acknowledged with a return salute. They introduced themselves as Sergeant Joe Hastings and Private Arthur Micklebaum, and offered to show us around if we were interested and if we had the time.

We were more than glad to accept their courteous offer, for they seemed most pleasant, polite and well-spoken young men. Apparently, they had been following us at a distance and wanted to meet Nobby, as he was a sergeant. I asked our newly found 'guides' if they knew what had happened to the gigantic carpet, but all they could say was that it had been rescued by their Command, immediately the place was overrun by their troops. They suspected that it had been shipped or flown to the United States.

They showed us the kitchens, the laundry, the air raid shelters and told us that all the machinery and appliances had been taken by the troops and the released multinational Jewish prisoners who had been enslaved by the 'Master Race'. Our GIs went on to tell us about the numbers of Jews who had perished whilst building Hitler's retreat and later in the appalling conditions in the concentration camp. Out of sixteen thousand at the outset, only a couple of hundred were rescued by the American Forces.

It was getting on towards lunchtime, so we suggested making a move to go down. The lift was summoned and as the brass doors opened, we now noticed a large trapdoor set into the floor. The GIs told us that there was another room below, for the élite SS Guards and the Gestapo agents, who were handpicked by Hitler himself to be his personal bodyguards. They were able to hear every word spoken by any occupant, even to a whisper.

As we descended down one hundred and twenty-five metres, we reflected on how many important people had been inside the lift, such as that pompous ass Mussolini, for instance. We wondered how many had met their death for speaking out against their Leader, after an interview, thinking that they were safe to talk. We stopped. The brass lift doors opened into the tunnel once more. Straight ahead, we saw a big brass double door set into the rock face and we asked our guides where it led. They told us that it was the garage that housed the huge Mercedes Staff car which Hitler used wherever he went. It was bulletproof and was his favourite mode of transport.

Also in the garage was stored the motorbike which Hitler's mistress, Eva Braun, learnt to ride, and after becoming quite skilled, rode up and down the tunnel. The tunnel measured approximately one hundred and twenty-five metres in length to the outer bronze doors.

As our group walked down the tunnel, as it was built on a slight slope, our voices echoed, and every so often we were shown where the listening devices had been placed. In a sense, it was a relief to get out into the fresh air again, although everything had been air-conditioned.

As we walked over to the wall surround of the *Parkplatz* to see the enormous drop below and the view of the nearby waterfalls, our American lads asked if we could give them a lift down to their PX stores at the village of Königssee. We answered with a grateful 'yes', and surprised the two with our jeep. They thought it was 'the tops' and vowed to make their jeep look just as good. With their viewing over, we got in and with a tight squeeze, we managed to survive until we arrived lower down beside the deep blue waters of the Königssee lake.

The village was small and most attractive, but full of GIs participating in all kinds of leisure activities. As we slowed down to a crawling speed, our two American guides were telling us about the story circulating that the Germans dumped vast amounts of gold, jewels, silver and objects of immense value, in crates, in the deepest part of the lake, which is supposed to be of unmeasurable depth. We thought that this story had only been put around in order to stop people trying to usurp the treasures.

We were directed to the American army PX stores and in the grounds was a restaurant, run by the American Forces. As the two GIs alighted on to the dusty gravel roadway, we thanked them for their courteous assistance and slowly gathered speed so that we would create as little dust as possible. The whole setting around Königssee was really delightful and one could imagine it to be a very popular place for families to visit in normal times.

Nobby found the winding road ending at a junction which, on turning left, brought us on to the main road back to Salzburg. We could now recognise our way and gathering speed, we soon crossed the border back into Austria and following the signs, reached our correct road to take us 'home'. Now we were on the lookout for somewhere pleasant to have lunch, as we were beginning to get hungry, especially Guss!

We found nothing to attract us until we came to Hallein. Here we found a very old inn, so we pulled up outside, happy in our anticipation of a good meal. We were not disappointed, for the food was of the highest standard; only the service fell down a little. The waiter kept going over to the windows every now and again to gaze at our jeep, which caused the other diners to have to attract his attention for their service, and sometimes ours too. However, we couldn't and wouldn't complain because the place matched the food it served.

We noted that there were many objects in and around the inn, which were made of marble and on enquiring from the waiter, we were told that there were several mines in the area where the marble came from, and now the industry was picking up again after the war years. It used to be exported to many parts of the world before the War. These little bits of information about the towns we pass through were always very interesting.

Feeling a great deal better for the rest and the meal, we were off again and climbing all the time towards Golling and the Lueg Pass.

As we approached the pass we saw threatening black clouds ahead and in no time at all, we were feeling a decidedly cooler air and a few heavy drops of rain began to smudge the dust on the windscreen. A few more miles, and the heavens opened. Torrential rain battered the jeep and the lightning was spectacular. We decided to stop at Werfen, for it was stupid to proceed any further as the roads were awash, and poor old Nobby couldn't see through the windscreen as the wipers wouldn't work quickly enough.

The little town ahead showed up a dominating mountain with a typical Austrian castle perched right on its summit. It looked so eerie as the flashes of lightning illuminated it and the town below. The boom of the thunder deafened our ears as the storm came nearer, bringing with it more even heavier rain.

We picked our way into the town and soon found a hotel. Nobby edged the jeep as near to the entrance as he could, which allowed Guss and me to dash inside. Guss asked the receptionist where we could leave the jeep overnight, and luckily we were able to leave it where we arrived. Guss grabbed an umbrella from the porter and went outside to give Nobby a hand with the grips. Making sure the jeep's safety switch was activated, the lads hurried in, finding the umbrellas being little to no use at all as the rain was so torrential. The road had turned into a river, soaking their feet.

With the usual Austrian efficiency, the staff wasted no time in selecting our rooms and offered to take the shoes, socks and trousers to the drying room, when the lads were ready. The lads had one of the double rooms with two single beds and I had a single room; both were at the front of the hotel and looked out on to the castle.

The men had quickly changed out of their wet clothes and had handed them over at the Reception desk, to be dried. They had found the little lounge which had a bright burning wood fire, giving us a good welcome. I had been lucky, for I managed to reach the inside before I had time to get soaked. On my way in to the lounge, I had ordered three double whiskies, to warm up our insides, for the

temperature had dropped quite considerably as the down-
pour began. We had been used to very hot weather up until
this moment. Perhaps it had been too hot, which resulted
in this storm. It went on unabated for several hours, finally
moving away to the west.

The following morning, brilliant sunshine filtered
through the lattice of the window shutters and once more,
the air felt hot and sticky. Flinging the shutters wide open,
we got a magnificent view of the castle and the town, which
seemed to be inviting one to explore its hidden secrets,
such as the old mines.

All the shoes and clothes had been dried and items
unwanted for the journey had been tucked away in the
grips, which now were waiting for us to pack in the jeep.
With a wave to some of the staff who had come to see us
off, we motored on through the streets and out into the
country beyond.

It was over our breakfast that we decided to return to
our 'home' in Klagenfurt by a different route. We would
follow the road to Eben turning left just before
Bischofshofen, then Altenmarkt, Radstadt and the
Radstadter–Tauern Pass to Tamsweg. Everything had been
to our liking with the scenery, for it was just so beautiful
and the road was fairly good, in spite of the many potholes.
However, as we neared Obertauern, the road almost
disappeared. The previous day's storm had washed many
parts away and the torrents of water had caused landslides,
bringing down huge boulders which studded the mountain
road.

In spite of the four-wheel drive, Nobby had quite a task
in keeping the vehicle on safe ground. Some parts were
very hair-raising, for the ground tended to sink with the
weight of the jeep.

We didn't relish the thought of ending up in a heap
down the tremendously steep drops to the rushing rivers

below. The summit of the pass was the worst bit, but with great dexterity, Nobby negotiated the upheaval and we slowly extricated ourselves from the mess. We could not have made the trip without the aid of the four-wheel drive.

We stopped at Tamsweg for a break and the waiter serving the coffees at the little café told us that the authorities were going to close the road to Altenmarkt im Pongau on account of the damage. The reports had come in that the road had been blocked by landslides so we were very fortunate to get through. Any other track or road we would drive on in future would be a piece of cake. We wanted to take the quickest route back so we decided to hop over the mountain road to the Turracher Hohe Pass, then Patergassen, Feldkirchen and the final stop at the General Headquarters, which was our temporary Command. The stretch from Predlitz to Patergassen was incredibly beautiful and perhaps would be even more scenic in the springtime.

We drew into the grounds of General Headquarters in the evening and I reported immediately to the Adjutant. The lads went to their quarters meanwhile to offload their kit and returned half an hour later to take me back to the Moser hotel.

Apparently, Colonel C.D. Colacicco at Salzburg had been on the telephone to my Major Advocate, whom I had not met, and related our mission to him. The Adjutant was keen to hear the results of our mission, being so involved in the first place. He informed me that I would be seeing a Major F.S. Williamson, KC, in the morning at 1000 hours. I was advised not to be late as the Major didn't like to be kept waiting. I assured the Adjutant that it was one of my principles not to be late, in fact, I was always too early. The Captain went on to inform me that the Major was one of the senior advocates in the Judge Advocate General's Department in southern Europe. He had been to a conference with the American counterparts at the Counter-Intelligence Corps Headquarters at Livorno, Italy. He had returned yesterday.

I was awe struck at the imminent meeting with Major Williamson, for I had never met a lawyer before to have any dealings with. Nobby was waiting to take me back to the Moser hotel and I asked him where was Guss.

'Oh he's in the bath having a good soak!' said Nobby.

I arranged for him to pick me up at the hotel at 0945 hours, which would allow me plenty of time to be at the Adjutant's office before the deadline.

That night, it was strange eating alone and I wondered where Jan would be. I had a good meal and began to feel the reaction of the past days and felt tired, so I went up to my room early and prepared my dirty clothes to give to the chambermaid for overnight cleaning. This was an excellent facility organised by our Headquarters. I didn't have many clothes, so what I carried with me had to be clean and ready for use.

Nobby was punctual and as I walked out to the jeep, I felt a feeling of trepidation. Nobby must have sensed that, for he said that I had nothing to worry about and he couldn't understand why I was not my usual cheery self. I didn't know it at that time, but it was Nobby who had met the Major at the little airfield just outside Klagenfurt. I didn't even know that Klagenfurt had an airfield. Nobby had got on quite well with the Major, for he complimented Nobby for having such a splendid jeep.

The atmosphere in the Captain's office was getting almost unbearable for me as the seconds ticked away towards ten o'clock and precisely on the hour, the Major appeared. The coming to attention and flinging a salute in recognition of his rank, seemed to break the tension and I began to ease, as I was bidden to do by my superior.

'Now, Captain Bell, your first mission went off exceedingly well, according to the full reports given to me by the Americans at Salzburg. I am grateful for that, as it has helped our relationship with them immensely. We need all the assistance we can get from our American counterparts, whichever field we operate in. Colonel Colacicco was most impressed with your team efforts.

'We have another assignment which we want you to do. There is an Austro-German by the name of Wilhelm Reisler, a civilian who was one of Himmler's henchmen. He was Chief Administrator of the Prison Service, which included the infamous concentration camps, stretching from the Rhine to the Russian-Polish Borders.

'Three foreign agents working for our intelligence fell into the hands of the Gestapo and were imprisoned in a castle at Linz, then transferred to Mauthausen, where they underwent the most terrible tortures until they died. Their bodies were cremated along with thousands of European Jews. Details are very sketchy but we know that Reisler is living at Graz. He is in his early forties, according to the prisoners released from that dreadful camp.

'If you are fortunate enough to find him and make the arrest, then bring him here to Klagenfurt and hand him into the custody of the Military Police.'

I asked the Major if I might have the same team and without any reservations, the answer was yes. I was delighted, and now having more courage after his deliberation, I mentioned that whilst we were up in the Tyrol area, we had heard rumours that a sizeable force of German SS troops were shielding a very high-ranking person and that they were very heavily fortified. The Major didn't seem at all impressed. He remarked that there were always rumours about pockets of German resistance being flushed out from time to time. However, I was glad that I had mentioned it.

I imagined the Major to be about thirty-three years of age and to have swept the board with trophies at his university for sports, as he looked the epitome of an athlete. He wore no wedding ring, so I assumed that he was a bachelor. His bearing appeared to me to be a little adventurist, yet very precise and inspiring.

Turning to the Adjutant, the Major asked if we had been well looked after for funds and petrol coupons and received a very satisfactory answer from the Captain and myself.

'Captain Bell, you will receive more domestic details from Captain Middleton, and good luck in your mission,' said the Major, and left the room as swiftly as he came, giving us no reply to our spritely salute as he dashed for the door.

Captain Middleton excused the Major's sudden departure by saying that he had to be in court in ten minutes, and that was downtown! At least, I had the rest of the day to organise the team and our method of tackling this problem. I went to the central Admin office to collect money, petrol coupons and food vouchers and then called up Nobby and Guss. We all went off to the hotel.

When I told them that we had to find an Austro-German called Wilhelm Reisler who was supposed to live at Graz and was in his early forties, and nothing else about him except that he had control of all the prisons and concentration camps from the Rhine to the Polish-Russian borders, they nearly collapsed.

'That's a tall order, Skipper,' they said in unison.

'Albeit, we have an immense task ahead,' I continued, 'and one which we must accomplish, as this guy is a brute of all brutes. He was one of Himmler's men, but he never was in the forces. He might of course, have changed his name or taken an alias as Vogle did.

'We will take our uniforms just in case they are needed but civvies are the order of the day. I would like you both to draw a pistol each, something fairly small like a Beretta, from the Quartermaster. One magazine apiece will be enough. We will establish ourselves in a fairly central hotel and hope that there won't be any Russians there. Nobby, you try to find out what you can from taxi drivers and garages. Guss, you make enquiries from the *Polizei* and wherever else the leads go. I will rummage around the civil offices, library and the markets. It is best we meet at the hotel. We will have to ignore each other if seen on the streets or in any building unless aid is needed. Should that be so, then a signal by a scratch of the hair over the right ear will be enough.

'Nobby, you will of course hide the jeep away and switch the safety on. I will see that you will have money. I'll give you that at the hotel. We will still require our best map and I should draw one which covers the district of Linz, for I have a feeling that we may have to go there later. Now, memorise our man's name and age.'

Guss remarked that after all his evil deeds he should be old and grey.

'Perhaps he is,' I replied.

The lads needed their freedom now to do what they wished for the rest of that day, and on our leaving, we arranged for the two to be at the hotel at nine o'clock, ready for our venture.

It was only a two-hour journey to Graz, and although it was a wet day, we easily found a good-looking hotel which was fairly central, called the Erzherzog Johann, on the Sackstrasse. It was not an expensive one but it was suitable for our stay. One can draw attention by staying in too cheap a place, as well as by staying in a very expensive one. I immediately got the manager on our side by showing him my little red booklet, and introduced the lads to him. He said that he would instruct his staff to be most discreet about our presence.

I was given a room on the first floor and Guss and Nobby had a single room each on the second. Although it was a very old hotel dating back to the sixteenth century, each room had a bath and shower. It was good to see that some places hadn't suffered from the ravages of war. Nobby had garaged the jeep safely and had joined us in the hall at the reception desk. The page was only a lad in his early teens and looked not strong enough to carry our heavy grips, so we carried our luggage up to our rooms.

I told the lads to come to my room as soon as they had made themselves comfortable, as I wanted to discuss our plans further. We talked about our ideas and the task ahead, realising that we had precious little to work on. We had the man's name and age. We knew his background and his home town. What we wanted was a photo. Guss mentioned that in the report, the released prisoners said that his age was about forty-two, or at least in his early forties. I wonder if there are any ex-Mauthausen prisoners existing who might be able to provide some clues to his whereabouts. Nobby's helpful suggestion gained a good point with Guss and myself.

'Guss,' I said, 'you take Nobby and pay a visit to the hospitals' sanatoriums or even the Mental Asylum if need be, and ferret out any ex-inmate of that infamous camp. I'll go to the *Rathaus* and begin there.'

Nobby gave a little snigger at the name. I must say that every time I thought about a town hall in Austria, I had to smile at its name in German.

The lads left once we were out in the Sackstrasse and I made my way past the Hauptplatz and along the very attractive Herrengasse with its old façades, until I reached the *Rathaus*. Once the porter had seen my red book, I got all the help I needed to see the right people. First, I was shown into the Office of Registrations and the female clerk brought down book after book for us to scan over.

There was only one Wilhelm Reisler but he had just been married was aged twenty-four. When I saw the name appear, I heard my heart thump. I quickly wrote the address down, for I thought we might go out to his home and verify whether or not our man was of the same family.

The clerk brought several more books out of cupboards and working carefully through by dates, we found that a Wilhelm Reisler had been born in 1904 in Graz. Father German, mother Austrian; enlisted in Brownshirts in 1936, in Munich; became Leader of 127 Storm troopers, April, 1938; August, 1938, was invalided out after a duodenal ulcer operation; became active Nazi Party Administrator in Linz in January, 1939.

Records stopped there. I was elated with this information and to make sure I had every detail written down correctly, I went over once more every word from the records.

I asked the clerk why it was they had so much information about the people of Graz and was told that they didn't do it now but it was a practice that the *Bürgermeister* insisted on, immediately the Germans were vanquished. I looked at one or two names in different parts of the tome and saw similar entries. I suppose this was to ensure that ex-Nazis and their collaborators – in whatever field – would not be allowed to participate in any civil administration bureau or local politics.

Unfortunately, there was no photograph available anywhere in their records, so I had to be content with the information I had. In any case, it might have been a very old one and would not have been much good.

My next call was at the *Kleine Zeitung* newspaper offices in the Schoenaugasse, where I hoped to find old copies of *Der Spiegel* or *Der Adler*. These two magazines were something like our *Illustrated London News*, which might have some article or photo of our man. Again the reception was more than accommodating but a little disturbing, for there were Russian officers visiting the premises who seemed suspicious as to what I was doing. Unfortunately, my little red book didn't have the text translated into Russian, otherwise I would have shown it to them. Being in civilian clothes and hearing me speak in English to the departmental heads more than likely put them on their guard. The two German magazines were often published in wider zones other than the *Vaterland* so it was worth a try, I thought.

At first, I was directed to the News office but when they understood what I was after, I was escorted to their *Dokumentarbericht Büro* by a middle-aged, enormously stout 'motherly' sort of lady. I saw she was married by the ring on her finger and wondered how many children she might have at home. I suggested we have a look at some back copies of their newspapers around the March – August 1938 period, for it was March 1938 that the Germans invaded Austria and Wilhelm Reisler had been making a name for himself with the Storm troopers. I found a copy of their publication in April, 1938, which showed a legion of Panzer Troops being 'welcomed' by the citizens of Graz. There was an extensive coverage of the occupation, giving a list of dissenters, along with pictures of Jews being rounded up.

I asked the woman if she could identify any of the Storm troopers lining the route. She carefully scanned the relevant page, aided by a powerful magnifying glass, and shuddered as she scrutinised the photo. Being forty-three years old at that time, she had terrible memories of that evil event.

There were pictures taken at a later date showing Hitler accompanied by Himmler, standing in the huge Mercedes Staff car, driving through the city in a triumphal cavalcade. We spent nearly the whole day in the archives ferreting amongst papers, magazines and various cuttings. One cutting showed a picture of some Nazis on a dais in the Hauptplatz in front of the Luegg House. They seemed to be a group of generals with some civilians, so I asked the good woman if she could identify anyone in that group. After a long and hard study, she shook her head in a negative reply.

As there was nothing more to be done, I returned to the hotel. It was late evening by the time the lads returned and came to my room to report. They first tried the asylum then the sanatorium and lastly, the two hospitals and at the last one, they found the record card of Wilhelm Reisler, dated June, 1938.

'Right, lads,' I said, 'let's go over the facts as we know them. While Reisler was a Storm trooper in 1938, he had an operation for a duodenal ulcer in June and in the August, he was invalided out. From that moment, he was a civilian but had some sort of promotion. We must obtain a photo of this man somehow, somewhere. You've tried the various *Krankenhauses*, the City Hall and the newspapers. Nobby, did you try the garages or the taxis?'

'Yes, Skipper. No one could come up with anything, quite disappointing.'

'I think we ought to go to Linz, do you two agree?' I suggested.

They both saw the point that we had not gained very much at Graz and figured that Reisler was too well-known, or that he had wanted to erase all traces of himself in his birthplace.

Nobby said that it was about one hundred and fifty miles to Linz, which should take us to lunchtime, as we had some awkward high passes to climb. We arranged to have breakfast together at eight. It was misty, dull and still raining as we left. Our route to Linz will be via the Präbichl Pass, Heiflau and Steyr. Under normal conditions, this should be a super route. We vacated our rooms, for there was every likelihood that we would have to stay a night or two at Linz.

We arrived just before midday as expected and found the city to be bigger than we imagined. Nobby drove around the streets a little in order to orientate ourselves for when we should go on foot.

We saw a picturesque hotel called the Drei Möhren which looked like an old inn, which suited us as we were fond of that type of hotel. They always served good food. Well accommodated, we parked the jeep and had lunch.

It was a good thing that the *Rathaus* was not far away, for it was still raining. We had to cross the big square which was very impressive with a baroque Trinity Column in the middle. The *Rathaus* faced the square. The moment one entered the building, one could smell the antiquity. We were immediately accepted, as I had shown the desk clerk my red book, and were ushered along corridors and down some stone steps leading to the basement, which gave access to the Records Office and the Archives Department.

The clerk made an internal phone call and ushered us into a large room with high desks and stools. A few minutes later, a man came in and introduced himself as Herr Seipel. He was a Deputy Librarian and looked a studious type but was completely without change of facial expression. However, he quickly became fascinated with my ID book and mellowed to our requests. There were rows after rows of shelving, filled with volumes of richly bound leather books of all sizes. Everything was neatly categorised.

We explained to Herr Seipel what we wanted and he willingly retrieved a heavy tome from several shelves away. Wilhelm Reisler was not under the Rs. I asked if he had any magazines which covered the period from early 1939–1945. Off he went to search and came back with a pile for us to look through. We each took some and silence reigned except for the rustle of the turning pages. Steeped in concentration, we didn't realise how the time was passing until Herr Seipel broke the silence to announce the Hall would be soon closing.

Coincidentally, at that moment Nobby found an article with a photograph of our man. It showed a group of German rank and file shepherding bunches of Jews – men, women and children – into lines five abreast, as they were made to detrain from the cattle trucks in a marshalling yard.

Several German officers and the few civilians standing by were identified by name, beginning from left to right of the picture. One civilian was Wilhelm Reisler. We were overjoyed and, hearing our mirth, Herr Seipel came over and saw the picture. Immediately, he offered to have some blown-up copies made for us, even though it was past closing time for visitors. Meanwhile, we went on looking at the magazines, especially those after February, 1940, when this photo had been taken.

Wilhelm Reisler figured prominently in many articles and consequently must have enjoyed some notoriety in Linz. There was a picture of a new part to the concentration camp at Mauthausen. German troops with their Alsatian dogs were 'guiding' columns of Jews into the accommodation blocks. Again, Reisler was prominent but his face was only partially visible.

Half an hour later, Herr Seipel came with the enlargements. They were extremely clear and would more than serve our purpose. We offered to help our librarian friend to put all the magazines back but he would not listen. He said that it would give him something to do in the morning. With that, we left to go for a welcome cup of tea.

We were recommended to go up the Landstrasse to the *Konditorei Wagner*, which is famous for its *Linzer Torte*. Whilst walking to the café, Nobby remarked that there were many more Russian military personnel about here than at Graz, which made us feel a little uneasy.

Over our tea, we studied the enlargements well, as we each kept one, and we discussed the dreadfulness of the evil suggested by it. I asked myself, what would a beast of a man like Reisler be doing now and where would he be living? Most likely he would want to be in a position of power, and yet he might lie low and take on an alias perhaps. I said to the lads that I was fairly convinced that Reisler was living in Linz and working at something which gave him authority. Usually, criminals revisit their places of crime, so I worked on that theory, that our man would not be too far away.

Nobby suggested that in the morning we should pay Mauthausen a visit, which we agreed to do. Now that we had a photo of our man, there was every likelihood that someone would recognise him and give us as much information about his deeds as could be remembered.

It wasn't far to Mauthausen but on the way, shortly after leaving the city boundary, we passed an enormous hospital and I got Nobby to turn around and drive in. I was sure we would get all the information which we needed from people at this place.

We were introduced to the Superintendent who accepted our identification and reasons for our visit. He immediately organised his staff to help us with any of our requests.

We were told by the staff at the entrance to some of the wards that those inside were suffering from acute mental disorders and were ex-inmates of Mauthausen. I asked the nursing staff if all the inmates in the big block we were in had been prisoners at Mauthausen, and I was told that nearly everyone in the entire hospital had been at that dreadful place.

Nobby couldn't enter some of the wards, for the state of those in care were too sickening for him to see. Guss and I went in to have a word with one or two, whom the staff thought might be helpful to us.

Tears rolled down some of their faces as we neared, not knowing who we were but only sensing that we were sympathetic towards their plight. The hospital was doing their best to give them every aid and comfort and treatment but memories could not be erased. These were indelible for the rest of their lives.

With the risk of upsetting some, I had permission from the doctors to show some patients the photo of Wilhelm Reisler. We had to have proof to the stories of the murder of the three British agents. Slowly, Guss and I went from bed to bed and from chair to chair. Unfortunately, one woman suddenly went berserk and a team of nurses had to rush to restrain the poor soul. Some sort of knock-out drug was quickly injected but even with that, she took a long time before she was overcome and silent.

We were so lucky in stumbling across several men, a mixture of Jews of various nationalities, who well remembered the three 'foreign prisoners' who had been paraded in front of a batch of naked Jews who were being forced into the gas chambers. This was part of the torture procedure which was always witnessed by Reisler. On other days, the three were beaten and left hanging for hours from rafters in the 'special room'. The Jews, in recounting the stories, cried, so we wanted to curtail our enquiries, but with a final question, I asked how they died. We were told that Reisler personally saw them being strapped on to the metal stretchers and pushed into the burning furnace. This was actually witnessed by one of the men we were talking to, as he was made to pull and push the stretchers in and out of the ovens. Thousands of the inmates of Mauthausen were burnt in this way, many still alive.

Now we had it established beyond doubt that Wilhelm Reisler was the beast and responsible for the many, many crimes at Mauthausen. We had every admiration for the nursing staff, for the poor souls in those wards were not a pretty sight but with their care and devotion, they would eventually be repaired in body and soul.

Joining Nobby again, we left the hospital and returned to the city. The three of us felt very queasy in our stomachs and somehow, very sad. As the jeep had been parked away, we went straight to the bar and had a stiff whisky, before going up to our rooms. It was a bath and a change of fresh clothes which raised my morale, for I could still smell that peculiar odour which permeates wards such as we had visited.

Meeting for dinner, we discussed what we had found and our plan for the morning. What we wanted now was, the whereabouts of this brute and his address.

'Remember lads, he could be wearing a moustache or a beard,' I reminded them.

The following morning, Guss and Nobby were detailed to go over to the city's steel mills and Chemical Works to see if they had a Wilhelm Reisler on their books. I would walk the town and try my luck at the bus station, the railway station and the Police. I tried the barber shops and was told that there are about thirty-seven in the whole city. Surely, I thought, that someone must know him. I persisted with my theory with the barbers, for they know so much about the citizens usually. I found one I had not been to and asked, if the man in my photo had a moustache, would he be recognised? The barber and his client had a look at the photo and said that they thought they knew the man, and then they thought not. Their unsureness gave me hope. I tried some shops and to get to some of them, I took a short cut through the Market. I stopped at a fine looking fruit stall and as I went for my handkerchief in my trouser pocket, the photo slipped out on to the floor. The fruiterer thought that it was some money and picked it up for me and when he noticed that it was a photo, he gazed at it before giving it to me. He had a look of query on his face and asked if he could see it.

'This is Josef Boeckl who owns Lindemann's *Herrenausstatter* on the Landstrasse,' he said. I said that I was looking for him as an uncle of his in the United Kingdom had died and had left him some money in his will. By now, a small group of other stallholders had gathered round hearing my broken German mixed in with my English and fingered the photo. Luckily for me, the fruiterer told them that I was here to give Boeckl some money from his dead uncle.

What the group didn't realise was that I had shaded in a moustache over the face of Reisler and slightly shaded a thick growth of stubble. I managed to retrieve the photo and made my diplomatic retreat. Once away from the Market, I criss-crossed the streets until I reached the hotel, making sure that I was not being followed.

The lads were propping up the bar with a lager apiece and I readily joined them. Even before I had time to order my lager, they said that they had been unlucky and nowhere was there a Wilhelm Reisler to be found. I told them my findings when we had secured a corner table and Nobby paid for a second round in celebration.

'We now know where he works,' I told them, 'but we must look the place over in the morning. One thing is certain. We cannot arrest him at his business. We will have to find out his address.

Nobby suggested that we look in the telephone directory and I just managed to stop him from jumping up to get one from Reception; I didn't want to draw any attention at all to what we were doing.

I suggested that in the morning, we would take a ride over to Urfahr after we had a good look at this outfitter's shop. It was a good day so we didn't need our raincoats. We strolled up the Landstrasse and saw ahead on the other side of the road an outfitter's called J.T. Lindemann, and written under the name, *Herrenausstatter* with a date, 1798.

Guss volunteered to go over and buy something in the shop. Nobby and I sauntered from shop window to shop window, keeping an eye open for Guss. We saw him come out so we crossed over to his side of the road and turned a corner into Bismarckstrasse and waited for him to join us.

'Skipper, that's our man in that shop all right,' said Guss. 'He has about a dozen staff manning the whole place and his tailoring department is on the first floor. It looks an old place, but it's well organised. You were right, Skipper, he has a beard and a moustache but is decidedly thinner than in the photo.'

'So you had to buy a shirt for that! Keep it safe, Guss,' I said, 'for that will be some souvenir in the future. It will remind you of the success of our mission at Linz!'

Nobby interjected and said that it was not over yet.

We went back to the hotel and Guss put his shirt in his room and joined us outside, as Nobby had brought the jeep round to the main entrance.

As we crossed the wide bridge over the fast flowing Danube, we saw the many barges and river craft competing for trade which was then sorely needed. The damage from aerial bombardment by the combined efforts of our RAF and the Americans was immense, but great efforts were being made to rebuild new areas. The architects would have a real bonanza.

We toured around the Urfahr district as our first guess and saw several post offices. There were blocks of flats as well as small villas. Fancying the last post office we came to, we stopped and Guss hopped off to look in the telephone book. A few minutes later, Guss came out with a big smile on his face and jumped into the jeep beside Nobby.

'Skipper, how did you know Reisler, sorry, Boeckl, lived in this area?' he asked.

'I didn't,' I replied, 'I only guessed because the fruiterer said that the outfitter nearly always came this way on his way home. I asked him if he went in this direction, would it be to the railway station or to the suburb of Urfahr? He thought that it would be to the suburb as the direction for the station was not quite right. So the suburb seemed to be the likeliest place.'

'The address is 63a, Böhmerwaldstrasse, Urfahr, Linz,' said Guss.

With this very important find, we returned to the hotel to think out our next move. Up in my room, we agreed that the police had to be called in now, as we would arrest the brute at a late hour or probably in the early hours of a morning, depending on how quickly the police could act on our behalf. One never knew what the reaction of our criminal would be when challenged by the law.

I told the lads that the three of us would go and we would see the Chief Constable or the Austrian equivalent, the *Polizeipräsident*. We would have to get him to organise a small posse and in any case, they would know exactly where the house or flat is situated. It was important that we knew every detail about the place, for we didn't want him to escape or to cause any trouble to the neighbours.

We reached the Central Police Headquarters on foot and had no difficulty in meeting the duty officer. He was of similar rank to mine so I had no fears of explaining our mission. During our talk, several phone calls were made by the officer and junior staff appeared in order to receive instructions. It was explained to us that the officer's superior would have to attend our interview as he would be responsible for this action. His staff were trying to locate him.

Twenty minutes later, the internal phone rang on the officer's desk and brief words were exchanged.

'Would you please follow me, gentlemen,' he said, as we were shown to the door and followed the officer to his Chief's room.

We told the whole story about Wilhelm Reisler, alias Josef Boeckl, and the demand that he be arrested and given into our hands to be formally charged and committed for trial in our Military Court of Justice.

There was no doubt that we had shocked the Police President, as he was known, and he went over again the details which we had put together. We showed him the photograph and borrowing a rubber from his desk, I rubbed out the facial shading and the moustache, which created a surprise. He was convinced that Boeckl and Reisler were in fact the same man. He told us that Josef Boeckl had acquired the business quite legitimately from a Herr Aaron Lindemann in 1940. Aaron was the great-grandson of the founder, Josef Tabor Lindemann. The plot was now thickening in the Chief's mind, but it was perfectly obvious to us that Reisler had arranged an alias when he had swindled the family out of the business before having sent them to the gas chambers at Mauthausen, or even further afield – to Dachau, perhaps.

The Chief confirmed that there were no survivors left of that family and as far as he was aware, this man called Boeckl had never given any trouble, so he had no file on him.

We commented to each other on what a crafty devil Reisler had been.

Nobby said, 'he deserves all he gets when we get hold of him!'

The Chief realised our request that the operation should be carried out with complete secrecy and vowed to co-operate fully with our wishes. He had seen my little red book and remarked on its power.

Several uniformed policemen came in carrying rolled-up maps and helped to spread them open in front of their superior. Surrounded now by us and his deputy and the officer in charge of the Urfahr District, the Chief formulated a plan of action to the agreement of us all. It would take place around 1 a.m. after firstly getting the signal from his agent on the spot.

An unmarked police car would pick us up at the hotel, so we would have to be ready. We would then be taken out to Reisler's address, where already the police will be deployed.

On the pretext that there had been a robbery at the shop, the police would awaken Reisler and once entry had been gained, the arrest would be made after the due warning.

A thousand and one things went through my mind as to what might go wrong, but I had to trust the police and hope that our man would be taken by surprise.

We waited at the hotel up in my room, because it was on the first floor, and supped cups of coffee brought up by the willing staff. We played cards and waited. The time was getting near to the arrival of the car so we quietly went downstairs and played more cards in the lounge. From where we were sitting, we could see the main door. It was 1.20 a.m. when the car pulled up outside and a plain-clothes policeman came in to accompany us. As we reached the bridge, another car followed and we were told that it belonged to the driver's Chief Constable.

The night was very still, slightly muggy and with no moon. We passed through several areas of three-storied flats with well laid out gardens and play parks between them. We skirted the Pöstlingberg hill and left the fairly well lit area to go into more sparsely illuminated garden and villa zone. The driver informed us that we had nearly arrived. We turned up a small unmade dust track, which looked to be a cul-de-sac, and stopped.

The Chief Constable's car had stopped somewhere else, for when we were led by our driver round some footpaths and villas, we met him at the gate to No. 63a. The villa had been converted into two flats. No. 63a was the bottom flat and 63b was the top one.

Whilst we were waiting for the police to get into their positions surrounding the villa, the Chief whispered to Guss that he had informed the occupants of the top flat what was going to happen and that they must carry on as if nothing contrary was about to disturb the silence. He also told us that when the door was opened by Reisler, he would be told by the officer that his shop has been broken into and a large quantity of goods had been stolen, and that he would be needed straight away to identify and evaluate the loss.

We saw dark figures creeping closer and closer, from hedge to hedge, then came the sound of a doorbell ringing. Nothing resulted, and after a second or two, another more prolonged ring was made. This time a light appeared in the hallway, showing through the frosted glass in the top panel of the front door. A figure appeared dressed in a silk dressing gown. The officer made his statement, as was arranged, and the occupant ushered him and the two Constables inside. The last Constable to enter left the door open and then we followed quickly and joined the four men now standing in the living room.

As soon as our man saw the Chief Constable, he knew that he had fallen into some sort of trap and immediately became very nervous. The Chief warned and asked our fellow if he was called Reisler. At the mention of his real name, he developed a nasty nervous tick in his face and sat down. The situation became tense and highly charged, but strangely Reisler answered quite coherently the many questions put to him by the Chief and ourselves. He was cautioned and told that he was being arrested and would be tried in a British court. We found it strange that Reisler remained passive but then we thought that the surprise had the effect of numbing him somewhat.

The Chief told Reisler to get dressed and detailed two constables to watch over him. Guss, Nobby and I went on a search of the flat for anything that might be useful to us for the courts. The Chief said that everything would be taken care of and if we wished for anything later, to contact his office. Whilst we were searching his writing desk, we heard an horrendous scream coming from the bathroom, so we all rushed to see what had happened. Reisler was slumped between the toilet and the bath, writhing in extreme agony. He had taken something which we guessed was cyanide or strychnine and was near to death. It was not a pretty sight but certainly an end to a terrible man.

A Constable was detailed to radio from the patrol car for an ambulance, and we watched the other police bring the dying body away from the bathroom and into the bedroom. We felt that in the end, Reisler would have met his death, but perhaps it would have been quicker and less painful than what he was experiencing now. The body twisted and jumped involuntarily. An officer had phoned the doctor who lived not very far away, and he was with us in a matter of a few minutes. By this time, there was no further movement from the body and the doctor carried out his tests and declared that Reisler was dead. Nobby said that we had been cheated, yet we all realised that an end like the one we had just witnessed was perhaps the best thing that could have happened.

I asked the Chief if we may see him during the morning later on, towards lunchtime perhaps as we wanted to get back to Graz that day if possible. An appointment was made for 1.45 p.m. I couldn't talk with him any further because he was asking his Constables why they had allowed Reisler to kill himself. The Constable who had followed him to the bathroom said that Reisler told him that he wanted to have a shit. Thinking that it was a natural function in his extreme shock, the Constable never put it to thought that Reisler would take his own life, and remained outside the door; for the sight of Reisler sitting on the loo, didn't appeal to him one bit! Nevertheless, the Chief was giving the poor man a real reprimand, partly I think for our benefit. I asked the Chief when I had a chance, to please have a full statement and report ready for me to take back to my Headquarters, and that was agreed.

The disturbance now caused by the ambulance and the local doctor's car arriving awakened the occupants of the villas close by, and the Constables who had been deployed around the area under cover had to visit the alarmed residents, and with brief explanations, allayed their curious fears. It was an understatement to say that they remained horrified to learn of their neighbour that he was a notorious criminal wanted for war crimes. He had been a model citizen and nothing would have put him under suspicion. They wanted to know more, but the police quietly told them that, as it was now all over, the best for them would be to return to their beds.

'Well, lads, our job here is over now, so let's get a kip before our journey home,' I declared, and Nobby and Guss agreed.

We said our thanks to the Police Chief and, after thanking his men too, we left the scene with the same policeman and car that fetched us. The irony of the result of our mission kept turning over in my mind. I was wondering whether Reisler would have received the death penalty or been given a life sentence. For his crimes, the death penalty would be the only verdict and now he had given it to himself. That was proof of his guilt and we were not sorry. The driver asked if we wished to be picked up at 1.30 p.m., but we said that we would come in our own transport and thanked him for his assistance and good driving!

The night porter was surprised to see us, even more so as we were sober, for he thought that we had been out to some club for 'live' entertainment. Nobby remarked that he wished he had, for he was always ready to meet nice young women for company.

We grabbed our keys to our rooms and left a message, to be called at 11 a.m. This would give us time to have a kip and to have a brunch before meeting the Chief Constable.

The hotel staff were excellent, for I was awakened by a loud knocking on my door, which persisted until I yelled out, 'Okay!' As soon as I was packed and ready, I grabbed my grip and went down to the Reception. While waiting for the lads, I paid the account and gave money for the tips to be distributed. The lads now joined me and we went into the dining room to have our meal.

'Did you manage to get any sleep, fellows?' I asked.

They both replied that they slept a little but were very disturbed.

'Skipper, do criminals like Reisler get their graves marked?' asked Nobby.

'No, Nobby,' I replied. 'They usually get cremated. There are always some fanatics who might just try to dig them up to give them a proper burial, so they get cremated and the ashes are scattered far and wide.'

'That is quite a nemesis,' said Guss.

'What in hell's name does that mean?' said Nobby.

Guss explained that it meant Reisler had received retributive justice in the end.

As time was drawing near to our appointment, Nobby showed us the way out of the back door into the yard where the jeep had been garaged, and we loaded up our grips.

Precisely at 1.45 p.m., we were ushered into the office of the Chief Constable. It was plush but displayed the optimum of efficiency. We were welcomed and put at ease while he mentioned to Nobby that his men would see that the jeep would be filled up with petrol before we left.

He then handed me a file containing papers which were typewritten in German and in English. He asked me to read over the statement in English, which I did and he followed, reading silently through the German version. Through Guss, he asked if I was satisfied with his report and if so, would I sign it in the space indicated. Having satisfied myself that the report was correct as to the events, I signed and handed the papers over to the Chief. He then signed under my signature and handed me the original, in English. He kept the copy in English. He then asked me to sign his German version, which I did, putting my signature over his and he then gave me the original, in German. He kept the copy which I also signed. All this was for formality, which suited us.

I was extremely grateful for all he had done for us and complimented him and his team. He still felt angry that his man, as he put it, had not kept a closer watch on Reisler, yet on reflection, he had to admit that he wouldn't have stayed in the toilet whilst the man was having a shit! One wasn't to know anything different at that moment. Recriminations could go on for long enough, but we felt that the conclusion was that justice seemed to have been done.

The Chief's uniformed men showed us where to go with the jeep in order to have it filled up with petrol, and while this was being done, we had a quick look at the map. It was just after 2.30 in the afternoon when we finally got away and on the road out of Linz.

'Nobby, do you think we can make Klagenfurt for eight?' I asked.

'Nothing to it, Skipper. You find the road for me and I'll get you there in time.'

Guss and I studied the map more closely and told Nobby to follow the same road as we came on, through Steyr and Leoben, then we change and go through Knittelfeld to St Veit, then Klagenfurt.

'It is a distance of about two hundred miles, is that okay?' I asked.

A big contented smile came from our driver, as the jeep roared along the metalled road. Shortly after leaving Linz, it began to rain, which was a nuisance, as the wipers made such a hypnotic noise. We made good time to Leoben where we stopped to have first a pee and then a good big cup of coffee and the inevitable Austrian pastry, rich in cream.

We followed the road out to St Michael and Knittelfeld with Guss driving this leg. Feeling well refreshed, we began a sing-song and in spite of the rain, felt very happy.

Chapter Four

There was a break in the clouds which helped to lessen the rain and so make our journey more pleasant. After some of the passes we have been over, the Perchauer Sattel Pass seemed a mere hump for our jeep. Guss was in his element behind the wheel, for he liked the feel of the jeep and its responsiveness. It was nearly seven o'clock when we pulled in to Klagenfurt. The lads dropped me off at the hotel with my grips and leaving them with instructions to pick me up at 0900 hrs. in the morning, they left to return to Headquarters.

There was no news of Jan, or any message from Headquarters, so I went up to my room and unpacked my grips, had a good shower and dressed for the evening. Even after a few days of being in civilian clothes, it seemed strange to be back in uniform. After dinner, I went up to my room and wrote out my report. I wondered if it would be Major Williamson I would see in the morning, or if it would be someone else.

Captain Middleton was expecting me but seemed somewhat surprised to see that I had my report already written out. He was going to ask me to write one for Major Williamson, who was not there. He'd had to go to Padua, in Italy, and then to another conference with the Yanks at Livorno. Leaving messages with his clerical staff, Captain Middleton suggested that we go over to the Officers' Mess for a long chat about our venture. Although it was not his department, he appeared most interested in our operations.

In reply to his questions, I related everything what had happened. I was waiting for the moment when he was going to break the news about my next assignment, but all I got was a word that there was nothing new for me just now.

I was given permission to have a few days' rest, to do anything that I wanted. Captain Middleton put a jeep at my disposal for me to get around the district and do a little sightseeing. My main interest was to visit Maria Wörth on the picturesque Wörthersee. With the weather now sunny once more, I took full advantage of the break and left the hotel early enough to have breakfast at the village's very attractive restaurant beside the lake. It was the kind of place one couldn't help but have a meal at, for the setting was unique to Austria. The building was an hotel consisting of two floors for guests and the third, which was tucked up under the eaves, for the staff.

Carved wooden balconies surrounded the building and supported well-stocked window-type boxes of begonias, and trailing ivies of fine leafed varieties, which gave the building a colourful appearance. I had the choice of sitting anywhere I wished out on the terrace to the restaurant, as I was the only one out there. Of course I chose a table right at the side of the shimmering lake, and looking down into the clear water, I could see the fish and only guessed that they would be delicious trout.

I was in no hurry, but with the usual Austrian efficiency a waiter came out to receive my order. I was pleasantly surprised to hear that I could have an 'English' breakfast, so I didn't give it further thought and accepted his offer with great anticipation.

I wished I had a camera, for the scenery was captivating. The blue sky reflected in the still water and the surrounding vivid green of the bordering fields, dominated by the majestic mountains tipped with early autumn snow. The pine forests and the attractive villas dotted about provided a painter's paradise. I counted my luck to be able to see such places.

Maria Wörth is a tiny settlement on a promontory and has two important churches dating back to the twelfth century. This little gem of a place I think I could call my favourite spot in the whole of Austria, of the parts I have seen so far.

I was so engrossed with my surroundings that I didn't notice the arrival of the waiter bringing my breakfast. It was the smell that attracted my attention first, for the bacon gave off an appetising aroma. It was usual for the coffee to smell rich in the country, for the Austrians have quite a reputation for their coffee. A small rush basket contained freshly-made croissants, still warm, and an earthenware pot was filled with butter of a deep yellow shade. My contentment was complete and I slowly enjoyed every moment of my good fortune.

Farther from this little place of beauty I didn't wish to go, so, I made myself comfortable on another terrace reserved for sunbathers. As the sunbeds were still available, I stripped to the waist to receive the sun's warmish rays. I rested and reflected on how fate had designed me to be here and for what reasons. The sun was fairly warm, in spite of the late season, but to expect the rays to cause a suntan was out of the question. The warmth was enough to cause a drowsy sleep, until I felt a slight shiver, as the sun was suddenly hidden by a large cloud.

I dressed and sauntered to the bar. There I met a group of officers who were putting in some hours before they had to entrain on the Medloc 'C' Route to Calais, on their way to the UK, either for leave or for demobilisation. They were full of their expectations at seeing Blighty again and wondered what the long train journey would be like. They were from various different regiments and the highest rank was Captain. The officers who predominated in the group, were from the 'Cherry Pickers', the famous Hussar regiment, which I knew in the campaigns in the Western Desert. We had quite a lot to talk about, although one or two had never seen the desert battles; but they had certainly seen plenty of action in Italy.

The train departure time didn't allow them to stay for lunch, much to the disappointment of all, for they had seen the fare which the hotel provided. They had to go to the railhead at Villach and I didn't envy them one bit. I think the hotel staff were sorry to see them go for they could have done with their custom, as there were only one or two Austrian families staying at the hotel.

After lunch, I took up my comfortable spot on the sun-bed out on the terrace, as the sun was still giving out a fair amount of warmth, and I just gazed at nature's wonder in front of me until I dropped off to sleep. It was early evening when the waiter came and wakened me. I had gone into a deep sleep, for I heard nothing for the several hours. I felt very refreshed, especially after having a good strong cup of tea. With the imprint of that wonderful picture of Maria Wörth still in my mind, I drove back to the hotel Moser.

The receptionist handed me a piece of paper with a message from the Adjutant that I had to see him as soon as possible. I somehow felt that I was going to receive orders for another mission. As I went back to the jeep, I thought to myself that I must count myself lucky that I had at least one free day. Captain Middleton was in the Officers' Mess, where I joined him. He had received a phone call from Major Williamson at Padua, that I had to proceed immediately to Padua where I would report to a Captain Reynolds for instructions.

The Adjutant advised me that clearance had been given for Sergeant Morgan and Mr Pless to be still part of my team. He said that they had already been informed and that I would probably find them in the Sergeants' Mess.

Sure enough, I found the two, who were engaged in a frame of snooker, so I watched until the black had been pocketed. It was Guss who won the frame, making the score two frames to Nobby and one frame to Guss. There were to be a few more frames to play but they realised that my presence had signalled the end of their fun and now work had to be done.

The lads had already packed their grips and had prepared the jeep for a long night's journey to Italy.

As there was more varied food at the Moser Hotel, I offered to treat the lads to dinner before setting off. We piled into the vehicle and with one last thought as to whether anything had been left behind by the lads, the okay, was given for our departure from the barracks.

Over dinner, we discussed what could be the reason Major Williamson wished us to be in Padua so urgently. We would never know until we reported to Captain Reynolds. I wondered if this captain, too, was attached to the Judge Advocate General's Department. We theorised throughout the meal and came to no conclusions, except that our meal was extremely good. As I had settled my account and vacated the room, the staff knew it was going to be our last night at the hotel, so they went out of their way to make everything A1.

The Russian contingent were extremely curious, especially when they saw Nobby in his battledress uniform showing the Sergeant's stripes. It was understandable that Nobby was a little nervous at seeing the Russians always looking over in his direction but we frequently gazed back at them – always with a polite smile, of course. We drank good Austrian *Apfelsaft* which is most refreshing and non-alcoholic.

When we got outside the hotel, the night was very dark and we were not sure if that was because there was no moon or because we were going to have rain. I had a quick thought of Jan van Halstaar and wondered if I would be lucky enough to meet up with him again.

The lights of Klagenfurt soon disappeared and as we came level with the turn-off to Maria Wörth, I mentioned to the lads what a gem of a place it was. The jeep now sounded in excellent form and relished the expert handling of the driver.

The road to the Austro-Italian border was long and steeply graded and as we came to the border crossing, the *Dogana* and the *Carabinieri* just waved us through, which was a blessing as it had now started to rain.

'Nobby,' I asked, 'did you not get the wipers fixed, to stop that hypnotic noise?'

'Yes, Skipper, I tried to and I thought that I had eliminated it altogether. I'll have to get a new motor at some depot when we get into Padua or some big city,' he replied.

I could see that it was becoming a sore point with Nobby, so I changed the subject.

Following instructions how to get to the Headquarters building of the Judge Advocate General's Department, we arrived early enough to see the night duty staff being relieved by the daytime staff. Nobby safely parked the jeep and I told him to take Guss off to the Sergeants' Mess for breakfast. I wandered over to the Officers' Mess and had a wash to freshen up. There was no one around when we arrived, as it was too early, so I took my time and waited for the cook to arrive to start the breakfast.

The aroma floating from the kitchen of bacon being fried soon stirred my appetite and I was just imagining the delight of a full English breakfast, when a Captain appeared and approached me.

'Captain Bell, I presume?' he said.

With the formal introduction over, Captain Reynolds suggested that we have breakfast together, so we sat in the lounge to await the opening up of the dining room by the Mess Orderlies.

The officer had a file containing some typewritten sheets of paper and withdrew the top sheet.

'You have done very well with your Austrian assignments, although the last one turned out to be very frustrating with the suicide of Wilhelm Reisler. He must have been a right bastard! You were to be chosen as the prosecutor at the man's trial. However, that is a closed case now,' he told me.

The Mess Orderly came in to receive the orders for breakfast and Captain Reynolds asked me what I would like. Without hesitation, I asked for a full English breakfast with tea. The Captain said that he would have the same but with coffee.

'Now, you were asked by Major Williamson to come here fairly quickly because we want this next assignment to be cleared up before the Autumn Court Session closes at the end of the second week in December,' he continued. Glancing down at the sheet of paper, Captain Reynolds began to brief me on my new assignment but was interrupted by the Orderly, who called us to the Captain's own table.

'We all have our own places here. Please, make yourself at ease,' he said, showing me where to sit.

I liked the man, for he spoke with clear-cut deliberation and with courtesy. I felt relaxed and ever so hungry, for the aroma of the frying bacon coming from the kitchen was titillating my appetite. I was eager to hear my brief.

'During the time of the Allied landings around Salerno, the Germans had recruited many diehard Fascists to spy and to create as much havoc behind our lines as they could,' Reynolds explained.

'In the bitter fighting, some soldiers got cut off from their units and with the swift counter-attacks by the Panzer

Divisions, they found themselves on the wrong side of the battle lines. One *contadini* family harboured a small group of Allied personnel, and the courageous daughter organised an escape route with the aid of a man called Georgio Bartinelli. He had been watching the farmhouse and volunteered his help. He assured the family that he was fighting for the Allies and when he could muster enough men together, he would form a Partisan group to fight the Germans.

'Unknown to the family, especially the girl, this Bartinelli was not only a German sympathiser but a local member of the *Brigata Nera*, the equivalent of the SS. He arranged the escape route for the group and during the night, led the party away from the farm. As they were traversing the fields and woods with the girl leading the way, Bartinelli suddenly opened fire with his sub-machine gun and, as he thought, shot them all dead. The girl managed to escape but was slightly wounded. She ran as fast as she could, not knowing in which direction she would eventually find our troops, until she was challenged by a British soldier who was on guard at a forward gunnery post.

'She was immediately taken care of and her story was related to the Battery Commander, who summoned a patrol of infantry to locate the bodies. When the girl retraced her route and found the spot, the soldiers came across the bullet-riddled bodies of two American servicemen, two British soldiers, one Air Force corporal and two Italians. The two young Italians were relations of the farmer and wanted to become partisans with Bartinelli. They were all duped and paid the price, poor devils.'

Captain Reynolds ordered another cup of coffee as the one he had went cold as he was talking.

'Do you know if the girl still lives at the farm, and do you have any address or details about the place?' I asked.

'No, we don't have anything, except that the girl is called Amanda Prevedini. As far as we know, she is not married, either,' Reynolds replied.

'If we are fortunate enough to find this brute, what should I do with him after his arrest?' I asked.

'Liaise with the Italian police and get him behind bars as quickly as you can, preferably in Rome. 'Don't let him out of your sight until he is in his cell and leave instructions that they must keep a strict eye on him until our authorities take him to court,' he replied.

I was about to ask Captain Reynolds where would I get petrol and so on, when he read my thoughts and escorted me to the office.

'Here you will find large denomination banknotes; petrol coupons; food vouchers for the NAAFI and the PX stores, and hotel chits which will be filled in by the hotel management, signed by yourself, and then the hotel will forward the chits to us for payment,' he told me.

I was handed a large envelope which contained all my 'goodies' for my trip.

'I'm sorry I cannot stay with you any longer as I have to get to the UK for lunchtime,' said Captain Reynolds.

'How the hell are you going to get there for lunch?' I asked.

'There is a plane waiting for me at the airfield just out-side Padua. Flying comes in useful sometimes, although I hate it,' he replied. Wishing me good luck, which I returned, Captain Reynolds then jumped into a jeep which was waiting to take him to the plane.

I felt a little stunned at the awesome prospects ahead and for a moment, just stood still watching the jeep disappear out of the yard into the street. Now, I must get the lads, I said to myself.

The lads were sitting around nearly asleep in the lounge of the Sergeants' Mess but on seeing me coming in, got up to hear my news.

'Skipper! We must be going a heck of a long way this time, because we have been given a trailer and it is full of jerrycans of petrol,' Nobby said.

'I think we had better go to the office, fellows, and will you please bring your map, Nobby,' I said.

'Sorry, Skipper,' said Nobby, 'I don't have a good map of Italy.'

'Right, then we'll go out and buy one,' I answered. I looked around the office just in case I could find a good map but there was no such luck.

Thank goodness the shops in Italy open up early! We found a good stationer's set back under a colonnade, right in the centre of the shopping area. There was quite a selection, but we had to purchase several in order to cover the areas we were going to.

It was at this point that the lads became less tired and more excited with the prospects of seeing much of the beautiful country. Back at Headquarters, we were offered a table to spread out our maps by the Duty Corporal who had just arrived. Opening the map showing the section of Campania, I indicated the location of Battipaglia.

'Gee, Skipper, that's a long way down,' Nobby remarked.

'Yes, this time we have quite a problem and much hard work,' I replied.

I told them the full story, as related to me by Captain Reynolds and thankfully, I was able to keep a copy of that brief.

'Now I know why we have a trailer full of petrol cans and that we have to work fast,' Guss interjected.

'That's right, lads. Are you refreshed enough? Have you enough cigarettes? Have you had a good breakfast? I see that you have both shaved, so you look refreshed!' I told them.

'We're okay, Skipper, all packed up and raring to go!' Guss remarked.

With that, we left the office and walked across the yard to the jeep, which was looking very businesslike with its trailer attached.

'Before we move off, are you sure you have everything you need?' I asked, for once we were on the move there was no turning back.

'Everything is fine, Skipper.'

Both lads concurred, so Nobby eased the jeep out of the yard and away on to the road south. We circuited the vast Cathedral Square slowing down just enough to have a quick glance at the magnificent building and then followed the road signs to Rovigo.

It surprised us that the Po Valley was so wide at this point. The river itself was very fast flowing and we had to cross umpteen bridges, many of which were still under repair from war damage. Now that we had the trailer behind us, we had to go more slowly than we had been used to, especially as it was fully loaded with jerrycans of petrol.

When we reached Bologna, we changed drivers and I took over. Until all of us had a sleep, I was not going to put more strain on the driver by having to do longish periods at the wheel. The two passes, Raticosa and Futa, were easily negotiated but one could feel the drag caused by the trailer. Nobby dozed off in the seat just behind Guss, who was also getting a little drowsy, and I felt that the sooner we get to Florence, the better.

I sensed my direction which should bring us to the Arno River and the famous Ponte Vecchio and luckily, I saw a restaurant fairly near to the bridge. Wherever one looked, there were American servicemen walking the streets and dashing about in their army vehicles. I wished it had been a wet day so that there wouldn't have been so many sightseeing, leaving more room to park our jeep and trailer. I drove around a couple of blocks and, as luck would have it, one of the Yankee buses reversed out of a parking lot and I was able to drive in. Guss gave Nobby a nudge to wake him, and after making sure the jeep was immobilised by the safety switch, we walked over to the forecourt of the restaurant and found a table, suitable for us to look out across the road and the river embankment to the Ponte Vecchio. Our position also allowed us to oversee our vehicle.

We were amazed to know how many *scugnizzi* there were, trailing after the soft-hearted and generous Americans. They were such appealing kids and really looked starved as well as being half-naked. Most of them wore no shoes and some boys dragged younger girls behind them, as if to intensify their plight. Once an unsuspecting American serviceman made a stop to give a child some chocolate or chewing gum, he would immediately be surrounded by yelling youngsters, all clamouring for an easy handout. As these groups on occasion got near to the jeep, Nobby anxiously watched in case they tried to steal a jerrycan from out of the trailer.

We hardly had time to sit down when an eager waiter came to take our order. The lads were now well familiar with our unwritten law that they could choose what they liked when eating out, so the deciding was made much easier and also, it was a little recompense for the type of work they were expected to do. Nobby was fully awake now and was scanning the map to memorise our next leg of our journey.

'Skipper, here's a town one heard about so often on the radio during the news reports during the War – Poggibonsi,' Nobby remarked.

'Yes, you're right,' I said. 'The Allies had a line right across Italy from Follonica, Perugia to Ancona and kept pressing the Germans back and back towards the northern part of the country. Forward elements, in breaching the German lines, would overwhelm their positions and when Arezzo and Siena fell, Poggibonsi became a key fortified position to hold off the Allied advance to Florence. Being a funny name, it sticks out in your memory, but you are right, Nobby, that area was heavily defended by the Germans. It is a miracle that here in Florence, there doesn't seem to be any war damage at all.'

While I was talking, the waiter came with our meal and we were offered Coca-Cola to drink. This was the first time that a restaurant had offered us the American drink, in our experience. We ordered it as we had to stay away from alcoholic refreshment!

As I glanced over at the map, I saw that we were only about fifty-odd miles from Livorno, where the Americans had their Headquarters commanding the entire central Mediterranean area.

'I think it would be a good idea if we went to Livorno, fellows, because Nobby can get a new windshield wiper motor unit from their Transport Stores and it will give us an opportunity to see the set-up they have,' I announced.

Nobby thought my idea was terrific and Guss said that we could have an early night to catch up on some sleep. Unanimously, we decided to stay the night at Livorno.

Feeling nice and comfortable after a superb meal, we rejoined the jeep and made our way along the banks of the Arno to the Ponte della Vittoria, which we crossed to get on to our road to Livorno. Just one and a quarter hours took us right past the vast complex which marked the American Headquarters. It was not difficult to find the Transport Depot, as trucks were coming in and out so often, that the security bar at the main gates was constantly raised up, as far as we could see. Nobby approached the Guardhouse and the complimentary salutes were given as soon as the sentry recognised an English officer. I showed him my little red ID book and he went to the window of the Guardhouse and spoke to someone. A Warrant officer came out to us and I explained what we required. With no hesitation at all, we were shown to a building which looked like a large hanger, which was the Transport Stores. The staff were most eager to help us and in quick time they fitted a brand new wiper unit and blade arm complete. I couldn't convince them that I wanted them to forward the costs to my HQ at Padua. They were only too delighted to do something for us for nothing.

As they put it, 'Geez, it's only peanuts, Man!'

Our introduction to the Americans left us elated at their cordiality and generosity.

We drove on towards the docks and southward to the better part of the town so that we could find a hotel for the night. We didn't come across one of the few hotels which could put us up for the night, so we went to the building near the docks which housed the offices of the *Polizia Stradale*. They regretted that they did not have many hotels but they could recommend us to go to a Signora Vergone at 156, Viale Italia, which was the main road out to Grosseto. We found the place without any difficulty as it was marked with a sign – '*Camera*'. We took that to mean something like our Bed and Breakfast.

It was a small but very pleasant detached villa, similar to our seaside bungalows. After pulling up outside the double gates, I went to the door. As the owner appeared, I asked if she was Signora Vergone.

'*Si, sono io,*' she replied. She seemed somewhat surprised to see an English officer, but then welcomed me with exuberance. I asked her if she had accommodation for us three for the night and she was so happy to oblige. She couldn't get us into her house fast enough. Nobby saw that I had met with success and reversed a little, then drove into the gravel driveway. Once we were inside, the house looked bigger, as it had three letting bedrooms, a lounge, dining room and two bathrooms.

The lads had a room with two single beds and I had a room with just a single bed. Without waiting for the *Signora* to get worried about an evening meal, we told her that we would take her out. She made us a cup of tea and served it up in her lounge. There, we saw framed pictures of a naval officer and as she saw us looking at them, she quietly told us that it was her husband. He was a commander and died during the battle at Taranto.

We had a super night although we made sure that we got into bed early. Signora Vergone made us a good breakfast the following morning and we made sure that the good lady was well recompensed.

Nobby had checked the jerrycans after refuelling the jeep and was satisfied that none had been pinched during the night. All packed once more, we pulled out of the drive and away on our long journey south. We soon passed Grosseto and Civitavecchia, where we stopped for a break, having done about one hundred and fifty miles. We were very thankful that we were able to bypass the centre of Rome, for we didn't want to get caught up in city traffic and then not easily find our route out again. It was all a bit complicated but we eventually found our way out to Velletri and Terracina. We had made several changes of drivers and some stops for refuelling and the emptying of our personal tanks!

With the nights closing in still further, we stopped the night at Terracina, having covered about two hundred and eighty miles since leaving Livorno. We felt our bottoms couldn't stand any more bumping, either. We parked the jeep and trailer in the police compound and walked to the only little hotel which looked closed up until we banged on the front door.

As we waited for someone to open up, one of the policemen came to help us and called, '*Alfredo! C'è gente! Apri la porta. Devi dormire a quest' ora?*' With another banging on the door, finally a man came and opened up. I thanked the policeman as he wandered back to his station.

That night was a disaster, for the meal was well below the usual Italian standard and the beds were as hard as boards. All night, the water system made strange noises in the pipes, and a loose window shutter somewhere banged every now and again as it was caught in the breeze. The only good thing one could say about the breakfast was that the bread was fresh. To accompany the bread, we only had slices of salami and butter. I left the owner in no doubt what our feelings were, for I thought that at least he could have tried to present better food. We had now dressed into our civilian clothes and having packed, we gladly left the dismal place and retrieved our jeep and trailer from the police compound.

Out on the road again, we headed south following the coast road. The scenery was magnificent for the atmosphere was coolish and visibility was just perfect. Looking out across the pale blue sea, we could see the Islands of Ponza, Zannone and Ventotene in the distance which told us that Naples wouldn't be very far away. Nobby suddenly saw a restaurant sticking out between two villas at the entrance to the little village of Baia Domizia and pulled up near the entrance. A young lad, about twelve years old, was washing down the tables that had been left outside on the pavement. When he saw us, he yelled, '*Papa! Ecco gli Americani!*'

With that, the lad flung his cloth down and ran into the restaurant. Guss and I followed the lad inside in order to identify ourselves and to enquire if we may have something to eat and drink. At first, we thought the lad had been frightened at seeing us arrive so suddenly but on the contrary, he was so excited with our presence. Perhaps he thought that if we were Americans, he would be able to get plenty of chocolate bars and other gifts that the GIs handed out to youngsters. The father welcomed us but left everything to his son, who was busy setting a table outside. In no time at all the boy had prepared everything, while we had gone to the toilets.

The size of the menu was nearly as big as the boy himself and with a big grin, he asked us what would we like. The seafood platter sounded good; everything would be very fresh here, as we were right on the edge of the sea. In fact, one could hear the rhythmic lapping of the little waves on the nearby rocks.

As we had to wait for our meal, we discussed what would be our best plan of action when we finally get to Battipaglia.

Nobby suggested that we should find out where the Prevedinis live and as they had accommodation for five or six people, they might be able to look after us whilst we search for Bartinelli. It was a very good suggestion which was accepted, providing there was the accommodation, for the escapees might have been hiding in a cellar!

'Certainly they wouldn't have been put up in bedrooms,' Guss remarked.

It was too early yet to formulate further plans until we get to the farmhouse with the Prevedinis.

With beaming face and mature dexterity, the lad brought our steaming hot plates of the delicious seafood with French fries. We had a glass each of white wine provided by the restaurant and once we had started to eat, the *padrone* came out to enquire if we liked the food. Once we had eaten, we wasted no further time, and in paying the bill we included a little extra for the lad, which drew even bigger smiles from his impish face.

Guss took to the wheel again, giving Nobby a break, and we soon saw the island of Ischia rising high up out of the sea. The very mention of the name Naples conjured up fantasies of spectacular scenery, music and the Isle of Capri. Driving round the headland, the view of the bay was incredible. A small cloud hovered above Vesuvius but it was so clear below that one could see little houses dotted about the bottom of its slopes. The thought of seeing Pompeii one day, perhaps, was intriguing but now we had only one ambition which was to find the Prevedini farmhouse. Guss had a job keeping his eyes on the road, for Nobby was pointing this out and that, especially the little harbours filled with small fishing boats and private yachts. We passed a plush restaurant called Zia Teresa and then skirting the Opera House, found our way out to Nocera and finally arrived at Battipaglia.

'We've made it, Skipper! Did you see the war damage still at Salerno as we passed through?' remarked Nobby.

I think that sight impressed Nobby mostly, because there was still so much damage to be seen in spite of the time lapse since the Allied landings and the subsequent fierce battles, for the Germans had been expecting our troops and were well dug in.

'Our best bet now, lads, is to find the *Questura*,' I said. 'They ought to be able to give us the address of the Prevedinis. Drive around a little, Guss, for we might just come across it.'

I was hopeful, but we saw every building of note except the one we were after. Guss stopped beside a *Carabiniere* officer and asked him. It was no wonder we could not find it by just driving around, for it was tucked away down a side street, without any visible signs that it was a Police Headquarters. However, as we arrived, several men came out, including one in civilian clothes, so Guss asked where should we go to make enquiries. We were directed to a door at the side of the building, but we had to leave the jeep where we arrived at the front.

Guss and I went in and Nobby stayed with the jeep. Being in civvies ourselves, we elicited an inquisitive stare from one or two policemen, and when they heard we were foreigners, more curiosity was aroused amongst them.

The Italian spoken by nearly everyone at the station was almost a different language but more musical. It was also spoken with the greatest emphasis of the hand movements as well as with louder voice. We were introduced to the *Capo* who we understood to be their boss but we couldn't identify his rank. We were immediately shown into a fairly large room, furnished with a big rectangular table, surrounded by about a dozen wooden chairs. As we entered, the Chief said, '*S'accomodi, prego. Ecco Signori, che vuole?*'

We took our seats then I asked if someone would keep an eye on our vehicle, as I wanted our driver sergeant to be here with us. That was quickly arranged and Nobby came in, delighted.

I said that I was wanting to contact the daughter of a *contadino* by the name of Amanda Prevedini. She lives or did live with her parents at a farmhouse in this area.

'*Momento, momento, Signori, prego,*' said the Chief and he got up and went out of the room.

Seconds passed then he re-entered carrying two folders. Behind him followed another policeman who introduced himself in English. He had a map which looked rather like one of our own Ordnance Survey maps and opened it fully on the table in front of us.

'*Dunque!*' he said, as he began to pick out the spot where the Prevedini family live.

'Oh, she still lives there, does she?' I asked.

'As far as we know, yes,' came the reply.

Nobby marked on our map the approximate location of the farmhouse.

'What is there so important about this girl?' the Chief asked.

I told him that the British want to give her a medal for the courageous work she carried out on behalf of the Allies when still in German occupied territory.

'*Bravo, bravo! Una cosa multo gentile,*' voiced the Chief.

I thanked the police for their help and we left for our destination.

We nearly took the wrong turning out of the small town and just saw the signpost to Montecorvino Rovella in time to save us having to reverse back, as there wasn't anywhere we could have turned. We went about five and a half miles out of Battipaglia on a narrow road with small farm dwellings dotted all over the countryside. There were ravines and small hillocks covered with little trees. The crops appeared to be a mixture of maize and vineyards.

Driving very slowly now, we saw a lane leading to a dwelling at the far end and thought that we might tempt our luck, so we turned off the road and slowly drove to the house. To our disappointment, it was not our house but we were directed there by the occupants, who seemed very curious. We had to unhitch the trailer to turn the jeep round and with it attached once more, we waved a farewell to the farmer.

The farmhouse we were directed to was well tucked away from the road and the path leading to it was completely unmade, just tracks on grass and stone surface. There was no gate nor fencing of any description but the field in front of the house had been recently scythed so we were able to drive on to the green and park.

An elderly man came out and I asked, '*Signor Prevedini?*' The poor man looked frightened but we quickly assured him of our good intentions. Still with some nervous scepticism, he called towards the open door '*Mamma, vieni qua!*' From the shadows of the doorway stepped a frail elderly woman with a saucepan in her hand. She had heard our jeep arrive but was a little afraid to come out to see who it was. We again reassured the couple that we were here with good intentions and in no way were we going to harm them or create any trouble. I asked in English whether we could stay with them for a few days and when they heard me speak English, they lightened up and changed their whole bearing. As we were talking out in the open, a girl of about twenty-five came from behind a haystack at the side of a cowshed and approached us.

'*Papa! Cosa vogliano i Signori?*' she asked. I offered her my hand and, in English, introduced myself giving my rank, then I introduced the two lads. As she had her sleeves rolled up, I caught a glimpse of a terrible scar down her right arm but I ignored it as I didn't want to touch on the subject at that time. Her father told her that we were wanting to stay with them for a few days and she responded with great joy. She said her name was Amanda.

We were invited into the house where there was an old cast-iron kitchen range set into the wall at one end of the room. A large kettle was simmering on one of the hobs and overhead was a small clock which had a loud tick.

They said that we must have come a long way to see them, and therefore it must be something very important.

I was a little anxious about leaving the jeep and trailer out in the open for anyone to see, so before talking about anything else, I asked Amanda if we could hide the vehicle somewhere whilst we were there. We all went outside to unload our gear and then Amanda showed Nobby a shed which would just about hide the jeep; but the trailer we would have to conceal under some hay. We had just finished as it got almost too dark to see anything further outside.

Getting back into the house, we realised how chilly it was outside and thought that perhaps it was now necessary to wear a sweater.

Amanda's mother was already busying herself in the kitchen, and her father was carrying logs of wood from a huge stack out at the back of the house, inside into another room.

Presently, we could smell the burning of wood and Signor Prevedini invited us to make ourselves comfortable in their 'best' room. As we entered, we saw an old stone fireplace big enough for me to stand up in. The room was sparsely furnished but several cushioned armchairs formed a semicircle around the fireplace. The floor was stone and highly polished with a red dye polish and looked unused.

The family appeared determined to make our stay as pleasant as they could. The crackling sound of the burning wood with its aroma, mixed in with the appetising smells coming from the kitchen, brought back many memories of my days with the partisans in the autumn of 1943.

Amanda came into the room with her father and told us that everything was now ready for our stay, and that they wanted to ask us so many questions. This was not unusual for Italians, as they are a race full of curiosity. The old boy opened up the conversation by asking each one of us our ages.

'Signorina,' I said to Amanda, 'three years ago during the German occupation and following the Allied landing on the coast in this area, a small group of Allied personnel got caught, being separated from their troops in the fiasco which followed the invasion. We know that you harboured them and risked the terrible consequences if caught by the Germans. The situation became untenable as the battles raged and you thought it better to try to get the group away and over to the Allied lines – wherever they might have been to your knowledge. Of course, you didn't know at that time that an Italian who offered to help you with this escape was an ardent Fascist and a German sympathiser.

We know his name and we know that he worked on a farm but we don't know how he found out about this group and what you were doing for them.'

'*Si, Capitano... questo uomo* – oh! I had better try to speak English again, as I have never spoken it since those days and I was doing very well!' said Amanda, and her eyes lit up as she began to recall those fateful days.

We read her message that she revelled in being able to play some part in fighting the Germans in whatever way she could. Every now and again, her father would shake his head as if he was agreeing with every word Amanda was saying.

'*Quell 'uomo era un bastardo,*' interjected Signor Prevedini.

'*Si, Signore, questa è la ragione che siamo qua.*' I told him.

'*Capitano*, said Amanda, 'I didn't know where he came from, but he seemed so nice and helpful and I was only too glad to have the help from one of my own countrymen. I didn't want to involve my father because if he went away from the house, my mother would have been left alone and more vulnerable to the German soldiers.'

I asked Amanda, 'What was this man called?'

'*Si chiama* Georgio Bartinelli, I remember his name well.'

'After the experiences she had, Skipper, it is not surprising she remembers his name,' uttered Nobby.

Amanda went on, 'I believe this man worked on a farm not very far away and roamed about spying for the Germans, and he must have seen the soldiers exercising or something; anyway he found out that we were hiding some soldiers and brought some food and wine and said that he wanted to help to get the soldiers back to their lines. He said that he knew the positions and knew how to avoid meeting the German troops.'

Amanda began to hide her tears as she related more of the episode. She felt that she had been badly duped and therefore, was responsible for the tragedy. She said there had been a break in the weather and Georgio had come in the afternoon and suggested that it would be a perfect night to make the escape, for the moon would give a little light for them to see their way across country. We listened intently as she went on.

'It was arranged that Georgio would come for us about two o'clock in the morning. I suggested that the soldiers should not wear anything very light coloured but if they did, they were to conceal the lightness somehow, for it would show up more in the moonlight.

'I stayed awake to watch out for Georgio coming, and just before two o'clock Georgio arrived across the fields from another direction to which he normally came, accompanied by two young lads who turned out to be my cousins. They wanted to join the partisans, who Georgio had said he was also joining.'

Again, Amanda wept a little and her father tried to console her. She continued, 'Georgio said that he would lead the way, as he knew every path to safety, and off we all went.'

'Exactly how many did you have with you, Amanda?' I asked.

'There were two GIs; two British soldiers and one airman and my two cousins. We had gone about three kilometres. We could hear the shellfire all round and machine-guns making their loud noises. We were nearing a little wood when suddenly Georgio turned round and fired his machine-gun straight at us. Not one other than myself was saved, and that was only because I pretended to be dead! He didn't even stop to see if anyone was still alive. I had to check, but my arm was hurting so much that I couldn't do anything for the dead. I got myself going in the direction from where the gunfire was coming and luckily landed right by one of your gunners.

'They signalled by field telephone to some other units, and so quickly a jeep arrived with four soldiers who had a look at my arm and put a dressing on it. They asked me if I would take them to where the shooting occurred and said that they would help me all they could. I did that and after some difficulty, we found the bodies as they had lain. It was not a pleasant sight, *Capitano*,' remarked Amanda.

'The soldiers were so kind to me. They gave me a drink of cognac and put my arm in a sling and held me to stop me from falling, as I fainted once or twice, I remember. They were anxious to get me back to the jeep but first they had to bury the bodies in a temporary grave. They had to work fast as the dawn was beginning to break. It was terrible, *Signori*! I will never forget that night. *Mamma mia!*'

The nightmare of that venture all came back to her and she darted out of the room, sobbing violently. The old man then spoke and told us how his daughter had suffered mentally as well as physically and would, in his opinion, only overcome this suffering whenever 'Il Bastardo' was captured. Guss said to Signor Prevedini that perhaps Bartinelli might be dead, but that if not we intended to find him and to bring him to justice. We tried to assure him that we would do everything in our power to find him, even if it took a long time.

The following morning, Amanda took us along dykes and fields, over little streams and alongside small copses until eventually arriving at the spot where the group was gunned down. There was a stone cairn erected, about four feet high, marking the spot.

Amanda said that the British had taken the bodies away after they occupied the area and chased the Germans northwards. We remarked together about the pluck this young woman had and how she had survived. On the way back to the farmhouse, Guss asked Amanda if she had any idea where this Bartinelli lived now. Had she ever heard of him? Had anyone in the area heard of him? All she could say was that she felt that he was still somewhere in the area of Battipaglia.

Safely back at the farmhouse, Amanda showed us where the family had hidden the group from the Germans and then brought us inside to the kitchen, where we had a coffee before making our plans to search for Bartinelli. Amanda left us alone to help her father with the many chores about the farm.

Nobby said that he didn't think Bartinelli would be in this area because he would be scared of being identified by any of the Prevedini family. Guss thought that he might take on an alias. I heard Amanda out in the yard talking with her dad, so I called her in as I wanted to ask her an important question.

'*Ecco me, Capitano!*' she replied.

'Amanda, has anyone ever asked you any question about the killings?' I asked.

'*No, Capitano,*' came the quick reply.

'Has there been anyone lurking about from time to time watching you or your mum or dad?'

'No. I only go to the clinic every now and again to get treatment for my arm muscles.'

'Where do you go for that?' I asked.

'I go by bus to Salerno.'

'Is there an animal market near here?'

'Yes, there is one at Battipaglia and a bigger one at Acerno.'

'If ever it was necessary to have you with us in order to identify this man, would you be willing to join us?' I asked.

Amanda jumped at the suggestion, for she was as keen to get hold of this fellow as we were.

'Amanda,' I continued, 'would you find out for us where the locals go for their dancing, and what other entertainment there may be which might attract our man to go there?'

'Battipaglia is the centre for the entertainment, especially on a Saturday night,' she replied.

Nobby perked up on hearing that word 'entertainment', for he was beginning to droop his eyelids.

I thanked Amanda for her help and we went on formulating a plan for our first move. Roaming the countryside on an individual basis, seeking information as to the possible whereabouts of Bartinelli, was ruled out. In Italy, any stranger is immediately spotted and comes under suspicion unless he tries very hard to be a good mixer.

Nobby suggested that he and Guss would take Amanda to the local hop at the village hall at Acerno or Battipaglia on a Saturday night; for that way, they might be able to look for Bartinelli.

I agreed with that suggestion. Perhaps when it came to the day of the Livestock Market, we would go together, again with Amanda.

Both these ideas we put to Amanda and she readily agreed to help us in any way she could. I gave Amanda some money and told her that she must let us know if there is anything we can do for them. She said that she would have to go into Battipaglia to do some shopping, for now she had an 'army' to feed. With a cheeky grin, she looked at us three up and down and perkily left the room.

Nobby and Guss went to the shed and got the jeep out. Nobby's usual thoroughness had made sure that the vehicle was topped up with petrol from the jerrycans. I briefed the lads to find out all they could about local dances, sales, and the days of the markets and so on, in fact, anything which might draw a local crowd.

It was a great feeling to accept that one could rely on the lads to do a good job. I had no fears that they might not do things as expected. Amanda came into the kitchen with a completely different hairstyle and looked very attractive in her 'shopping' clothes. The moment she stepped out into the yard, both lads gave her a duet of wolf whistles, which greatly amused the elderly couple, who were watching for the lads' reactions. They thought the world of their daughter.

After the three had gone, I asked Signor Prevedini what I could do for him and he showed me a big wooden tub which was about twelve feet across and three feet high. There were grapes inside, possibly thousands of bunches of beautiful black fruit. I was asked if I had ever trodden the grapes and I was glad that I was able to give him an affirmative reply. I didn't wait to be asked. I took my shoes and socks off and, rolling up my trousers high enough to avoid the level of the fruit, I stepped over the edge of the barrel and nearly fell right in! I had underestimated the depth, so I quickly got out again. Signora Prevedini had been watching from the window at the rear of her kitchen and came out laughing but suggesting that I take off my trousers.

My underpants were very decent, so remembering my days long ago with the Italian family while escaping from the Germans in 1943, I stripped off my trousers and had another go at vaulting the sides of the big tub.

'*Bravo, bravo Capitano,*' yelled Signora Prevedini as she watched me begin to tread the grapes. It was a job I enjoyed for I could eat them as I worked. The juice began to show over my toes as each time I trod heavily down. It was not easy work on one's own, as there is so much of the fruit, but the end result was always so pleasant.

Every now and again, I was rewarded with a glass of the wine made from the same type of grape and produced in 1941. It was absolutely delicious. After my feet had been in the juice, I wondered what the taste would be in time to come!

It seemed ages that the three had been away and I felt relieved when I heard the jeep arriving at the house. The lads had a good laugh when they saw me in the tub.

I broke off my work in order to listen to their findings. They had bought a good deal of food, chosen by Amanda and they showed me a scrap of paper which they had used to write down various dates for market days, local dance functions and a three-day visit by fairground people. I asked Guss to look after that list of information and suggested to Nobby to put the jeep away as soon as it was unloaded.

Signora Prevedini had prepared a light lunch of polenta and cheese, so when the lads had finished what they had to do, we had our lunch outside on benches near the wine tub.

The lads had already made themselves available to help treading the grapes and joined me inside the tub. It was quite a new experience for Nobby, and Guss asked Signor Prevedini if it was not too late to tread these grapes. The poor man had to admit that he was a good month behind time this year but nevertheless, he was going to have a try, so we worked harder to help him get the grapes crushed as quickly as we could. He had a contraption to channel the liquid away and when this had all been done, the seeds, skins and stems were collected and shovelled into a crusher and compressed until there was a solid rectangular 'cake'.

Having accomplished our task for the farmer, we washed and dressed. As it was getting too dark outside, we went into the kitchen, which was always the general living room as well. Guss brought out the piece of paper with all the dates he had written on it and we talked about the probable places where we might get a glimpse of our man.

The Livestock Market at Acerno would be in two days' time, so we planned to go there with Amanda. As we put this suggestion to her, she agreed it would be all right and then she mentioned that she had to go to Salerno in the morning for her treatment to her arm. We told her that we would take her, which brought great relief, as it was always such a tedious journey by bus. She had to change twice and wait ages for the buses to come, for they were never on time.

That evening, the Prevedinis tried to show us how to play cards with their very strange card types. I had seen them before being played by the partisans and the *contadini* and could never understand their systems. They had a set of dominoes, so we played with those.

The following morning it was teeming with rain, so we were content to be going to Salerno for something to do. Amanda guided Nobby well and we arrived on time for her treatment at the General Hospital. There was now no need to warn Amanda to be ever vigilant, for she knew she had us to champion the cause of capturing the Italian murderer. We sat in the jeep and watched the coming and going of those requiring treatment, or visiting. To just watch the people was interesting enough and for all we were to know, our man might be one of them, for we still didn't know what he looked like.

We watched carefully as Amanda emerged from the main doorway, in case anyone was staring at her, in the sense of being recognised. It was still pouring down with heavy rain, so we made our way to the centre of the town. As I saw a women's dress shop, I asked Nobby to pull up outside, and then Guss and I took Amanda inside the shop and we said that she could choose a dress for herself.

Amanda carefully looked around and tried on several before she chose one. She thought that she had finished, and then I told her she could choose a dress for evening wear, like going to dances and special occasions. She was speechless, and with tears in her eyes, she tried to follow the *vendeuse*, as she unhooked one or two dresses from the rack. The joy in Amanda's face was never to be forgotten. Happily suited with a superb dress which fitted her extremely well, Amanda watched as the female manageress folded the two dresses neatly into a cardboard box, which Guss took charge of. The price was not all that outrageous but in any case, it was a mere detail in recompense for her services to us.

It was still pouring down so we dashed for the jeep and Nobby then drove us around the town and over to the infamous Red Beach where the landings were made by the Allied forces. Even in the torrential rain, the beach seemed to cry out in pain as if it was pleading for the riddance of some of the destroyed relics of war. Amanda took a great interest in the tour round, as she had never seen this part of her country. The coastline was beautiful, even looking through rain-splashed windows of the jeep.

Back in the centre of the town, we parked the jeep and making sure it was safely locked up, Amanda took us to the best restaurant for lunch. From the outside, it didn't look inviting but Amanda assured us that the food was unbeatable. As we got in, Amanda glanced around, looking for a possible identification. It was becoming a habit now wherever we went, for we had to chance a sudden sighting of our man by Amanda. I was anxious as to whether she would know the man if she saw him but she always assured me that she could never forget his face.

The à la carte list was formidable but Amanda suggested that we should try their *Frutta di Mare* dish, which was reputed to be the best in town. The lads agreed to the suggestion but then they would never turn down anything, as both of them had voracious appetites.

On the way back to the farm, we noticed the advertisement for the Autumn Fair at Battipaglia, which would last for three days, beginning Saturday, and lasting through

Monday and Tuesday, in a week's time. The adverts were all over the town. Any *festa* in Italy is a good excuse for having a good time, especially in the countryside.

The following day, the three of us helped Signor Prevedini to chop wood, clean out the grape vat and bottle the wine into flagons of enormous size. Signor Prevedini attended to his grape seed presses which he said that all the stems, seeds and grape skins would ultimately be used in the process of making grappa, a very potent liquor. Amanda busied herself around the house and as she had done our washing for us, was ironing the items.

Suddenly Guss saw a head pop round a largish rock up the rise towards the little copse about one hundred and fifty yards away, and managed to catch Amanda's attention as she came to the clothes line for more items to iron.

The two of them went into the house and managed to go right round behind the man and, coming up from behind, challenged him; but he turned out to be the son of some neighbours who was just curious as to who we were. He had just as much a fright as us, in the first instance. Amanda explained the reason we were visiting was to gather information for a story about the Allied landings and the subsequent battles in the area. The youth, aged about nineteen, was satisfied with the story and went home.

It was a cold and misty day when we went off to Acerno to the Livestock Market with Amanda and as we arrived, Nobby parked the jeep as much out of sight from the throng as he could. We arranged for Amanda to go with any one of us separately, while the others would just mix with the crowd but always with an eye open, in case of a possible sighting and recognition by Amanda of our man.

We walked around the fairly extensive market and watched the crowd beside the auctioneer. It was fascinating to watch the man and the response of the buyers to his rapid patter. I am sure if I had touched my ear or nose in any way, I would have been landed with a young heifer! It was strange that neither of us had caused any interest at all, so we felt quite at ease roaming about.

Every now and again we four would meet in passing, and Amanda would slip her arm into the next in turn and briefly tell us if a recognition had been effected. Amanda toured round the whole area several times but there was nothing to report. Drawing a blank, we returned to the farm. The following day, we repeated the same drill at a little village higher up in the mountains called Lioni. Again we drew a blank. The market at Battipaglia was the next place to hold their market day, so we tried the same drill and nearly walked Amanda off her feet. She never grumbled once, which on one occasion put Nobby to shame, until she realised that he was only pulling her leg. The rapport between the two lads and Amanda was now like that between brothers and sister. Nobby always was the tease and Guss played the pranks on the girl.

Time had passed very quickly, without any of us realising that we were nearly at the end of the week. Nobby and Guss took Amanda to the local hop at Acerno on the Friday night and enjoyed themselves, in spite of still having no sightings of Bartinelli. While they were away, I chatted to the two old folks and improved my Italian, although grammatically I was getting nowhere fast! I vowed that I would learn the language properly one day, so that I could speak with anyone fluently and correctly. It was such an easy language to learn, so musical and articulate.

I decided that in the morning, we would go on a recce to see where the fair was established at Battipaglia and how big it was. When the three returned from the dance, I put the idea to them and told them that we four would go to the fair in the evening and have some fun as well as to seek out our man in the crowds, maybe.

It was a bigger fair than I had expected as it contained all the usual sideshows, carousels, big wheels and the dodgems. There was the Death Rider, the motorcyclist who looped around a big drum and was caged in. He was supposed to be doing sixty miles per hour and at one point, took his hands off the handlebars – great stuff!

We could hear the engine noise coming from that drum, so we watched. We were keeping the actual rides until our visit in the evening.

'What is worrying you, Skipper?' Guss asked.

'I have a feeling that we may need some help soon from our friends, the police,' I replied.

'Neither of you have any firearms, and what happens if Amanda does recognise Bartinelli?'

'I don't think you will find him here, Skipper' chipped in Nobby.

'I think he would have forgotten completely about the whole thing by now, and certainly wouldn't expect to be caught after all this time,' exclaimed Amanda.

Back at the farmhouse, I got the lads and Amanda together and told them that I wanted to have things all sorted out as to how we would capture our man if he was recognised.

'Firstly, we will have to be very sure that the man you identify is the Bartinelli and no one else,' I told them. 'You must not give yourself away that you know him, Amanda. Without attracting any attention, and at the first opportunity, you must point him out to us. Once we have seen him, then we will take action.'

I felt a funny feeling inside that we were going to have success at this fairground, but from which quarter was anybody's guess.

We didn't bother too much about our dress that evening, as we were going to go strictly in 'casuals', but we asked Amanda to make herself as pretty as she could so that she might attract our man. No Italian likes to see a young woman on her own and invariably makes a pass or asks if he can accompany her.

The night was very dark so the brilliant coloured lights at the fairground looked great and, coupled with the conflicting tunes from the various organs fighting to be heard above the shrieks from the girls on the dodgems and the 'Caterpillar', drew the crowds in ever-increasing numbers. After safely parking the jeep, I gave the three of them enough money to pay their own entrance fee, which was going to a local Church charity for war-crippled children.

I kept a close watch on Amanda all the time but it was difficult not to draw attention to the fact. Guss took Amanda on the 'Caterpillar' and played at some of the sideshows. Then it was the turn of Nobby, who took her on the big wheel and more sideshows on the far side of the ground. The music coming from the organ pipes at the carousel and from the other star attractions was almost deafening.

Everybody was in a very festive mood which added to a very happy night. To see the crowds thoroughly enjoying themselves was great and although I didn't think too much about the possible outcome, I was nevertheless a little bit nervous – and yet hopeful.

I was watching the crowds surrounding the rectangular area which held the dodgem cars and the scramble when each session came to a stop, and after several sessions, which never lasted long, I saw Nobby with Amanda grab a car. They were oblivious to all who were around them as they excitedly waited for the electricity to be switched on and their car to move. The amount of shoving and pushing to get a car was hilarious to watch and to find out who were the victors. Nobby held on to the girl as their car was being buffeted by the others; they tried to gyrate, but often got caught in a jam and had to be released by the attendants.

I went over to join them as they got out of their car, and we were just pressing our way between the spectators standing on the surround when Amanda suddenly gripped my arm tight and looked across the grass alleyway at a round stall. It was one where one rolls a coin down a slide and it has to land on a big number to win a prize. The whole circle of the stall was packed with people playing and watching. Amanda whispered in my ear very excitedly, 'That's him there, *Capitano!*'

I looked in the direction and gathered that he was the man who was running the stall. I mentioned to Nobby out of earshot of the crowd to study the face and he broke away and joined the circle in the background. For all the world the man could have been Tyrone Power's younger brother. He was the spitting image of the American film star.

Amanda was trembling with a mixture of fright, hate and anger, and I had to say sharply, '*Zitto, prego!*' I was sure she was about to call his name. It would have been disastrous for us if she had spoilt our plans.

We got away from the stall without creating any undue attention and wandered off to find Guss. We walked about between the different shows when we spotted him having fun at the coconut stall. We went up to him and watched his last three shots with the wooden balls and he success-fully got one down, so he claimed his prize. As he turned away he saw Amanda and me and came over. We told him that Amanda had seen Bartinelli at the coin slide stall. There was no doubt at all, it was him. I told Guss to have a good look and remember his face well, and when he had memorised it, to join us at the jeep.

Just as Guss was turning to go to the stall, I called him, for I hadn't told him where to look, and said, 'He is the guy who is in the centre running the show!'

I felt excited now and, taking Amanda's arm, I made my way with her to the jeep. Nobby had been watching us and followed, keeping a little distance behind. Once we were all in, Nobby drove off out of the grounds and back to the farm.

The Prevedinis were waiting up for us and had some coffee ready with pieces of their polenta cake. When we told them of our good fortune, they wailed half with joy and half with fear of the consequences. They asked over and over again to Amanda, if she was sure it was Bartinelli and not some other poor fellow.

'*Mamma mia! Mamma mia!*' was all Signora Prevedini could say. She was obviously shocked by the news and I suppose, worried now about her daughter having to go to the trial. Amanda assured them that there was no doubt at all that the man was Bartinelli.

I had a fitful sleep that night, for not only was it extremely humid and threatening a really good thunderstorm, but I was formulating a plan for the next moves to make.

I must have been in a deep sleep when Guss came to waken me, as he had to shake me very hard until I realised what was happening. The moment I heard the church bells tolling, I knew Sunday had arrived and more than likely, the Prevedinis would be going to Mass. I had my wash in the water trough outside in the yard next to the shed where the jeep was garaged. It was invigorating to say the least but I felt fine after it. I didn't shave that morning, for there was no hot water available and as I had a tough beard, the cold water would not have been too pleasant! However, now and again it was quite a treat not to shave.

We had been spared an overnight storm although it had rained a little, making the air much fresher. We had our fresh bread, cheese and coffee and sat about in the yard outside, discussing our plans for the next move to get Bartinelli.

'Tomorrow, we will go to the *Questura* and obtain their assistance in the arrest,' I announced. I don't want to go too soon as I wish to keep the element of surprise. I propose to go there at about 10.30 tomorrow night. Now the fair shuts down at midnight and by then, most of the public will have had their fun and have gone home. Monday night will not be as busy as they were last night, for instance.

'I'll get the police to make a formal enquiry first from the boss man, while his men are positioned in and around the grounds but far enough away not to be seen. We will make the arrest and if there is any trouble, then the police will be on hand to help out.

I think that if we do it ourselves, there will be less likelihood of disturbance or even panic by the public who linger on.

The Prevedinis asked us if we would like to go to their church, but with good grace we declined, and Nobby cleaned down the jeep and did his 'checks'. The trailer was now up on its tyres more, on account of losing some petrol from the cans into the jeep. We agreed to get the empties filled again before going back up north.

In the afternoon, we four had a good long walk, nearly to Contursi, which we could see in the distance. I could very easily live in this beautiful country and I felt that I could enjoy the nature of the Italians. During our walk, we found many mushrooms; we had to open up our handkerchiefs and knot them together in order to carry them home for our evening meal.

That night, we chatted altogether in the big kitchen. We must have touched on hundreds of topics, from maladies, local government, farming, education and, of course, the inevitable subject – sex. It always has to raise it's head! Then came a long discussion about the war and politics.

The Italians love talking about politics and invariably get very heated about their opinions. What I like about 'family' discussions is that usually they end up with a sing-song, for after a time, most of the company are fairly 'happy' with the quantity of wine that has been drunk during the evening.

That Monday night, Amanda wrapped up well as she prepared to come with us to the police station. On arrival, we went in and I showed the *Carabiniere* officer on duty my ID booklet. I was in full uniform, so was Nobby. The duty officer seemed perplexed at seeing members of the British army in his town – after all these years – as if we were leftovers from the days of the battles! I did explain that we had been home and had returned after a good meal!

He gradually understood my leg-pulling and then became very serious when I demanded to speak with his superior. He flustered a little and rang up his boss.

With words a thousand to the minute, he gabbled down the line, '*Si, Maggiore. Si, Maggiore. Prego? Si. Lui e un Capitano Inglese dal Servizio Guidiziaria. Grazie Maggiore.*'

Banging the phone down, he turned to us and told us that the Major would be coming here in a few minutes.

We waited in the hallway and literally it was only a few minutes before the Major arrived. More *Carabinieri* soldiers arrived from different parts of the building and salutes were flung in eagerness as they saw their revered superior.

Nearly the whole building was illuminated within, as room after room had its lights switched on in case the Major chose the room he desired for our meeting. Nobby nudged me and said that it was like a comic opera. I had to be more serious now that a room had been chosen and the Major's staff had collected some chairs for the company.

I showed the Major my ID booklet and after he studied it carefully, he leant over the table and offered his hand for me to shake. We told him what our mission was about and that we had the victim here with us who could truthfully identify the man. We told him where he was and that we wanted to make the arrest – but with their co-operation, of course.

The Major called a junior officer and gave instructions to go immediately to the fairground and, without causing any suspicion, to seek verification of the name of the stall attendant in question. Amanda was getting very nervous now. We thought it was because we were in a police station surrounded by many uniformed men.

'They always look "military",' she commented, after I'd asked her if she was all right.

In no time at all, the *Carabiniere* Junior Officer came back and had the verification. Amanda was right, bless her. The Major now addressed Amanda, '*Signorina...*' and he went on to ask her what was the Christian name of the man, how old was he, where did he live.

I interrupted the questions and answers, as I saw that Amanda was reliving her terrible ordeal over again. She mentioned the death of her cousins, too. I wanted to know from the Major if we could keep Bartinelli in the cells here overnight, and I got the assurance that he would be well looked after in solitary.

It was now time for us to go to the fairground and on arrival, we parked the jeep conveniently but out of sight of the public eye.

We walked around a little and were surprised to see so few people left. Here and there in the shadows we caught glimpses of the Major's men and we had the advantage of walking in the shadows too, for the bright lights of each stall tended to blind the occupant within.

Amanda stayed with me and the lads took up their positions and from three points, we slowly approached the 'coin stall', as I called it.

As I came into the light at the edge of the circle, I challenged the man; '*Siete Georgio Bartinelli?*'

'*Si,*' came the reply and with that, Nobby and Guss vaulted over the side behind the man and grabbed his arms before he could do anything.

Nobby had the handcuffs and slipped them on. There was no struggle at all. The man was too dumbfounded to speak or cry out. The Major then appeared and told him in his own dialect what he was being arrested for. Several members of the public who were left in the grounds were keen to stare at the happenings but were ushered on and out of the grounds by the policemen who had been standing by.

Not even the fairground boss came to see his employee being taken away. The Major instructed one of his Warrant Officers to take charge of our prisoner and to lock him up safely for the night. I said that we would follow close behind. So as not to distress Amanda anymore, Guss and I went into the station and signed the papers and left instructions that we would be taking Bartinelli with us to Rome, sometime tomorrow.

I wanted to get my hands around his neck and wring it, for he looked so suave and good-looking. On the way to the farm, we remarked to Amanda how it was possible that a man like Bartinelli could be so twisted in his mind to do such a crime. How fortunate we were to have Amanda to remember what he looked like after all this time! We all had to admit that once seen, his face would not be forgotten.

Back at the farmhouse, Amanda couldn't get in fast enough to tell her parents all what had happened. She burst into the kitchen shouting, '*Papa, Mamma! Il Capitano a arrestato Bartinelli e lui non a protestato!*'

The three of us followed Amanda inside and we were welcomed with a big kiss and plenty of hugs from both the old folks. Excitedly, Amanda described how the arrest came about and now, because of the relief she felt, she began to sob heavily.

Guss and Nobby were the champions to comfort her and soon had the brave girl feeling better. Signor Prevedini rummaged in his wine cellar and brought up several bottles of his good red wine, plonking them on the table. The old lady fetched her best wine glasses out of her glass fronted cupboard and we all toasted to our success and the future happiness of the family.

We had a wonderful evening, apart from having to tell our good hosts that we would be leaving in the morning.

Captain Bell
photographed in Rome,
1946.

Flight Sergeant Arthur Banks. RAF VR.

The Gestapo HQ at the Citadel in Parma. During the German occupation a huge Swastika flag was draped above the door.

Inside the Citadel. Captain Bell's cell was situated on the second floor next to the doorway. The interrogation room was on the left of the doorway on the ground floor.

The remains of the wall where Bell stood in front of the firing squad.

Sergeant Morgan stopping for lunch with the official interpreter, Gustav Pless, en route to Milan. *Note:* the smashed windscreen caused by a bandit's bullet.

Pless and Morgan in front of the best hotel in Milan. The central station is visible in the background.

The outfit sitting very perkily on the way back to Padua from Milan.

Chapter Five

Everything had been packed and the jeep and trailer readied for our long journey northwards. Signora Prevedini had made some bread roll and salami sandwiches and the old man gave us a bottle of his special red wine, to help us on our way. Guss told them, in better Italian than mine, that Amanda need not worry anymore and might not be called to the trial for some while yet. If she was called by our judiciary or that of the Americans, all expenses would be paid and she might even be awarded compensation for her injuries.

'Amanda, you will be able to bring your mum and dad with you, when you are called to attend court, even if it is held in Rome or Livorno,' Guss told her in Italian at my request, so that her parents could understand as well. The poor souls had very mixed feelings about that.

Our stay at the farm had been fairly lengthy and we had felt so much at home with the family that we were really sorry to have to leave. They stayed well out into the open as we slowly bumped our way down the grassy track, waving to us. As suddenly as we first saw the farmhouse, so it now disappeared as we got on to the road to Battipaglia.

Georgio Bartinelli was handed over to us in handcuffs and I signed the Possession document and we quickly left the Police Station and made our way on the coast road through Salerno to Naples. The type of handcuffs that had been put on our prisoner was quite different from ours as they kept the hands much closer together, which was a good thing for us. We placed him on the offside of the jeep behind me and Guss took the inside rear position. That was because if our prisoner did try a break, he would probably get hit by a passing vehicle or one following behind.

One thing was for sure, we were not going to let our man escape. I had my revolver very handy and well out of range of any possible grabbing by Bartinelli.

When we reached Naples, I asked Nobby to take us to the *Questura* Headquarters, where we were able to give our prisoner a short break and I was able to telephone the CIC Headquarters in Livorno and my HQ, at Padova.

The police attended to our man's needs very well, which included some food and drink, and we also were given special treatment. The senior officer on duty told us that they had received information from their Battipaglia Station of our exploits and in consequence, had looked up in their criminal files, the full account of the alleged offence. As Bartinelli had killed two Italians as well, they were envious that we had arrested the man first. I told them that they could do what they liked with the prisoner after we had finished with him, if he would still be alive as most likely, he would receive the death sentence.

Nobby was also given fuel and with our jerrycans once more topped up, we secured our prisoner once again inside the jeep and moved off.

We didn't want to miss the placid sights of the little harbour with the famous Zia Teresa's restaurant commanding the view over the yachts and fishing vessels. The sea neared the road's edge in parts, inviting us with its stillness to stop and test its true Mediterranean appeal. Our journey was long and difficult enough with having our prisoner to look after, so we merely slowed down to wonder at the beauty of the Posillipo area. With aching longings to see Naples again, we looked back at that wonderful coastline and the Pozzuoli bay and then lost them out of sight. I could see that Bartinelli was now becoming moody and fidgety, so Guss and I warned him to behave, or he would be in great trouble.

Our next halt was at Formia. Guss changed over with Nobby and I sat behind the two, to strictly guard our man. The further away we drove from Naples, the more despondent Bartinelli became. We were grateful that the roads still had relatively little traffic, for we were able to make very good headway. We had covered 86 kilometres and had a further 153 still to do to get to Rome and the Regina Coeli Prison.

Our prisoner continually protested about his innocence but his feeble excuses and protestations fell upon deaf ears with us. He would be given plenty of opportunity to defend himself in our court, wherever that might be situated. He could even end up in an American Forces Court. We discussed these matters between ourselves during the journey as well as many things we felt we would like to do to this bastard in our hands. Nobby couldn't bear the arrogant look shown by Bartinelli from time to time. His extremely good looks really got Nobby's back up, for I think Nobby could not equate those features with his evil mind.

When we reached Anzio, our road passed alongside the British War Cemetery so I got Guss to stop near the entrance. Making sure the handcuffs were well secure, we got Bartinelli out of the jeep and took him over to the hallowed area and showed him the hundreds and hundreds of neatly positioned grave stones. He remained pale faced and stern but not the slightest emotion flickered to show any remorse. The British War Graves Commission had done and were still doing a tremendous job in the laying out of the tombstones and the care of the sacred ground. It was appalling to see how many graves there were and to know that this man beside us had added a further seven good lives to the total.

It was at these moments that one felt like taking retribution on the spot, thus saving a great deal of time and expense but, thank God, we are not born that way. Our inbuilt code of honour and justice forces us to act in a civilised and humane manner.

Nobby roughly pushed Bartinelli into the jeep again and sat next to him and I took the wheel for the last leg to Rome.

Lights were already beginning to show in the distance indicating that we were approaching the city, so we slowed down in order to get our bearings and to find someone who could lead us in the right direction for the prison.

Everyone we stopped beside to ask the direction turned out to be not from the city, but the countryside. They were heading into an area where there was a carnival of sorts. We drove deeper into the outskirts and we found the River Tiber, and in the distance we could see the enormous dome of St Peter's. As I drove up wide avenues, I saw ahead of us a Police Constable on point duty at a large junction, and standing on the pavement nearby was his colleague, so I pulled up beside him to ask our way. Our enquiry caused astonishment, which made the constable peer inside the vehicle. With a wave of a white gloved hand, he directed me to take third left out of the piazza and straight down to the Tiber embankments when I should turn left again into the Trastevere district, which is the oldest part of Rome. I should then be able to see the prison which runs parallel to the Viale Trastevere.

Following those instructions, we rounded the policeman on duty, who was well illuminated by an overhanging light suspended by steel cables anchored to all corners of the piazza. His white helmet stood out the most. The Viale Trastevere was a long and wide road and once we had begun its length, we could see over the rooftops the multi-floored building of the Regina Coeli Prison. Its dome in the centre stood up like a boil, which gave us a landmark to aim for. Bartinelli was at the point for trying to make a break, so Guss held on to him. The heavy wooden iron studded doors opened wide and we were suddenly bathed in bright spotlights. I showed myself and my ID booklet to the guard, who then took it to the office at the side of the archway. A barrier had been dropped which just came level with the top of the radiator. Behind this was another door, with no breaks or 'personal' doors, just very solid. The all-clear had been given and we were directed through to the Admissions Gate. Here we had to stop and leave the vehicle. Guss took Bartinelli inside the office with Nobby in attendance and I followed in company with the officer.

One of the prison warders unlocked the handcuffs on Bartinelli and gave them back to me. I made sure that the keys were given too, for sometimes, this small but very necessary item was forgotten, with every embarrassment!

Intake sheets had to be filled out with the nature of the offence and so on, and while this was being done, an officer came in from another office with a small piece of paper the size of an envelope. The officer read out a message which was typed on the paper, that Bartinelli's lodgings had been searched after his arrest and his personal effects would be forwarded on. Documents seized in an old motorised caravan included a membership card of the *Brigata Nera*. This infamous Fascist band of criminals were equal in every way to the SS and Gestapo. This tied in with the details we were given at the briefing at Padua. One could easily picture the man dressed in the all-black uniform. The *Brigata* wore black shirts with two pleated pockets at either side on the breast and long sleeves, and trousers which looked like jodhpurs tucked into high black jackboots. Their hats were black and looked like a cross between a shako and a kepi but without the peaks, and had a tassel dangling down the side which was fastened from the centre. Beretta pistols were the usual side arms, carried in a black leather holster attached to their black belts. All members of the *Brigata Nera* appeared to have been recruited from the criminal elements throughout the country, for their deeds could only be assigned to that type.

The documentary procedure was tiresome but I suppose necessary and the finger printing routine was in duplicate, which extended the waiting period in the office. Finally, the clearance was given for the prisoner to be taken to the cells. As it was a section well away from the general blocks, Bartinelli was able to reach his cell without being noticed by other prisoners, and the warder opened a heavy steel door to a sparsely furnished cell. It had a wooden sloping bed, two blankets, a table and chair and a slop bucket. The man had to be pushed inside by the warder, and the door clanged shut with a metallic echo which resounded around the courtyard cloister, made louder by the stillness of the night. A shiver ran down my spine, for it was not so long ago that I had been in a similar position – but far worse – in the hands of the SS and Gestapo!

Back in the office, I was able to ring my seniors at Padua and the Americans at Livorno, telling them what I had done and seeking their next instructions.

I was ordered to return to Padua as soon as was possible, so leaving the prison, we drove back into the city centre and along towards the Via Salaria. It was now time to have a meal, and hawk-eyed Nobby spotted a brilliantly lit restaurant ahead and pulled into the car park adjacent to the building. There were about four waiters to each table, or so it seemed as we strolled to our seats, and the reception was equal to any we had so far, even in Austria.

The large folders showing the à la carte and table d'hôte were presented to each of us and the wine waiter busied himself with his list. The restaurant was fairly crowded and our entrance had created a little extra chatter and speculation. However, we were too interested in the large selection of dishes to worry about any impression we had given to the other diners. The atmosphere appeared very friendly, especially after a trio of musicians who had a very extensive repertoire strolled from table to table, delighting the patrons with their Neapolitan songs.

We were delighted with this interlude from our official duties and for a good hour and a half, we almost forgot that we had a journey ahead of us of at least 310 miles. Nobby offered to drive the first leg of the way, so he went easy on the wine while Guss and I shared nearly a whole bottle of Frascati.

Having refreshed ourselves, in every way, we made for the jeep and prepared for our long night's journey. Nobby would drive as far as Siena, then Guss would take over and drive to the Futa Pass, halfway from Florence to Bologna. I would drive the rest of the way to Padua. We all agreed on the schedule of drivers and hearing the sweet drone of the engine as Nobby started up, we knew that our faithful vehicle would give us no trouble during the night.

Once out of the city, the roads became more empty and darker so the vigilance had to be kept to the maximum, as the Italian drivers enjoyed their speed and had the habit of driving down the centre of the road! There was always the ox-drawn carts of the *contadini*, which would suddenly enter the main road from a field, and the odd Italian long-distance lorry, swaying with its load and lack of new parts. How some of the vehicles ever managed to hold out for the whole of their journey was incomprehensible. It was not unusual to see several aged trucks left partly on and off the road with mechanical failure, or with their steering gone, having careered into a ditch. During the German occupation, they had bled the Italians dry of all transport spare parts and to obtain new tyres was a dream for the poor souls.

Just five kilometres from Siena we nearly ran into a herd of sheep. The hapless animals had escaped from a lorry which had slewed off the road into a deep ditch on a bend. Several animals were in a bad state and the farmer and his driver were trying to put them out of their misery. The two men seemed to have been hurt but with minor injuries, luckily. We had to help them to get the sheep 'penned', in order to clear the road, as the farmer would lose more by other road traffic ploughing into them.

Such diversions helped to keep us fully awake, and with our uninhibited singing, the night soon passed away and Padua became only a few miles away. I drove into the yard behind the offices at Headquarters and roused the two lads who were on the verge of falling into a deep sleep. Bleary-eyed, they tumbled out of the warm interior of the jeep and grabbed their grips. I told them that I didn't want to see them until four o'clock in the afternoon and to get some sleep. I took my grip and went to the office to report in with the night staff.

A jeep used for general duties was ready to take me to the Leone Bianco hotel in the Piazzetta Pedrocchi, which was used for the accommodation of officers. A room had been booked for me and at the reception desk, I found a note from my senior officer, giving me instructions to report to HQ, the following day at 0900 hrs. Now I felt the strain of the journey as I tried to relax and it was only after getting to my room and seeing a big comfy bed that I realised how tired I was. I had a quick shower in the tiniest closet and then dived under the voluminous duvet.

It was after one o'clock in the afternoon when I awakened, probably because I subconsciously felt and heard my stomach rumbling. I hurried with my ablutions and as it was very cold outside, I wore my trench coat over my uniform, as I went in search for something to eat. The cafeteria at the Social Club opposite the hotel was closed so I had to go further, to the shopping arcade in the piazza nearby. Looking at the shops as I was making my way to a coffee bar, I came across a shop selling lambskin pelts for coat linings.

The window dresser had done an extremely good job, with posters of male and female models wearing coats that had been lined with the skins. Those that were on show looked extremely cosy and warm. I didn't need to be tempted further, so I was hooked on getting my coat fully lined. Inside the shop, the manager showed me some pelts and after working out how many I required, I selected those I wanted and being assured that I would have my coat ready in two days, I placed the order and left my trench coat with him.

Even before I had eaten, I dashed back to the hotel to get my greatcoat, as the weather was decidedly chillier now. There was quite a difference in temperature between Battipaglia and Padua.

I wasted no more time in getting to a coffee bar, where I had a delicious toasted cheese sandwich and coffee. That was enough to quell my hunger for a while.

I walked on, window gazing, and at a chemist's I replenished my stock of razor blades, soap and other toiletries, and made my way back to the hotel. I rang the clerk in the office at HQ, and asked for transport to take me to Headquarters, as it was now getting near the time to meet the lads.

I went straight into the office of Captain Reynolds and was surprised to see Major Williamson sitting beside him at his desk. I saluted his rank. The friendly, most informal attitude of the Major made me completely relax and ready to answer any of the questions which I knew he would ask of me.

'I am sorry I have asked you to carry out your assignments in a hurry, but we must try to get through our cases, as many as we can, well before Christmas,' said the Major, opening up the interview. 'You have been most successful with your team and we have yet one or two more which we want you to handle'.

The Major offered me one of his Senior Service cigarettes and, as the three of us were smoking, he lit each one with his lighter.

'I am really pleased to meet you again, Captain Bell, and with this next case, we want you to be the Prosecuting Officer as well,' he continued.

Suddenly, I felt very nervous inside, for I have never had any training whatsoever in law. I have never been inside a courtroom! I tried not to let the Major see my anxiety and puffed just that little quicker on my cigarette.

'How did you find Bartinelli?' he asked. The question was suddenly sprung at me.

'I didn't really, Sir,' I replied. 'It was Amanda Prevedini who spotted the man. She had carried the mental picture of the bloke all this time and as soon as she saw him, she knew him to be the right man.'

'How did you work out where to find him?' the Major asked.

'Sir, we tried the dance halls nearby and the local livestock markets, for we felt that he would still be in the area, as his home town is Battipaglia. Then I thought that most likely he would have to live at home or in digs in or around that area if he did that. He would not want to be living at a permanent address and therefore, would make a living touring about. It was a chance trip to Salerno when we saw a poster advertising a visiting fair and I noticed the dates that it was coming to Battipaglia.

'Something inside me was saying that we should pay this fair a visit, and so it was arranged. It was an ideal place for a man who had a motive to hide away, yet to earn himself a living. Working at such a place, he would be least known. He'd have no permanent address; need not require references; could travel about to avoid detection.'

I was about to carry on when Captain Reynolds chipped in.

'Did Amanda go with you on your visit?'

'Yes,' I replied. 'She was just pushing her way off the dodgem car rides on to the surrounds with Sergeant Morgan in tow, when through a gap in the crowds, she spotted Bartinelli in the centre of the "coin stall" and just froze for a second, gripping my arm tight.'

It was quite interesting to relate the story now and to realise how simple an answer can be to what might appear to be a very difficult problem, that of finding the man.

'You will of course write out your report as to the circumstances of the arrest,' said Williamson, 'and what assistance the Italian authorities gave you, if any.'

'Certainly, Major,' I replied.

'You don't need to go into too much detail, just the circumstances leading up to the arrest, where you took him and where he is now,' said the Major as he gave his briefing.

'I have informed the CIC at Livorno, sir, because they are interested in their side of the story too,' I remarked.

'Yes, now I am coming to that, Bell. The Americans have asked me to lend you to them as they have a very difficult case. I have told them that perhaps we will pass you over after we have completed the next two assignments, if you are willing.'

I was intrigued at their request and no doubt would hear more about that later. I told Major Williamson how well I thought of Pless and Morgan and added that I would expect Morgan to get some recognition for the part he has played.

'I am delighted you have got on so well together, but sad to say, Bell, you will be losing Morgan after this next assignment, as he is going back to the UK for demob. You will be keeping Pless for a while at least,' he said.

I felt very sorry to hear this news.

'Now, Captain Bell, there is a second lieutenant formerly in the *Brigata Nera* named Cerati. He is twenty-two years old. He is to answer for his war crimes against a Flight Sergeant Arthur Banks of the Royal Air Force. Banks was brutally tortured, time after time, until he was shot dead. This brave young fighter pilot was shot down whilst on a mission over the Po valley marshland and the Fascists, when they captured him, handed him over to the *Brigata Nera*. They incarcerated him at Ariano and at another prison later, at Adria. This man Cerati, it is alleged, took part in some of the tortures. There is a full indictment which will help you to prepare the case for prosecution. Find him first and get him inside, the sooner the better!'

Major Williamson handed me the Cerati file to study and for me to make my own notes, for the file had to remain in the office.

The total population of Italy, and the thousands of Cerati's listed, made me mentally panic for a moment as to where we would start to find him. There was no address nor even his Christian name. I didn't want to ask a silly question in front of a leading barrister, so I let the questions on my mind pass.

I thought that surely somewhere hidden amongst the masses of words in the file, I would find some clue to his possible whereabouts. Major Williamson asked me if I had enough resources and back-up by the Italian authorities. I told him that the co-operation from the police was first-class and that the Identification booklet we carried was perfect for the job. All in all, we could not have a better organisation. With a wink, the Major passed the sly remark to Captain Reynolds, that I was enjoying my work. I couldn't help but assent to that remark.

'Where is Bartinelli now, Captain Bell?' the Major asked.

'He is in the Regina Coeli Prison, in Rome, sir,' I replied.

'Oh well, we'll get him up here for his trial. You'll see to that, Captain Reynolds. You'll probably have to get the Italian police to transport him in a van. I'll talk to you about that later after I have spoken to the Americans,' said the Major.

With that, I felt the interview was coming to a close and felt that perhaps Major Williamson was waiting for a question or two from me. I sensed a hiatus in the proceedings and struggled to find a question that I could ask without causing any embarrassment, but I couldn't so I broke the spell by offering my seniors, a cigarette.

This apparently had the desired effect, for the Major suggested that, as I had to make preparations for the next trip, I better get going. Captain Reynolds told me that I could get all my usual papers, coupons and money tomorrow, as the office had not the time to sort out my last details and to prepare for the next assignment. I was relieved to know that I would have a day or two free before going off again.

Once out in the yard away from the stale cigarette smoke in the office, I found the two lads waiting for me, as they had found out from the Clerical Corporal, that I was in with the Major.

Guss had a camera slung over his shoulder and I mentioned that it was a pity he did not have it with him on our previous trips. He said that he could not afford one then but as he had just received a substantial pay rise, he went with Nobby into the city centre to buy one. It was a beauty and his manner showed that Guss was extremely pleased with the acquisition.

I told the lads to get the jeep and we would go over to the Pedrocchi Club and have a game of snooker. That suited them fine, for like a flash, they were arguing as to who would be the victor. The vehicle spaces for car parking were marked out in white paint at an angle, just outside the Pedrocchi Club, so it was handy to park the jeep, especially as it was just across from the Leone Bianco hotel.

The bar at the head of the Snooker Room was very comfortable so we started our evening by having a few drinks and chats.

I told Nobby that I had been informed that, after this next trip, he had to return to the UK for demob. This engendered further conversation and a little gloom, for we had been a tight-knit trio and had got on extremely well together. Nobby said that we should not get too sad or he would be able to beat Guss and me easily at the snooker table!

We seemed to have played frame after frame, when we suddenly realised that no one had approached us to have a game. It seemed the Italians were not interested in snooker, only pool, or bagatelle. Nobby and Guss drew equal and I lost to both of them, which gained them a fiver each. That evening passed without thought of any differences between rank and file, for we felt really good friends. The leg-pulling was tremendous, urged on by the effects of the alcohol we consumed. It was a unique situation really, a good test of each character.

As we had such a happy evening, we decided to finish off our brief stay at HQ by having another evening in like manner. The lads would meet me at the Club, in civvies this time, at about 7.30 p.m. the following day. The lads went back to HQ and I had only a few steps to go to my hotel.

In the morning, I sorted out my clothes for the new assignment and as one or two pairs of socks were wearing through, I put socks on my shopping list, which also noted a gift item intended for Nobby. After lunch, I collected my trench coat from the lambskin shop. It was superb, and the lambskins had been sewn in so well that one couldn't see the joins. The whole of the coat had been lined, with the exception of the sleeves, even to the collar. The manager explained what I should do when the skins became soiled, which was to lightly dust them with talcum powder. With the pelts being from baby lambs, the coat didn't weigh as much as I thought it would, but it was so snug and warm. I settled the account and wearing it, I went off to do my shopping. I found a good leather shop not far away and bought a handsome leather wallet, which I wanted to give to Nobby on our last night together.

I thought that a small party would be appropriate, perhaps at the Pedrocchi Club, and would mention it to Guss. I had purchased all my requirements, so I went back to the hotel and got stuck into writing up my report for Major Williamson.

Half past seven soon came around and I didn't realise that I had missed a meal. I changed into my sports trousers and sweater and went over to the Club and met the lads who were waiting for me at the bar.

'Hello, Skipper! What are you drinking?' asked Guss.

I told them that I had missed my tea owing to being so engrossed with writing up my report for the Major and now was ready for a good meal. The lads heartily agreed, so I suggested that we leave to go in search of a good restaurant and then come back here to have some snooker.

Luckily, we didn't have to go very far, for there were two or three good restaurants under the arcade in the piazza. We happened to pass the shop where I bought my lining for my coat and showed the lads the lamb pelts in the window. I told them that I would show them my coat when we got back to the Club. The lads wasted no time in scrutinising the bill of fare and I ordered the wine. We all had different food and had chosen so that we could have a taste of the others' dishes. I remember on one occasion in Austria, when in doing this swopping, the lads changed each other's dishes in the end. The only course they never swopped was the sweet course.

It was very noticeable, and much appreciated by us all, that we didn't discuss anything relating to our trips or the next assignment over the meal. We talked about many things, which included stories about our families back at home. Guss had interesting tales to tell of his younger days before the War and the Nazi invasion and rape of his country. He had been a Boy Scout and loved the movement and remembers seeing some of the Scouts who tried to resist, being shot.

With stomachs full, we strolled over to the Club and as the table was free, we began our snooker game.

I was the first to challenge Nobby and we made it the best of three frames. The winner would play with Guss.

It was by sheer luck more than skill that I was able to beat Nobby, so we set the table up and tossed a coin to see who would break off. Guss won the toss and opted for me to go first. The later the evening wore on, the more hilarious the frames became. We were completely without knowledge of the technique of the game but nevertheless, it was most enjoyable and passed a very pleasant evening. Guss took all three frames and then, with victory ahead, he challenged Nobby. As Guss was in top form, he took the first frame and Nobby squared with the second. Guss struggled at first in the third frame, then had one or two good breaks which clinched him the third frame, making him the overall winner and winning him the prize of forty cigarettes.

As it was already very late, we went our ways to turn in, arranging to be at the office at 0830 hrs., ready to start our journey. I asked Nobby to inform the night duty clerk that I required transport to fetch me at the hotel at 0800 hrs. to take me to HQ.

It was a bitterly cold morning so I was able to try out my coat with the new lining. The driver who called for me was on time and we soon sped off to HQ. As I was transferring my kit to our own jeep, Captain Reynolds saw me in the yard and asked if I would join him in the office. Nobby and Guss stored away the remaining gear for me and remarked how well the coat looked. Of course, it did not conform to Regulation Standards, but we were given a certain licence to dress befitting our special type of job, and eccentricities were accepted within reason. I felt good that morning and eager to get off on our search for Cerati.

The door to the Adjutant's office was open, revealing two more officers standing beside his desk. I was immediately introduced to Captain Arthur Brown and Captain Reg Nichols. They were two members of the War Crimes Investigation Unit who had other territories and assignments to deal with. I was longing to have a chat with them but realised that Captain Reynolds was in the process of briefing them on their next assignments. The two were older than I, and looked far more experienced in legal matters, as I gathered from their conversation with the Adjutant.

Their awaiting transport was an ex-German army Staff Car, repainted in our field green colours and carrying British number plates. They commented on my trench coat as I walked into the office and as I took it off, they remarked what a good idea it was, and asked me where I had it made.

They were in a hurry to leave, so in parting, I said that I would be pleased to see them again in order to exchange experiences. Their driver had been talking with Nobby and Guss and as he saw the two officers hurry out of the building, he ran to open the car doors. They left with a tyre screech on the cobbled yard and vanished. With a shake of the head, Nobby indicated that such an exit was unnecessary.

The Adjutant settled himself in order to discuss more about our last mission and to receive all the relevant documents for our next trip.

'I see,' he said, 'that you have written a full comprehensive report, which will please the Major, especially as you have been able to get a report from the *Questura* in Battipaglia and Rome. You know that they have forwarded the documents that they found in Bartinelli's caravan. Did you know that he kept his membership card for the *Brigata Nera?*'

Captain Reynolds then showed me the card which also carried a photograph of the man, although it only showed his head and shoulders, but wearing his cap. I was delighted with that, because we couldn't have had better proof. Now it was up to Amanda and the Prosecution in court, to prove the man guilty beyond doubt of having carried out that dreadful crime.

Chapter Six

Once more, I was loaded with all the 'goodies', as we called the items of Italian money, petrol coupons and, of course, our pay. The Adjutant told me he hoped that we would be successful in capturing Cerati. It would be some recompense for the airman's family to know that a little justice had been done. With all the documents tucked under my arm, I left the office to join my crew outside in the yard.

'Where are we going, Skipper?' They both asked, as if they were twins, and I gave them the Indictment to read. Silence remained for a few seconds after the last line had been read.

'The bastard!' cried Nobby.

'Hell, let's get him, Skipper. It is beyond belief what people can do to others!' remarked Guss.

'I think we will begin by going to Rovigo, to look that castle over. We will take with us one or two *Carabinieri*. I will feel better having them with us,' I remarked.

We boarded the jeep. Guss sat behind Nobby hugging his newly acquired camera.

'Rovigo is only twenty-five miles away due south, so it should not take us long to get there,' I said, and pointed it out on the map to the two lads.

We made straight for the centre and enquired for the directions to the central police station from a taxi driver. We had to swing round the whole square and along several avenues until we came to the railway station. Opposite was the police station with its front facing the square and the one side running down a cobbled street.

We halted at the entrance and Guss and I went in to engage their assistance. The officer on duty willingly ordered two of his men to accompany us. After a lengthy explanation of our mission and squeezing them into the jeep, we drove off to the outskirts of the town. We came across a very old castle, which looked to be at least several hundred years old, and we were assured that this place had been used by the *Brigata Nera* as a prison for their victims.

Guss took a snap or two of the outside. The main doors had been blown away by bombs or shellfire during the German retreat. Taking great care against falling masonry, we went inside the prison on a tour of the main building and the dark dank dungeons. What a dreadful place it was! Everywhere, the air stank of stale urine.

Following the story of the airman, I wanted to see the other two prisons where, under the *Brigata Nera*, the poor man underwent the horrific tortures. We drove to Adria and looked that prison over and then went on to Ariano nel Polesine. At the latter, we slowly went from room to room. The wooden door to one room still had burn marks which looked like those made by stubbing cigarette ends. We suspected that it was this door that the poor man had been trussed up to and had his armpits burnt by the lighted cigarette ends.

'Skipper! Come and have a look at this,' came a call from Nobby, who had been wandering from room to room.

He was standing in a fairly large room with no windows. In the centre was a wooden table covered in dust, with one leg left at a crazy angle.

'Could that be the table the airman was tied spread-eagled to, and those two women carried out that horrific torture? Thank God they were caught! It is a pity they were not shot instead of being given life with hard labour!' said Nobby, who was incensed over the story.

We had seen enough and the stench was becoming nauseating, so we returned to the *Carabinieri* headquarters. It was a relief to have their co-operation, and they willingly allowed us to look through their files from the autumn of 1944 to the end of the year.

We found numerous entries of partisans who had been arrested and passed over to the *Brigata Nera*. Who knows what had become of them? Like the SS and the Gestapo, the *Brigata Nera* had overriding command and complete freedom to do what they liked. It was very noticeable that the present *Carabinieri* were very ashamed of their soldiers under Badoglio, for they were all Fascist fanatics.

'We've got to find out what the Christian name is, for Cerati is a fairly popular name,' I said to the lads.

Guss said, 'I fancy going back to the castle again with the police to make a thorough search of the dungeons in case we find a date or initial or something which the poor inmate had scratched to gain help.'

Guss was sincere in his remark but a thought struck me that if the two women were serving life, they would still be in prison and would therefore, be available for questioning.

I guessed that they would be at the Women's Prison outside Padua and I asked the senior officer to ring through for me to find out. Having no names to go on, we had to rely on the nature of their sentence, which would be recorded in the Prison Register.

There was a long wait, and hearing the officer at our end getting very angry and shouting down the phone when he at last heard someone at the other end talking, it was obvious to us that those at the prison's Administration Block were far from co-operative. When the verbal fury had died down and the earpiece replaced, we understood that the two women were there. I discussed this with the lads and we decided to go back to Padua and visit the Women's Prison.

The *Carabinieri* asked us to let them know what the result was as we left them, and we thought that they were genuinely interested as they were very helpful and courteous.

The huge almost medieval-type prison had a small drawbridge before the enormous iron studded arched wooden gates, which remained shut whilst we rested on top of the drawbridge. We expected the bridge to collapse beneath us as it didn't look safe. With eerie creaks, the doors opened and we drove into a cobblestone yard. It was semicircular, with a door to the left and another to the right. We stopped dead just inside, not knowing which door would accept us into the compound proper.

A peculiar looking man came from a small door set into the big one on our left, and demanded to see our documents. I showed him my ID booklet and Guss whispered that he was sure the man couldn't read! He handed me back my booklet and waved us towards the left-hand door, which opened as we approached with the jeep. The Administration Buildings formed a square around a courtyard which was just big enough for Nobby to swing the jeep and trailer round to face the way we came in.

The Prison Governor was a tall slender woman with a very pleasant face but, as was to be expected, she was very officious. We made our quick judgment of her by the way she dismissed her staff. She offered us the Spartan accommodation and wasted no time in asking us what it was we required.

Presenting her with my ID booklet, I told her that I wished to interview the two women who were convicted for war crimes against Allied servicemen and had, to our knowledge, also committed many crimes against their own countrymen. Nodding her head in agreement, the

Governor phoned her instructions to a subordinate and proceeded to ask us how we found out that the two women were at this prison. We told her that we had received full co-operation from the police at Rovigo.

'We are having great trouble with the two of them,' the Governor told us. 'They continually fight with the other inmates and have attempted to kill two of my warders, just before Christmas last year. I have made arrangements for one of them to be transferred to a safer place outside Verona.'

The phone rang and it was our okay that the scene had been set for our interrogation. The Governor led us down narrow passages through umpteen doors, which required unlocking and re-locking as we went through in file. Finally, we came to a room which was split into two halves by a three-foot wall, above which was an iron grille covered with a huge sheet of plate glass.

From a sitting position, at head height there was a section of louvered glass which one could talk through. A bench had been placed for us to sit on. The woman prisoner whom we wished to interview was brought in guarded by two sturdy women warders, who made the prisoner sit on a single chair in front of us. The Governor told the woman that if she answered our questions to our satisfaction, she would receive some special privileges. What those special privileges would mean was not our business and for sure, I was not going to give her any special favours.

She looked the most revolting woman I had seen for a long time. She had long black matted hair and appeared to be wearing hardly anything at all under her prison uniform, a striped blue-grey calico dress. I asked Guss to ask the woman if she would give me the name of the officer who was in charge of the prisons at Rovigo, Adria and Ariano nel

Polesine. She looked up at me but pretended to know nothing.

I then began to tease her. I asked if she enjoyed her days at Adria and Ariano Polesine with the *Brigata Nera*. This brought an instant reaction. I then created a mental picture of the men who commanded those prisons and how sexy they looked in their smart uniforms, how young and virile. Poor Guss had a job to keep up with the interpreting.

'They must have wanted lots of female company, and as they had complete freedom, your attentions to their sexual needs would bring you rich rewards,' I suggested.

She didn't mind one little bit about the questions that I put to her.

'Go to it, Skipper. She is beginning to warm up now,' remarked Nobby.

'If one doesn't have some fun amongst men, then life is rather dull isn't it?' said the woman.

'You cannot get any sex here with men, can you? So you have to create your fantasies, with your lustful memories. Do you remember the young officer who was in charge of the prison? He was really a special man, so handsome and full of vitality, remember him?' I said, teasing her, although she didn't realise it.

'You have the wrong guy, Mister, for the Governor of that prison was a puny man. I tried to have sex with Emilio Cerati but he was no good, so we left him alone,' she said.

'Did he enjoy watching your prisoners squeal when they were being tortured,' I asked her through Guss.

'*Si*,' came the quick reply. 'Do you remember the English airman you played with? Was Emilio in the room at the time of your enjoyment?'

The woman looked straight at me and like a witch, she yelled out that she would like to have me alone and began scratching her crotch. The two wardresses grabbed the prisoner's arms and yanked her off the chair and pulled her outside the room. I was grateful to have that barrier between us.

At least, now we had the Christian name and it remained for us to find out where he was now. Her admission that prisoners had been tortured and that Cerati watched on occasions, gave us more information to work on. A few minutes later, the door opened again on the other side of the room and the second prisoner was brought in to be questioned by us.

'*Dunque*,' said Guss as he opened the interrogation. The woman was in complete contrast to the former. This one was hefty and clean and with short hair. She smoked with the cigarette dangling in her mouth. She eyed us all, whereas the other one just glued her eyes on me. This one appeared to be on drugs, as she took everything very light-heartedly.

Guss now teased the woman still further with fantasy pictures of those days, with sexy young men at the various prisons, especially at Adria and Ariano. He could see that he was getting her all worked up.

'Men!' she said, 'they only like it when you are rough with them!'

'Did you like those days with the men of the *Brigata Nera*,' I asked.

'I enjoyed my days with anyone I could get hold of at Ariano, Adria, Rovigo, Venice or Bologna for that matter. We had special fun at Rovigo, for, that was where the Command kept their foreign prisoners before they were disposed of,' she told me.

I felt sick with anger at those callous remarks and the filthy way they flowed out of her mouth.

It wasn't hard for us to imagine what those two women must have been like amongst the defenceless prisoners and to what extent their sufferings had been. With Flight Sergeant Banks, we knew but what might have happened to the many many more prisoners who went through their doors.

I quickly asked her, in my best Italian, where Emilio Cerati lived. '*Lui! Era un giocattolo poverello! Un vero bambino!*' she explained. She then jumped up and made for the door. The two guards grabbed her arms at the door and as one unlocked it; the prisoner turned to eye us once more and was led away out of sight. We left the room too, but much more comfortably!

Thanking the Governor of the prison for her assistance, we left and hoped that it would be the last visit to that awful place. We returned to Rovigo and called on the *Questura*, who kept better records. They were extremely helpful and found for us a Register of Members of the Fascist Party for the whole of the area, which included Venice, Verona, Modena, Bologna and Ravenna. It was quite a book. We turned the pages with eager anticipation of finding the name of Emilio Cerati and there it was, with the address at Alessandria. I asked if that would be his real address, and he affirmed it would be, as the Fascists would check in order to verify if other members of his or her family were members of the Party too.

With grateful thanks, we left the station and found our way out of the town and headed towards Milan. Just about ten kilometres outside Rovigo, we saw a hotel, for that was the wording painted on the side of the building. As we got up to it, we realised that it was more of an inn than a hotel.

It was a good job we had taken the chance to have our lunch before returning to Padua before visiting the prison, otherwise we would be starving by now. As Nobby drew into the car park at the back of the building, for the front stood right on the roadside, the smells coming from the kitchen were very appetising. The car park was fairly full of cars which made us wonder if they were belonging to guests who were staying at the inn, or just for the food.

However, undaunted, we went in and found a little window to a tiny office at the end of a small hallway. Just above the window was a gong, which Guss struck. A young child of about ten years old ran into us and yelled, *'Mamma, vieni qua! C'e gente!'*

The youngster looked at us, not knowing quite what nationality we were but certain that we were not Italians, and brazenly asked if we were English.

One could see that the lad had been well inducted into the life of running a good restaurant with the added business from the sleeping accommodation. While we were waiting to speak with the youngster's mother, I asked Nobby and Guss if it would suit them to stay here. And as they looked into the dining room, they quickly said yes.

Thank goodness there were rooms for us and we quickly got our grips from the jeep and after locking it up safely, we were shown to our respective rooms, which looked out on to the car park. That perhaps was better than having rooms which faced the main road.

After washing off the dirt of the day, we made our way downstairs and were shown to a table which had been cleared and reset for us three.

Their speciality seemed to be Spaghetti Bolognese, so as we all liked it, we chose that and we ordered Lambrusco wine to go with it. On the other side of the house, opposite the dining room as such, was the bar, better known as the drinking room; so after our meal, we joined the locals and during the later hours met some British troops from Padua, who were transporting heavy tanks and machinery to Milan.

We had a great evening, ending up with the squaddies and their NCOs joining in with the Italians in a sing-song. The rendering of 'Catari' would have turned Caruso in his grave, but amongst the Italians, one or two voices would have been accepted for radio.

If the room had been less filled with cigarette and tobacco smoke, perhaps the 'choir' would have had a better chance. The military convoy moved off and left us alone with the jovial locals. As the wine was now starting to take effect and we had reached a reasonable time to call it a day, we gave the drinkers our salutations and made our way upstairs.

To our astonishment, we were welcomed the following morning with a bacon and egg breakfast. Each had an individual small frying pan type of dish which the bacon and eggs had been cooked in, and fresh cobs of bread. Over our meal, Nobby had brought in the map so that we could plan our route. I suggested that we should go and visit my old friends Signor and Signora Ferrari at Fontanellato, the couple who had looked after me after we escaped from Prison Camp in 1943.

The lads jumped at the idea and I was anxious to see my old friends again, especially as Guss had his camera and could take some good snaps.

We took the road to Ferrara, then on to Modena, discovering that we would have to pass Parma. I suggested to the lads that we stop there, as it was at the Citadel in Parma where I was taken when I was recaptured by the Fascists and put into the hands of the SS and Gestapo. As we were so near to the place, I wanted to take some photographs which would help me with my book. They thought that it was a great idea and willingly agreed.

When we arrived at Parma, we asked one or two locals for directions to the Citadel. This perplexed them somewhat until I mentioned the old fortress which was the SS and Gestapo Headquarters. Then they knew of it and warned us that it was ill-omened.

On previous trips, I had revealed little bits of my experiences when I was with the partisans in 1943 and the subsequent incarceration with the SS, so the lads were prepared for what was to come. We eventually found the dreadful place and left the jeep on the roadway, before the bridge. It was a solid stone affair, spanning a wide moat filled with stinking water. Guss lent me his camera so that I could take the photos which would suit me best for my records.

I pointed out to them where the huge Swastika flag had hung over the entrance and what fear it gave us prisoners as we passed underneath.

The two thick wooden doors were shut but one had a personal door set into it, through which we could enter an alley. The arched alley ran for about sixty feet. There were two doors to our left and two doors to our right. The second to our right nearest to the courtyard opened into the interrogation room. Nobby examined the other doors which he found locked and stopped beside us at the only door open. I mentioned that this was the room which I could remember going into but could not remember coming out of.

'So this is where the bastards pulled your teeth out, Skipper,' said Guss.

There was a pause for a moment as I couldn't answer straight away. That moment came flooding back.

'Yes, Guss and Nobby, this is the room and that is where they had the chair,' I said.

The two of them could see the bolts still embedded in the concrete floor which had held the chair in place.

We walked out and into the big courtyard. Quite a bit of the citadel had been damaged by either our bombing or shellfire in our forces' advance, but there was still enough of the place to see the cell block, although the stairs had been blasted away. The wall which victims were placed against to be shot was partly standing, so I took a photo of that as well as the position of my cell and the infamous torture room.

The lads couldn't get over the fact of how inhuman the Germans were. The sheds where hundreds of foreign and Italian prisoners – men, women and children – were herded until they were eliminated at the SS soldiers' pleasure made Nobby vomit, and Guss kindly helped him away from that wretched scene. Little did they know that, as they turned to walk away, they were treading on the mound of the mass grave which engulfed the bodies to be covered in lime.

That stench remains in my memory to this day. I felt a cold shiver as I stood where that poor Italian had been shot and where I had stood in front of the firing squad on that evil day in 1943. I looked again at the window of my cell and just as so many horrible memories came flooding back, Guss came and pulled me away asking, 'Are you all right, Skipper?'

Guss well understood my feelings and the reasons why I wanted to see the place again and said how fortuitous it was that we were able to take some snaps for posterity.

We joined Nobby again at the jeep and saw that he was okay once more. As we had seen enough, we didn't look back as Nobby slewed the vehicle round and headed back into the city centre to find the road out to Milan.

Guss found where Fontanellato was on the map and asked if we were going to visit that place as well. I told the lads that we had better get our job done first and then we will visit my old *contadini* friends and to see the prison camp where we escaped from. Who knows, we might even be able to meet up with some of my old partisan friends.

We stopped for lunch at Fidenza and motored on, this time non-stop until we arrived at Milan. It was an enormous city, and it seemed to us to be the biggest we had seen so far. We had to stop many times to ask the way into the centre and eventually, we came across the main railway station at the head of a large square. Nobby had to be careful that the wheels of the trailer didn't get caught in the tramlines, for the trams appeared to go along most of the main avenues and streets. We found a very good-looking hotel in the square and stopped right outside. There was no bother getting rooms, as the receptionist told us that business was very bad. Our presence created some interest, which brought good service. Our grips were taken from the jeep by two youngsters in hotel livery and taken to our rooms. We each had single rooms on the second floor overlooking the piazza.

Although it was late in the afternoon, we went in search of the main *Questura* offices and found them in Via Fatebenefratelli.

They had quite a set-up there and were very busy, but we were able to reach the office we required with no difficulty. My ID booklet stirred things up still further and their willingness to assist in our enquiries was extremely good.

Guided by a policeman in civilian clothes, we were led along clean terrazzo paved corridors, one after the other, until we stopped outside an office marked *Colonello W.A. Verzocchi*. The policeman knocked and we were ushered in, to be met by an extremely well-dressed middle-aged man in civilian clothes. We had expected to find a man in uniform. The policeman placed some chairs for us and remained in the room, standing behind near the door. In perfect English, he asked if he might see my ID booklet, which he had heard about.

'News travels fast,' I said as I handed it over to him.

He smiled and said that the desk had phoned him and told him that I was on my way to his office.

The Colonel asked me to tell him the story about Cerati. I related enough to get him on our side and to obtain his full co-operation in my endeavours to find Cerati. I was not at all interested in the fineries of police protocol but determined to keep the conversation purely on the matter in hand. The Colonel read my message and, luckily for me, tuned into my wavelength.

He made a phone call to one office, then another and a third, and then returned to us to ask what sort of transport did we have and how did we get fuel and where did we stay. Halfway through answering him, knocks came on the door and various people entered, each with pieces of paper in their hands.

As a result of all the movement between offices, we were informed that an Emilio Cerati lives with his family at a council flat at Alessandria, which was ninety kilometres from here.

'He was a member of the Fascist Party from 1941 and joined the *Brigata Nera* in June, 1942. He was promoted to Second Lieutenant in January, 1943. The flats are situated near the Stadium off the Viale Teresa,' said the Colonel, and went on to say that Cerati knew that the law was catching him up, as they had him inside for causing a disturbance, but he got off with a fine. It came out in court that he had been a member of the *Brigata Nera*.

Colonel Verzocchi received more messages from his police staff and soon had his desk covered with pieces of paper, each with cryptic messages scrawled in ink and pencil.

'When do you wish to pick him up?' asked the Colonel.

'I think I would like to make the arrest in the early hours of the day after tomorrow. I believe that at about 0400 hours is the best time,' I said. 'Everyone is fast asleep at that hour, usually.' I gave him my reasons and suddenly he excused himself because of an interruption.

'I have a message here from our force in Alessandria, to say that most likely Emilio Cerati will put up an armed fight before he is taken. Apparently, he and his family have constantly warned the neighbours that one day, should the law catch up with him, he would put up an armed resistance.'

I told the Colonel that under no circumstances did I want the man wounded or killed, and said, 'I will be here at your car park at precisely 0300 hours.'

'That should do fine, and I will arrange to have enough men and I will lead the convoy,' the Colonel stated. 'When we get there, we will be joined by a section of the Alessandria Police and I will disperse the men around the flats. We must be sure that he doesn't escape nor put the neighbours in danger.'

'Where will you take him after his arrest,' I asked.

'I will be getting him in at the main prison in Milan.'

The Colonel picked up the phone again and gave his orders to his subordinate at the other end. Satisfied that so far things were working well towards our goal, we departed and returned to the hotel.

The following day, I joined the lads for breakfast and they said that they would like to go into the city to have a look round. That was fine with me, for I wanted to get some letters written and to have a look at the city on my own for a change. We agreed to meet at the hotel for the evening meal. As they were leaving, I warned them to watch their money and the camera, for the street urchins were most clever in pickpocketing, and that applied to the more grown-up characters, too.

My letter writing took me all morning and then I had an early lunch. The railway station façade was most ornate and of course, it had to be absolutely enormous. The Italians seemed to love building places of enormous size and once inside the station, it was fascinating, for one was diminutive in comparison. I took the tram across the square and journeyed into the city centre, passing the Opera House.

I alighted at the piazza in front of the Duomo and gazed at it in wonder. The galleries nearby attracted me with their many shops and coffee bars and restaurants, which show very expensive meal tariffs. I was fascinated with it all and could have spent much more time looking around the centre. It is strange how time flies when one is sightseeing. I was not the only one in uniform looking around, for the Americans and our own countrymen were well in evidence.

That night, I had dinner on my own as the lads had not returned. I didn't worry for I felt that they would be somewhere enjoying themselves, especially as Nobby would soon be returning to the UK. I turned in for an early night's sleep as we had to get up very early the following morning. The reception desk did a good job in awakening me by phone and I didn't take long with my ablutions and dressing.

Downstairs, there was no sign of the lads, and all was quiet. I began to feel a little uneasy, especially as time was getting on and I knew it would take us about fifteen minutes to get to the *Questura*. Something told me to have a look outside and as I reached the pavement, there was the jeep, Guss and Nobby waiting for me.

'Where have you been, Skipper?' came the cheeky question, and with big smiles we piled into the jeep and off we went, reaching the police station on time. In the courtyard were four trucks, open at the back and each containing six fully-armed policemen, in a military-type grey uniform. The moment we came into their view, the Colonel came across and asked me if I would take up a position next to last in the convoy. That was perfectly all right with me, and so he jumped into the leading truck and got moving.

That night was a very cold one, but clear, and the police in the open trucks looked half frozen, poor fellows. We wasted no time and as the roads were clear of traffic once we were out of the city, we were able to make good progress. In spite of the open roads and the speed we were travelling at, it seemed ages before we saw the lights of

Alessandria in the distance. Now I began to hope that with all this armoury, things were not going to go wrong. We turned down one road from the outskirts and into another, past a piazza called Matteotti and along more side turnings until we came to an area which looked like the one we were concerned with.

The convoy broke up, with one or two disappearing around the corner and behind the block of flats nearest to us. The police from the other two trucks fanned out in and about the gardens and staircases of this block nearest to where we stopped. Slowly and silently, the police moved closer and closer until they had to climb some stairs.

A wretched dog barked, which triggered off a succession of barking from other dogs in the vicinity, and one or two lights appeared at the windows of the flats nearby. The Colonel gave the signal for his men to move up the stairs and to get closer by those on the ground floor. Three police were now outside Cerati's door and I stood with them waiting for the Colonel. Cerati was written on the door-plate.

The Colonel withdrew his pistol and with the butt, banged on the door hard and bawled out, '*Polizia! Apri la porta!*'

Getting no immediate response, he banged again and bawled his command a second time. The three policemen unslung their sub-machine guns and held them in readiness. Again the Colonel bawled out, '*Polizia! Apri la porta!*

This time, amongst the cacophony of barking dogs, we could hear voices from within and then the door opened. Like a flash, the three policemen rushed inside and switched on the lights as they went from room to room. '*Alzati! Alzati!* I heard them say to someone in a small bedroom.

I pushed past to get a look at the person the police were talking to and I was astonished to see a weedy-looking bloke rousing himself from a deep sleep, absolutely scared out of his mind as to what was happening to him. In his stupor, he was slow to react to the demands of the police, so they assisted in getting him up and out of his bed. He stood naked with only his underpants to cover him and began to shiver, more from fright than the cold.

The Colonel turned to me and said, 'I told him that I was arresting him for war crimes and to get dressed as we are taking him to Milan Prison.'

Now the wailing started by the parents and sister, who were in their living room, huddled together.

'They tried to plead with the Colonel that their son was innocent, but thank goodness, the Colonel brushed them aside,' he explained.

I had to hide my amusement upon seeing the puny bloke and we had such a force to carry out the arrest. The police did a thorough job searching the flat for any weapons, but found nothing. Cerati's bed was turned inside out but again the police found nothing.

At first, the young man began to be aggressive and used foul language when replying to the police instructions. When he saw me and my uniform, he changed his tone and became more morose.

While the man was getting dressed, watched by about a dozen people including his family, his mother was packing a few clothes and toilet requisites in a bag and bawling out aloud all the prayers she knew, just for our benefit!

The cruel deeds perpetrated by this man more than outweighed my feelings of sympathy for his family.

Not a moment more was allowed the man after he had got himself dressed. His personal belongings, which he was allowed to choose, were now ready in a bag and so the police escorted him out of the flat and down the stone steps towards the vehicles. Close neighbours, who had been watching the scene from their bedroom windows, hung out to shout their encouragement; '*Corraggio, Emilio!*'

As he felt that he had some people on his side, he began to shed tears, as if he was play acting to the gallery. Guss told him bluntly to shut up. I felt like kicking his backside. The Colonel asked me if I wanted to have the prisoner with me, but I thought that as it was so cold and the man was only wearing a light raincoat over his clothes, it would be more humane to have him with us in the closed jeep, instead of sitting out in the open at the back of the truck; he agreed and we pushed the man inside our vehicle.

Cerati was now terrified and protested loudly, making his voice echo in the still early morning air. Lights came on again in the flats and the police had to shout out to the occupants that there was nothing to be curious about and to go back to sleep. Guss and Nobby felt like punching the man, for his antics were getting the two of them irate. I managed to grab one arm and slung him into the jeep but leaving one leg dangling down the side. Nobby grabbed it and quickly made the limb follow the reluctant body into the vehicle.

The Colonel told us that they would lead the way back to Milan and they would go straight to the main prison. The convoy didn't take long in moving off and we too had to be in hot pursuit, to keep up. During the journey, the lads gave the prisoner a verbal hard time, telling him that if he didn't co-operate fully with our questioning, he couldn't expect any mercy from us. He remained impassive and almost childlike, holding on to his meagre bundle of personal items.

The convoy was relentless in its drive back to Milan and as we approached the outskirts, early risers for work were criss-crossing the streets and junctions on bicycle and foot, causing the leading vehicle to use its siren.

After many twists and turns and tyre squeals on the tram lines, we arrived at the prison gates, which opened without the convoy actually coming to a stop. After the Colonel had dismounted from his vehicle, the rest of the convoy dispersed, and we were never to see them again. He came over and asked us to bring the prisoner inside the Administration Offices. There was some formality at the 'Reception' desk which had to be dealt with and meanwhile, Guss and I chatted to the Colonel, who was obviously very pleased with the outcome of the assignment. I mentioned that I would file a full report on the excellent support given by himself and his men. This seemed to please him, for his co-operation was absolutely genuine.

We waited in the visitors' waiting room for the signal that our prisoner had been through documentation and was installed in a cell alone. We had long said our goodbyes to the Colonel and now we were escorted by a warder to where Cerati was locked up.

Through Guss, we told him that he would be staying here until his trial. It could take months and where it would be held, we didn't know. We would be coming back to interrogate him further about the terrible crime committed against Flight Sergeant Banks, of the British Royal Air Force. At that last remark, Cerati began to weep and plead his innocence that he knew nothing of what happened. I was in no mood to interrogate him then, but made it quite clear that he would be seeing me later that day.

Guss and I retreated to the courtyard where Nobby was waiting, being questioned by the off-duty warders as to how he had obtained such a nice looking jeep. He enjoyed this admiration and attention. I informed the office that I would be back later in the day as I would be interrogating Cerati for his involvement in the crime. The prison authorities knew the reason why we had arrested Cerati and gave us their full support to our demands.

We went in search of our hotel near the main railway station and were surprised to find how difficult it was to locate. By the time we had seen the directional signs, we had travelled a good distance in and about the city. We didn't mind, for we were having a good look at its magnificent buildings and piazzas. We eventually found the hotel, The Excelsior Gallia, which had looked after us extremely well, and offloaded our grips and odd items of tackle, in preparation for a longish stay.

The hall porter showed Nobby where to go to garage the jeep, which turned out to be behind the hotel but to get to it, he had to drive to the first turn left off the huge piazza, and down about 100 yards to an entrance between two blocks of private dwellings. We waited in the hall for Nobby to join us and meanwhile, the hall porter had our grips taken to our respective rooms.

This time, we had far better rooms, although not on the same floor. The lads shared a vast double room en suite on the first floor facing the piazza and I had a single room, with bathroom. In normal times, the hotel must have been one of the highest class, but the Germans had done nothing to help maintain its standard. It had been stripped of many refinements, so we were informed.

Nobby wasn't long away and soon joined Guss up in their room. We decided to leave Cerati alone for a day; as he was in solitary, it would give him time to think about his predicament. We spruced ourselves up and in battledress uniform, Nobby and I, with Guss looking very smart in brown with a leather battledress type of jacket, joined at the coffee bar. The decision to take the tram into the centre of the city and have a good walk around was readily accepted. We talked about the various places we wanted to see and one or two luxury items we might purchase. Nobby wanted to buy his mum a nice present and Guss was always on the lookout for something he could send back to his family far off in Czechoslovakia.

I wanted to buy a camera and a replacement film for Guss's camera, as I had used most of it when we were at Parma. Well refreshed with coffee and croissants, we made our way across the piazza and had a look inside the station first. Everything was on a grand scale.

What impressed us most was the cleanliness. Enormous marble and terrazzo designed staircases faced each other from either end of the building. From the top of one of the staircases, one looked down on to the main concourse and the commuters were dwarfed by the size of the place.

Crossing most of the piazza to get to the tram stop, we took our lives in our hands, for the little traffic that was seemed to pick us out as good targets. It was quite a novelty to ride in a tram, and it gave us the opportunity to absorb our surroundings. The famous La Scala Opera House we passed nearby, then the tram weaved its way around part of the Piazza del Duomo, where we alighted. The Duomo was magnificent, especially the bronze doors which, tragically, had shrapnel holes torn into them. The workmanship of these doors and the stained-glass windows, the masons' carvings and the interior woodwork, all provided awesome fascination.

It was well on lunchtime when we emerged from the Duomo and felt that the time was very well spent. We crossed the piazza and went into the galleries, which held its abundance of pricey shops and restaurants. We came across one good-looking restaurant called Savini which had an inviting look about it, so we went inside and were extremely well received. It was only after we got into the place, that we realised how cold it was outside and the draught through the galleries was no incentive to linger long in the passageways.

The food couldn't be bettered anywhere. We felt that the quality of the food was of the highest order and we resolved to visit Savini's another time. The service was superb, even to bringing a phone to the table so that I could ring the prison to tell them that I would visit Cerati in the morning, instead of this afternoon.

'Well done, Skipper,' remarked Guss after the important phone call; because the two lads made a bet between themselves that I would forget that I had made an appointment with the Prison Office for the afternoon. However, for their loss, they had to pay for the next meal! With great reluctance, we left the comfort of the restaurant and went shopping.

Loaded with our purchases, we finally had had enough and took the tram back to the Piazza Duca d'Aosta and alighted opposite our hotel.

Having already informed Headquarters at Padova of the arrest of Cerati, I was given a free hand to find, if I could, the Captain of the Company of the *Brigata Nera* who had controlled the whole region, and was Cerati's superior. We could well understand the desire of HQ to net the complete lot who were responsible for Flight Sergeant Arthur Banks's death, but it was to be a tall order nevertheless. We couldn't possibly do this before we had to lose Nobby – but we would at least try.

The following morning, we went off to the prison and were allowed into Cerati's cell. When he saw the three of us enter and the warder remain outside, he became very frightened and uncooperative. Guss interpreted for me as I flashed the questions at the prisoner.

'Who ordered the two women to carry out those cruel tortures?' I asked.

There was no reply.

'How old are you?'

'*Ventidue anni,*' came the muffled reply.

'Then you will look forward to your life sentence – and in your country, life means life!' I told him.

The Italian began to shout his pleas of innocence, which fell on our deaf ears.

'Who was your superior at Rovigo?' I demanded.

Like lightning, he flashed back the name, Bruno Zamboni. That bit of information I was very grateful to have, for at least we had the full name this time, to work on.

'What were your duties at the prison at Rovigo and Adria?' I asked.

With his head bent down between his hands, elbows resting on his knees, Cerati sat on his iron bed, completely apathetic. 'I was promoted to be the Keeper,' he replied.

'Does that mean you were in charge and had the authority to stop any prisoner from receiving bad treatment, in your charge?' I put the question to him to test his ego.

'*Si, Capitano,*' he asserted, and Guss translated his continuing reply. In this way we had established that this young man had been promoted to Lieutenant in command of the Adria and Rovigo Prisons by this Bruno Zamboni.

'What was Zamboni's rank?' I demanded.

'*Colonello,*' came the weak reply.

The questions and answers went on and I wanted to know where the Colonel came from. I put the question to Cerati time and again but got no response. Then I resorted to harder questioning, and told the prisoner that the Russians were coming, as they had many of their men tortured by the *Brigata Nera* after capture. I said that they knew where Cerati lived and would be coming to get him. This cell would not stop them and knowing them, he wouldn't see a courtroom.' There was a moment's silence, then a weeping session began. We allowed this act to continue for several minutes, hoping that he might think we were softening up a little.

Guss told Cerati a tale about the Russians who were advancing rapidly across Europe and were now into Austria. He didn't tell him that there were only delegations of them in Vienna. Guss went on to frighten the man still further about what the Russians do to their captives for perpetrating war crimes. Now and then, he would ask Cerati for the name of the home town of Zamboni, but got no reply.

The warder came and asked if we were all right, which gave me the chance to finish with the interrogation. I told Cerati that I would be back, but not when. I gave strict instructions that no one would be allowed to see him other than my team. He was to be kept in solitary until he was required to be moved to the court, wherever that might be.

I had to keep the severity of the crime uppermost in my mind and not to surrender to any softening of feelings. Back at the hotel, I received a massage from HQ that Nobby had to report back in three days' time. As far as I was concerned, Cerati could stay in gaol until I was ready to go back to question him further. That decision didn't stand for long, however, for I was anxious to know the home town of his bastard Colonel.

After telling Nobby the news about his forthcoming departure, we wanted to finish off our missions together in a spectacular way.

We decided to go back to the prison and question the prisoner further. Again, we were left alone with Cerati and this time, we hammered home the fear that the Russians were now only a few days away and would not hesitate to carry out the same tortures on him as he allowed and helped to do to Flight Sergeant Banks and others at that prison. I wanted to know all about Zamboni. Guss pumped the questions one after the other and then suddenly, the prisoner broke and told us that Bruno Zamboni came from Bologna. He had forced Cerati to do the tortures and allowed the two women, who used to have sex with anyone they chose and were watched over by himself, to help him. He was frightened by Zamboni, for he was told that if he didn't do what he was ordered to, he would be shot.

This was Cerati's tale of woe, and at the end of the interrogation, the man was sapped of emotion and, almost in a faint, flopped on to his bed. We left, leaving him to speculate as to his ultimate fate.

Chapter Seven

We returned to the hotel and over lunch, I suggested to the lads that I would like to take them to see my old friends, the *contadini* who had looked after us immediately after our escape from *Campo* 49. The little hamlet called Parroletta, just outside Fontanellato, would be only about seventy miles away. The lads jumped at the idea and suggested that we take them some presents. They were now getting as excited as I was, for I had not seen the farmers since the days in 1943. It would be a chance to take some photos for our families to see back home.

We went into the city after lunch to do the shopping for the two families, the Maris and the Ferraris. It was difficult to know what they would require so we bought a block of two hundred and fifty cigarettes apiece for the men and perfume for the women. The lads spotted a film which looked exciting, but in Italian, which they wanted to see, so we spent a couple of hours inside a cinema behind the galleries. After dinner at the hotel, we lounged near the bar and chatted over a thousand and one subjects. We also agreed to get up early and have a good long day at Fontanellato.

There was no difficulty in finding the village signpost after we left the main Milan to Bologna road and we were speculating as to what we were going to find when we got there. The two farms which we were going to were actually situated at Parroletta, three kilometres outside Fontanellato. The road was just about wide enough to take the jeep and as we swung round the last corner out of Parroletta, we came across the house of Mari. The front door came on to the roadway, so we pulled up a little way beyond it.

On hearing the jeep stop outside their house, Signor Mari came out and couldn't believe his eyes when he saw me. He immediately recognised me, and called his wife to come and see. It was a tremendous moment for me to see the two elderly folk again and to be able to thank them again for all their sacrifices and help they gave us officers when we escaped from P.G.49, in 1943. Over one of his best bottles of wine, we celebrated the reunion and we gave our presents to the two wonderful people. The lads were surprised to hear the story from Signor Mari as to the number of times the Germans came to look around the area for escapees. They also told us about the Fascist farmhand who constantly kept his place under observation.

'So that was the time when we were nearly caught in the maize field, remember?' I said.

Mari could hardly forget, as it was he who had eventually distracted the man and led him away. Apparently, that same man was caught by the local men of the area and shot, after the Germans fled the country.

The lads excused themselves as they wanted to look around and to take some photos. Meanwhile, I sat chatting to the Maris in very bad Italian – but at least it was conversationally adequate.

I wanted to have some snaps which I could keep for posterity, so I got the couple outside and took a good snap of the two with their dog. I took a snap of the path that the Colonel and I had to run along to get into the maize field, to hide. Unfortunately, the maize had been harvested but it didn't need much imagination to visualise what it had been like.

Signora Mari realised that she didn't have any accommodation to offer us for the night and suggested that we went over to the Ferrari's, as their house was bigger with more bedrooms. Of course we well understood her predicament and we made it easier for them by telling them that we would come again in the near future to chat over old times.

I gave the two quite a substantial amount of money in recompense for all they had endured on the Colonel's and my behalf, as well as the cigarettes and the perfume. They were overwhelmed and couldn't thank me enough – but I still didn't think it was enough for all they did for us. After all, but for the loyalty and courage shown by the Maris at that critical time, I probably would not have survived to tell the story.

We sadly said our goodbyes and went off to the farm of the Ferrari's. They heard us coming, and from their side window overlooking the drive, they saw the jeep and immediately understood that it could only belong to me. They ran out of the house as we drew up; Signor, Signora and Alda their daughter, who had grown quite a bit since I last saw her. The reunion was tremendous, and extremely emotional between all of us. They were the salt of the earth, bless them.

I introduced Guss and Nobby to them and they accepted them just as if they had known the lads as well as they knew me. Nobby unhitched the trailer and pushed it alongside the barn. We all went inside and sat around the wooden table in their only living room-cum-kitchen. The atmosphere was terrific; very festive, and Signor Ferrari brought out his good wine, joking that it was made with the effort of our feet in 1943! I assured the lads that the Colonel and I had washed our feet in the trough outside. The two darted out to see if it was still blocked up!

A thousand memories came flooding back of those fearful days and Signor Ferrari told us of the events of their lives, after we left for the mountains.

Whilst the menfolk were talking and exchanging experiences, Alda and her mother were busy upstairs preparing the rooms for our sleeping. Alda had grown up quite considerably in the three years. She was a real young lady and a great help to her mother. Aldo, her brother, who was ten years older, was living at Genoa, as he had a job with a petrol company. Signor Ferrari mentioned that we might be lucky in seeing him, as he expected to have him back home for one of his breaks.

It was far too dark now outside to have a look around but we were shown the cowshed and even now, the chickens were allowed inside the kitchen, as before. I can well remember Colonel Peddie being so shocked when he first set foot inside that kitchen and saw the hens pecking about the floor. I asked the lads if they were bored with all the talk about the family and myself. They both said that it was very interesting to hear a corroborated story and to actually see where some of the action took place.

Signora Ferrari had a very big fire going in the kitchen range and a very large flat frying pan with high sides held a mixture of food which would defy identification. We badgered the good woman to tell us what was in the pan but she wouldn't yield. Like a good 'mother', she told us to wait and see. The aroma was tantalising.

Ferrari told us that they heard about a band of partisans up in the Monte Cisa area who were fighting the Germans and when I told him that the partisans were the ones I was with, he winked and gave me a hard slap on my back. Whether or not he really knew that I had been their leader didn't matter, as long as he felt that I had something to do with them and the actions proved beneficial.

I asked if it were possible to meet some of my partisans, who I remember lived in the Po valley, and I suggested that it was more than likely that I would have to come this way again during my work. I said that I would try to let him know when that might be, so that messages could be sent to anyone available from the partisan group.

The idea thrilled the old man and he said that he would do everything possible to send word around. Several bottles of red wine had been consumed while we were waiting for the dinner to be ready. Alda had been busy making a speciality 'cake' from maize flour and coffee. The night was very cold outside but inside, the kitchen was really cosy with the oil lamps and the glowing fire in the range.

The time had arrived when Signora Ferrari swung the frying pan away from the range fire and called us to be ready for our meal. The three of us quickly washed our hands in the earthen trough beneath the window which looked out on to the yard, and hurried to take up our seating positions, as directed by Signor Ferrari. More wine was plonked on to the table; this time it was white and we were assured that it was one of the best vintages. The tasting proved that!

Signora Ferrari asked each one in turn to come up to her with the plate that had been set in front of each setting. A big scoop dolloped out a portion of the fry and Alda served the mashed polenta from another pan. When all of us had been served, Signor Ferrari said Grace. He then raised his full glass and asked us to join in a toast to the reunion. We did just that and even Alda, who I remember didn't drink much, enjoyed the glass of rich wine.

We had a hilarious time over dinner, for Nobby had a cockerel's head and talons amongst his mixture, and Guss had part of a hedgehog in his! However, in spite of the strange ideas, the food was unanimously claimed to be most delicious and filling. The polenta cake was a great success as Signora had filled it with whipped cream.

We all helped with the washing-up and the clearing away of the table, for Ferrari had brought out some more red wine. The kitchen was full of tobacco smoke. Thank goodness he liked the American Camel cigarettes which we brought him! Alda retired to bed and we continued putting the world to rights.

We had reached the stage when it was difficult to find our way out to the 'bog', which was across the courtyard, and trying not to disturb the cows, for we had to pass them in their stalls in order to reach the yard. The fun came when Nobby put his foot right into a pile of dung. It was a good thing that neither of our hosts could understand the remarks Nobby made. The boots were left outside to be cleaned in the morning. Nobby's last remark was, 'This rustic life is not for me!'

Signora Ferrari showed us to our rooms. The lads were to sleep in Alda's bedroom. Alda was sleeping with her parents. I was to sleep in Aldo's bedroom. Slowly, the oil lamps were extinguished downstairs and with a last call to us to know if we were all right, the upstairs lamps were put out as they were required no more.

Of course, the family were up early as the cows had to be milked and the chickens fed. We roused ourselves after sleeping soundly and had our shave and wash in the cold water tub at the back. The water was freezing cold, which quickly dispelled any hangover we might have had. Signor Ferrari was in very good spirits and pulled the legs of Nobby and Guss unmercifully, especially when he saw Guss trying to wash himself with his vest on.

I asked the family if anyone wished to come with us into the town, as we were having a chunk of cheese with the home-made bread cobs and coffee. The offer was declined as they had too much to do around the farm, but *Signora* gave me a short shopping list, as we had made her larder empty of some things. I told them that I wanted to go and show the lads where our prison camp was and also, as I had never seen the centre of the little town, I was eager to take some snaps. I also wanted to try to see the nuns at the convent next door to the camp, who did our laundry and left little notes of encouragement inside the ironed clothing.

As we entered the town, we were amazed to see a medieval castle situated right in the centre of the piazza. It was surrounded completely by a deep moat full of water. There was only one entrance which was gained by a stone bridge connecting the castle to the piazza.

It was an unbelievable sight, which immediately took our vivid imaginations back to the twelfth century. The architecture of the castle was unique, for nowhere else had we seen one similar. Around the square and under a covered walk were shops and coffee bars and a restaurant. There was no raised pavement from the road level, just large stone flags set under the arches and joined with the cobblestones of the roadway. Our presence caused a stir, and soon we were swamped by the locals asking us many questions.

The very young wanted to climb all over the jeep and those with bicycles were eager to show us the way out to the convent. For their safety, we had to decline their offers but some went on ahead. Nobby and Guss stayed with the jeep at the entrance to the convent, while I went in. At the main wooden doors, a window was opened and a nun appeared. As soon as she saw the visitor was a man, she quickly shut the window and silence returned. I knocked again on the door. I called out that I wanted to speak with the Mother Superior as I am from England and I was an ex-prisoner at the orphanage next door.

The window opened again and then shut tight, and slowly half the door opened. I was motioned to follow the nun who led me into a bare room. The room smelt clinically clean and through a small open grille, I was confronted by several nuns, with the Mother Superior in the foreground. The excitement created by my presence was genuine, and I was able to deliver my thank-you on behalf of all the ex-inmates of Campo Concentramento 49.

The pushing and shoving by the nuns wanting to get a closer look at me behind the Mother Superior was like a scrum in a Rugby match. However, the meeting gave me a great deal of satisfaction, for I wanted them to know how grateful we all were for their co-operation and guile under great difficulties of being found out by the Fascists.

I rejoined the lads and I showed them the camp and where I slept and all the places where we tunnelled. They were very struck with everything they saw. Luckily, the authorities hadn't done a thing to the building since we left, except to take away the guard huts and the barbed wire fencing. Our cameras took snap after snap. There was a strange feeling walking the corridors again and lots of memories came back, even to the day of our escape. Satisfied that I had recorded all I wanted on film, we returned to the piazza in the town. We shopped for the things which Signora Ferrari required and bought some extra cheese and wine for them.

Back at the farm, we told the Ferraris what we had seen and what I did at the convent. They were very pleased. Signora Ferrari and I regularly teased one another, and with a little tussle of words, I made her keep her money for the food.

Later that afternoon, Signor Ferrari took us over to his neighbour who had a cheese factory. We had met him when we were on the run and he gave us some of his cheese to take with us when we left the farmhouse to go up into the mountains. He and his wife were very kind people but I felt sorry for the Ferraris, as they were treated more or less like serfs. I hated class distinction.

That evening deserved a special celebration, for it would be the last one spent as a team together before Nobby had to go back to the UK. Also, we would have to leave in the morning early, so we made the best of things. The Ferraris made special cakes and we had roast chickens for our evening meal. We emphasised that we would be back as often as we could, depending on where my duties took me.

The parting from Parroletta was very touching, for the Ferraris genuinely treated us as extra members of their family. Giving us clear directions for our way out across country to the road to Mantova, Signor Ferrari came to the end of the drive and cried at our parting. I had hidden a bundle of banknotes between the sheet of my bed and the under-blanket and hoped that it would be sufficient for their needs for quite a while. It was my own money so I didn't feel bad giving it to them.

The river Po was widening to a very substantial fast flowing river. Once on the other side we felt safer as the bridge we crossed didn't look safe at all. We motored through Legnago and only then, did we see the sign posts to Padua. Nobby found an ideal spot beside one of the tributaries feeding the Po river, where we had our picnic lunch. The nearer we were getting to Padua, the less I liked it, for I felt it was going to be the end of an epoch which could not be matched. The comradeship had been exceptional yet never had there ever been the slightest lapse into familiarity. The credit for this was due entirely to the intelligence and training of Sergeant Morgan. The spirit of *bonhomie* had been maintained, without the loss of any discipline at any time, and I vowed to myself that Major Williamson should be told, in order to add my report of the conduct and ability of Sergeant Morgan, when his Discharge Papers would finally be served. The atmosphere during the last hours before reaching Padua was tense between us, for each one realised the coming to an end of our unique team.

Nobby pulled into the yard at Headquarters and dropped me off outside the offices. He and Guss took the jeep and trailer round to the garages, after I told them that I would see them later in the day. Captain Reynolds was pleased with our mission and informed me that Major Williamson has ordered me to fetch Cerati from Milan and to bring him to the prison in Padua. I was delighted, and asked if I could have Sergeant Morgan and Pless to accompany me. I knew Morgan had to go back to the UK for demob but just one more trip of say three days wouldn't be amiss. I argued my point in an almost pleading way and was told that perhaps a decision would be made in the morning.

The following morning, I was in the office before the Adjutant and was able to coerce the Corporal Clerk to give me the details of the demob transportation movements for Sergeant Morgan. Luckily, the railway warrants had not been made out. I waited, for I knew the Adjutant would not be long and on his arrival, he had good news. Sergeant Morgan had a stay of one week only. Unfortunately, we had to give up our jeep. Captain Reynolds then suggested that we move off in the morning and that he would send Sergeant Morgan and Pless to pick me up at the hotel at 0900 hrs.

Sure enough, the following morning Nobby and Guss arrived in an open jeep with trailer, and clothed suitably for the cold journey ahead. At least it would be a direct one, this time taking the main road through Verona and Brescia. Nobby was delighted with his extended departure time from Padua but, like all soldiers, he had his moan about losing his favourite jeep. Milan was about one hundred and fifty miles away, so we had not much time to dawdle. On arrival in Milan, we went straight to our favourite hotel, The Excelsior Gallia. I took a good snap of the two lads with the jeep in front of the hotel, with the station in the background. We had a super welcome from the hotel staff and after offloading our grips, we went off to the prison and made arrangements for the collection of Cerati, in the morning.

The lads wanted to go into the centre of Milan to do their own thing, whilst I wanted to write some letters and to make out my report. They said that they would make their own way back by tram so I took the jeep to the hotel. I knew what they were after but who cared, for they were free to do what they wanted as long as they didn't get into trouble with women; they were known to steal everything from the soldiers.

The following morning, the lads were downstairs with their grips all ready. I plonked mine beside theirs and we went in for breakfast. The two of them had spent a very enjoyable evening, having found two good types who didn't steal their wallets! In fact, according to Guss, they didn't ask for any payment. 'It was just for love,' he remarked with a sigh.

Nobby said that it was perhaps a good thing that he was going home soon, otherwise he might get serious, as his had been a 'smasher'.

On the way out to the prison, I asked Nobby if he wouldn't mind passing the station so that I could post my letters and in doing so, we nearly came to having an accident with a tram. Nobby thought that a crossroad was for vehicles but unfortunately, it was reserved for trams only!

As we slowed almost to a halt outside the gates to the prison, they opened enough to allow the jeep to get through and into the yard. Guss and I went into the office and showed my ID booklet to the staff, who we had not seen before. They were most curious to see a British officer and to know what was his business requiring to be at the prison. The Senior Warder of the group in the office, rang through to his superior and received some strong language back, down the phone. The commotion that followed indicated that the staff who were on duty should have been informed of our appointment and had the prisoner ready to be handed over to us, upon our arrival.

Apologies came to us from all directions and it took about a quarter of an hour before Cerati was paraded at the office door. He wore a light raincoat with a cream coloured scarf around his neck. The raincoat was completely inadequate for the weather, as it was crisp but dry. In the jeep, it would be extremely cold once we were motoring. We were asked if we wanted Cerati handcuffed, but looking at the prisoner, we reckoned he wouldn't dare to try to escape with us three always beside him.

We bundled him into the jeep, which was now closed, and made our way out of the prison and on to the road to Brescia. It seemed that we were never going to distance ourselves from Milan, for the outskirts sprawled in ever-increasing circles. Finally, we were out into the country and humming our way along a fairly good road surface. The weather brightened, so we stopped and put the hood down.

Cerati had been warned that if an attempt would be made to escape, he would be shot without any warning. Guss took a snap of myself, Cerati and Nobby, for we wanted to have a snap to show our folks what a type we had arrested. It was clear right from the start that Cerati had no intentions of even giving cheek, never mind trying to escape!

We couldn't help having contempt for this spineless being, for he seemed to smarm his words and actions, like a fawning child. Nobby said that he wouldn't mind betting that he was a homosexual and wanted to give him a thorough good hiding. Cerati tried his best to court the softer side of Nobby's nature, which angered Nobby all the more.

Coming to the outskirts of Padua, we skirted round north of the city, as the prison for the male population was to the north-east. We were extremely relieved to arrive at the main gates and to be able to hand over our captive to the authorities, for if the journey had taken any longer, Guss or Nobby would have easily beaten the daylights out of him. Feeling happily relieved of our burden, we returned to HQ.

We had not even had the time to draw a sigh of relief, after the engine had been switched off and whilst we were getting our grips, the duty Corporal Clerk met us and announced that Nobby was going off early the next morning.

The three of us followed the Corporal into the office and then we got all the details. Nobby had to be ready to leave with Major Williamson at 0700 hours, as he was to accompany him on the plane to Klagenfurt. Then he would be driven to Villach where he would board the troop train on the Medloc 'C' Route to Calais.

Although we had been expecting the move, the news came as a bombshell. I suggested to the lads that we might have a Going Away Party at the Pedrocchi Club and they gladly accepted, so we arranged to meet at seven, in civvies. The clapped-out jeep which was used as a runabout took me to my hotel. I think Nobby was quite glad to drive our jeep back to the garages for the last time.

Once up in my room, I ran the bath and prepared myself for a good long soak. As I lay in the comfort of the hot water, I thought of the forthcoming trial of Cerati and how I was going to tackle the job of Prosecuting Attorney. After a good deal of straight talking to myself, I felt better and feeling the water cooling quite considerably, pulled the plug and stepped out to dry with nice warm towels. My cast off used clothes were in small heaps, so I tidied up, making a bundle for the morning's collection to be laundered. Feeling good in clean clothes and in my favourite sports outfit, I went downstairs to meet the lads, taking with me the present which I had bought for Nobby.

The bar, which was our usual meeting place, was fairly empty but it was still too early to expect many people. I had time to arrange a table but I thought it best for the lads to choose their own meal. Looking resplendent in their immaculate sports gear of thick twill grey trousers and barathea jackets, the lads looked like two models fit for Bond Street.

'We thought we would outdo you, Skipper, for once,' remarked Nobby as he approached, for he could see the look of astonishment on my face. Guss gave a broad smile and said that it was all Nobby's doing.

'When and where did you buy those good-looking clothes?' I asked.

'Guss walked me from the galleries in Milan up a fairly narrow street which looked the equivalent to our Bond Street for shops, and we saw this Man's shop,' said Nobby. 'God, Skipper, it was pricey!'

'Nobby didn't want to buy anything but I did, so I got him in just the same,' said Guss.

'Who bought first?' I asked.

'Oh, Guss did, but then I saw how good he looked in what he chose that I felt I would be out of it and in any case, the clothes would come in handy for when I got back home and into Civvy Street, especially suitable for Christmas parties,' replied Nobby.

'You both look great, now let's go in and eat and we can do all our drinking afterwards.'

We had a super night with a great meal and good wine. I was able to present Nobby with my gift at a moment he least expected anything, and it stumped him for words. I gave a little speech to thank him for the extremely good driving, and to thank him for his temperament and his comradeship, which never went beyond the limits between non-commissioned and commissioned officers.

Nobby unwrapped the present and sat in silence for a moment, not knowing what to say. As he looked inside the wallet, he saw the folded white £5 note. I was glad I did think of a wallet for him, because he said that he was going to buy one before returning to the UK.

A firm handshake from him told me of his feelings and we drank each other's health. Nobby knew that I had made out my report for Major Williamson on his conduct for the records and he would be told of the report's contents before leaving the unit, by the Adjutant.

The breaking up of our team that night was difficult to accept, but we were trained not to be sentimental in the forces. This rule was not always easy to keep to. As they left to return to HQ, I mentioned to Guss that I would see him sometime during the next day.

★

The trial of Emilio Cerati, the twenty-two-year-old second lieutenant in the *Brigata Nera* was soon over for him, and he was committed to prison for two and a half years. I learnt a tremendous amount of the law during that trial and was most grateful for the opportunity to undertake the tremendous responsibility of Prosecuting Attorney. I felt that the sentence was not enough, but then the Bench decided that considering all the evidence, they could not increase the penalty.

★

I overslept the following morning and whilst I was shaving, I had a thought of Nobby and where would he be. I wondered who would I get for his replacement and knew that it would not be long before I was to find out.

Chapter Eight

The usual runabout jeep came to pick me up at the hotel to take me to HQ. The Adjutant, Captain Reynolds, was in his office, so I asked to see him, so that I could get my new assignments. The first priority was to try to find Colonel Bruno Zamboni of the *Brigata Nera*. I had all the details, such as they were, and I was given a new driver but still had my young interpreter friend, Guss.

I thought it would be a good idea to meet my crew, so I went off to the Staff Quarters and the garage and nosed about. It was not long before I heard Guss talking to a mechanic beside a jeep in the garage. The motor pool for the unit was quite large really. As I approached, Guss introduced Driver Brian Dixon of the Royal Army Service Corps, saying that he would be our driver, and then he pointed out the jeep and trailer which had been assigned to us. It had a hard body top to it and on the radiator was the JAG disc in white letters. I told them that I was glad to see that we had a closed jeep this time, for the winter was really settling in.

The following morning, my new crew picked me up at the hotel and we went off to Bologna in search of Zamboni. We went to the *Questura* but they had no one on their files. They'd had their documents burnt by the Germans during their retreat; in fact, most of their building had been destroyed. As they could not help us, we then went to the Army Barracks outside the city and got no joy there. We got rooms at the Al Cappello Rosso, which was a fairly small hotel.

The next day, we set off for the market and made some enquiries there. One or two had heard of the name but didn't know where he was. Snow was now falling, so we tried to keep under cover as much as we could. We went to the railway station at the top of Via Marconi and asked many people, from porters to those in the offices. No one had heard of Zamboni.

As we made our enquiries from one to another within the station, we noticed an elderly man now and again coming up to us within earshot, and suddenly he called out behind us, '*Capitano! So chi è!*'

Guss asked him if he wouldn't mind accompanying us to the bar just across the piazza, which he willingly agreed.

It turned out that the man had been a barber up until last year. His shop was near to the Duomo just off the Piazza Maggiore. Zamboni had been a client of his. Guss asked him to tell us all he knew about the man.

'*Senta!*' he said. The Italians always started their conversations with that word 'Listen!' He proceeded to tell us some interesting facts. Guss translated his story well. Apparently, during the German occupation of Italy after the Armistice, Zamboni was promoted to Colonel of the 14th Brigade of the *Brigata Nera*, which commanded the whole area for a radius of two hundred kilometres. He was a ruthless man and every time he came into the shop for a haircut, he would boast of his adventures with his prostitutes. If there was anything he didn't approve of, he would immediately become enraged and would bang his fists hard on the arms of the chair.

Guss asked him if he was ever frightened of him. '*Si*,' he said.

'*Abitava in quel'albergo là,*' said the old man, and pointed out the hotel down the road, where Zamboni lived. The barber went on to tell us that, during the German occupation, when the Allies were nearing the city, the Germans laid some landmines at the approaches and one day, Zamboni got himself blown up by one of them and was taken to the Infirmary on the Viale Carlo Pepoli, where he nearly died.

Guss remarked that it was a pity that he didn't die.

Guss asked the old boy if he knew the whereabouts of Zamboni now. He told us that, the last time he had come into his shop for a haircut, he said that he was leaving Bologna and was going to live with his sister up in the mountains at Merano.

The man kept looking at his watch and we felt that we had all the information we required, so we said that we were going to the centre and could we give him a lift. He declined and told us that he was waiting to meet a young woman. Guss was dying to ask him about the young woman but thought it better not to and we left him.

Brian went off to get the jeep and drew up as close to the bar as he could so that we wouldn't get the snow on us. Following the barber's directions, Brian got us to the Infirmary in good time in spite of the slippery roads. It was quite a big place. Guss and I found the main entrance and sought out the office which would be the most useful for the information we required. On the door was a plaque bearing the title '*Registrazione Administrativa*'. We knocked and were ushered inside.

A middle-aged woman in a white coat was sitting behind a desk and as we entered, she got up to greet us and offered the hospitality of her office. I showed her my ID booklet, which drew raised eyebrows, and she said she would help us all she could. Guss then told her about Bruno Zamboni, an ex-colonel in the *Brigata Nera*, who was brought in there after being blown up on a German landmine.

'*Momento, prego,*' she said and picked up the phone. Gabbling down the phone, she gave her instructions to the person on the other end and presently, a woman clerk came in with a file. It was true that Zamboni had been a casualty and his life was saved, but only just.

'He will be on crutches for the rest of his life and will suffer from injuries to his chest,' she told us.

With grateful thanks to the woman, we left and made our way out of the city. The snow had stopped falling and the roads were now even more dangerous with the slush. Brian drove very cautiously but it was difficult to compare his driving with that of Nobby.

We found a very pleasant looking trattoria at Crevalcore and had a substantial meal of Spaghetti Bolognese. After lunch, we got as far as Verona where we stopped the night. The snow was now becoming quite thick. The following morning we were off again but it was getting colder and colder. Each of us were thankful for our heavy overcoats and I was especially thankful to have my trench coat lined with the lambskins. The feet took the brunt of the cold, unfortunately.

The snowploughs had been busy in the early hours and had cleared the road to Trento. The windy, fairly narrow road to Bolzano proved more difficult to negotiate but Brian coped extremely well. We only had another twenty-nine kilometres to go so we struggled on. The snowploughs were doing a great job but sometimes we had difficulty in passing them, for the road was not all that big, even without snow!

We talked about whether or not we would be lucky in finding Zamboni and if we were, would he be in a fit state to get him inside a prison.

At last the snow stopped falling. We found the local *Carabinieri* station without any trouble and were able to obtain the address of the Zambonis. We were about to go out to the jeep, when the officer in charge asked us who it was we were seeking. I showed him my ID booklet and he softened and reduced his authoritative tone. He then told us that Bruno Zamboni had died in February that year. He offered us coffee in his office and allowed us to warm our feet on his radiators, which were boiling hot!

We chatted about many topics, his job and ours and we again heard mention of the story of the band of German renegades somewhere up in the Alps near the Austrian borders. According to the latest news, the *Alpini* Troops who had been sent up in that area to locate this band, had been able to capture some of the escapees, and under interrogation by the Italian and the Austrian authorities, they confirmed that their leader was Martin Bormann himself. That to me seemed very logical but I wanted to know more. Unfortunately, the officer didn't have any further information.

I asked him where would be the centre for the troops who would be sent up into the mountains, and he told us that the central barracks was at Udine. I wanted to get this information to my Headquarters, so I was given the phone and I rang the office. Captain Reynolds had gone on leave, so I spoke to a Captain Manners. I related to him all what I had heard, then he asked me to phone him back within half an hour. During that time, we offered the *Carabinieri* some of our cigarettes and drank more mugs of their coffee. We warmed ourselves up and listened to the weather news.

The radio was very encouraging about the snow, so we felt that, wherever we might go now in the mountain areas, the roads would not be so bad. I rang the office again and was told that I must investigate further. I was instructed to liaise with the Italians and the Austrians if necessary and when more precise information was available, to let HQ know. I told Captain Manners about the result of the Zamboni affair, and he said that he would make a note of it.

He wished me luck and instructed me to keep HQ well informed.

We got down to Trento all right and as I wanted to get to Udine by the quickest route, I asked at the local police station what the road was like to Belluno. As it was fairly good, we took that road and found the road information not as accurate as we were led to believe.

With a struggle up on the heights around Primolano, we made Belluno before dark. We dumped our kits in the hallway of the Dolomiti Hotel and I went out to give Brian a hand to fill up the jeep and to garage the outfit. Meanwhile, Guss had done the necessary to get the rooms and to arrange where we could have a good meal, as the hotel didn't have a restaurant. It was only a small hotel but the rooms were comfortable. Having freshened up, we went out on foot and found a trattoria on the Via Matteotti. As Guss and Brian had never eaten truffles before, we indulged and the outcome was that they thoroughly enjoyed them. After that, we had veal steaks and ended up with a coffee gâteau.

The following morning, we left fairly early and motored on through Vittorio Veneto and Pordenone, finally making Udine. It was bustling with soldiers from the *Alpini* regiments and the *Bersaglieri*, with their colourful plumes in their hats. We found out that Udine was their garrison town. We didn't know who to ask first for their Headquarter Offices, so we asked the first soldier we came to stop beside.

Following his precise instructions, we came to the main entrance to the barracks and stopped at the Guardroom. I showed my ID booklet and excitement reigned among the guards and during the phone calls that followed. We were directed to a building straight ahead of us and shown where to park. We were right in the midst of the *Alpini* troops' barracks.

IMPORTANT MESSAGE FROM
YOUR METER READER

I CAME TO READ YOUR METER BUT MISSED YOU. CAN YOU HELP?

Sorry I missed you on..... 3/10/13

can you call or text me within the next 24 hours on,

tel: 0845 071 9646

text: 07767852335

with your: ◯ Gas Reading   ◯ Electric Reading

WE REALLY NEED YOUR METER READING – WHETHER YOU PAY BY DIRECT DEBIT, QUARTERLY OR ONLINE. IT'S SO THAT WE KNOW EXACTLY HOW MUCH ENERGY YOU'RE USING – SO YOU DON'T END UP PAYING FOR MORE THAN YOU SHOULD.

SSE   Southern Electric   Scottish Hydro   SWALEC   Atlantic

008049

DEAR

ADVICE ON HOW TO READ YOUR METER

Electricity Meters

If your electricity meter looks like this, you would write 94695.

| 9 | 4 | 6 | 9 | 5 | 5 |

If your electricity meter looks like this, you would write 063129.

| 0 | 6 | 3 | 1 | 2 | 9 | 7 |

Electricity Meter Reading

Please enter your electricity reading below:

Gas Meters

If your gas meter looks like this, you would write 7519.

| 7 | 5 | 1 | 9 |

If your gas meter looks like this, you would write 07519.

| 0 | 7 | 5 | 1 | 9 |

Gas Meter Reading

Please enter your gas reading below:

Guss pointed out the Officers' Mess and the Administration buildings, so we chose the latter and walked in. Obviously they had been warned of our coming, for we were greeted at the door by an NCO, who led us to his Commanding Officer. I told him that I wanted to know what was behind the rumours about Martin Bormann being up in the Alps with a little army of his diehards.

He said that they had captured some of the Germans from the group and under interrogation they had given information that their leader was Martin Bormann. They were picked as the best of the SS troops who used to guard Hitler and now they found it difficult to stay any longer up in the mountains. They also revealed that arrangements had been made for Martin Bormann to go free, if his troops surrendered.

The Austrian authorities, liaising with the Italian Government, agreed to let Martin Bormann go wherever he wanted to, without interference. The Brigadier agreed with my comments and found the arrangements most unusual. I said that I would like to keep in touch with him as to the developments and I wrote down his phone number. He said that he would be very pleased to keep me informed. I gave him one of my best salutes, to keep the mutual respect, and left his office feeling somewhat puzzled as to the politics of the situation.

Guss was like me, thank heavens, sorely perplexed – and we needed a stiff drink to sort things out!

We asked the lads at the Guardroom where was there a good bar and they directed us towards the centre of the city. We found the one they suggested, which allowed us to park the jeep right outside the place. We picked a table so that we could keep an eye open for the jeep, especially the trailer, as it was loaded with the jerrycans of petrol. For starters, we downed a whisky apiece, which warmed us up.

'Guss, what do you make of it all?' I asked, as I sat down feeling all keyed up.

'I would like to know the reasons for allowing the sod to go free without interference!' replied Guss.

'I would like to have a further chat with that Brigadier. I want to know where exactly the bastards are camped out,' I said.

As Brian had been left out of the meeting, we explained to him what had transpired. He felt like us, completely baffled. However, I did think that perhaps the various authorities might be planning to see Martin Bormann go somewhere and to eventually catch more of his followers, who were equally criminals who need to be brought to justice. It all might be part of one huge strategical manoeuvre. I put this theory to the lads and they toyed with it but concluded that I might be right.

We got ourselves in at the San Giorgio Hotel and safely parked the jeep and trailer. Before going to the barracks the following morning, I rang the Brigadier's office with the number he gave me, and found that he was out. I was put over to the Major who asked me to come and have a chat.

We stopped again at the Guardroom at the entrance to the barracks and were directed to the Admin block. Parking the jeep almost in the same position as yesterday, Brian was left to look after the unit. Guss and I went into the offices and met the Major. He showed us a map of large scale which was hanging on the wall. It showed the whole region of the Corinthian Alps and the Dolomites. The Major pointed out an area where the German troops were believed to be encamped.

He said that according to their latest intelligence, Martin Bormann was expected to move out within the next couple of days. As far as they could tell, his route would be as follows: Dobbiaco-Toblach; Auronzo di Cadore; Ponte nelle Alpi, near Belluno; Treviso; Mestre; Chioggia;

Ravenna; Rimini; Pesaro; Ancona; Ortona; Vasto; Foggia; Cerignola; Barletta and finally Bari.

'Ah!' I said. 'That's where he is making for.'

'*Si. Pensiamo che lui va in Argentina,*' replied the Major.

Guss was writing down all those names of the towns that the Major was reciting. At least now we had the approximate location of the Germans and also the proposed route of escape.

'What kind of vehicles will he have to do that long journey with?' I asked.

'We believe his transport is good,' the Major replied. 'He has a car and he will be escorted by two repainted ex-army vehicles. According to the intelligence reports, he has been advised to travel as much at night to start with and then to go like hell until he gets to Bari.'

Guss said that he would not like to be in his shoes.

I didn't give the Major any idea as to what I was going to do but I was determined to give all the information I had to HQ and then see what they wished me to do. I had difficulty at first getting through on the phone but eventually I made contact and the voice at the other end acknowledged what I had said and instructed me to follow any leads but under no circumstances should I apprehend. As the situation was now getting to the critical stage, I rang off and thought that I would phone later; perhaps then I would be able to speak with someone of higher authority. The phone line was very bad and I couldn't get the name of the person with whom I was talking.

I asked the waiter if he could recommend a good restaurant and he gladly gave us the directions, which suited us, for I wanted to get out of Udine as quickly as I could. He told us that there was a good place at Tricesimo, only a few kilometres out of town. It so happened that the place he recommended was on our way to where I wanted to go. I was determined to find out if all this talk about Martin

Bormann was true. The only way was to go as far as I could near to where his redoubt was reputed to be.

At Tricesimo, we lunched extremely well and were able to buy food which would last us for several days. The only items we couldn't get were hot drinks, so we had to buy the Italians' equivalent to our thermos flasks. I reckoned that Martin Bormann had it all worked out and that he was going to travel on one of the darkest nights and in vehicles that would cause the least suspicion to anyone en route.

After a very gruelling drive, taking turns at the wheel, we made the sanctuary of the police station at Dobbiaco-Toblach. It was a tiny place but our welcome was completely friendly and totally unexpected. The *Carabinieri* and some *Alpini* troops were packed inside the building and the hubbub was raucous to say the least. As far as we could see, every room was full of tobacco smoke and the dull electric light bulbs didn't help us very much to pick out who was in charge. As soon as the crowd realised that the newcomers were not of their tribe, the noise abated and through a channel which had been created, a figure appeared wearing some insignia of an officer. As he advanced, he saluted and I responded in like manner. With the compliments over he guided me and Guss over to a corner and asked what was our business. I showed him my ID booklet and he read it carefully and handed it back, giving an order to his lieutenant.

It was fortuitous that we arrived just at the moment messages were being exchanged over the field telephones about the movements of the Germans. They had been sighted approaching Brunico-Bruneck and were moving fast towards Monguelfo-Welsberg.

'That is the village next to this one,' I said, and I got the affirmative.

Without the slightest hesitation I moved, with Guss tailing me closely. We jumped into the jeep and Brian reacted to the instructions perfectly. We drove out of the village southwards and saw a gateway just off the road. There was a tree at the entrance. We manoeuvred the trailer and then re-hitched it to the jeep in readiness to pull away quickly.

We had just finished this parking business when Brian spotted some headlights approaching. He restarted the engine and we jumped in. To our annoyance, they were the *Alpini* vehicles so we switched off and got out again to listen for any distant engine sounds. The silence of the night was only interrupted by the gentle rustle of the leaves beneath the denuded tree beside us. Our vantage point gave us some view of the road when it was illuminated by the lights of any vehicles, but once they had passed by, the night remained extremely dark in spite of the surrounding snow.

We seemed to be waiting an interminable time. The only disturbance was made by Brian, who had to leave the driving seat in order to have a pee.

Our feet were getting very cold and to be sure that the engine would start immediately, Brian made it run for a minute or two at intervals. Behind a ridge some distance away we saw the reflection of vehicle lights in the sky. Then they disappeared, only to be seen again as the vehicles progressed along the twisty road towards us. Guss remarked that his heart was now beating fast and I had to agree with him that mine was doing likewise. Brian had the engine running but no lights were shown. With the passenger door wide open, we were ready to make a dive into the jeep.

'Are you all right, Brian,' I asked, hoping that he was not going to be scared of driving on the narrow roads with the snow making things more difficult.

'I'm okay, Skipper! You don't have to worry about me,' came the cheerful reply.

Distances were very deceptive, for the lights of the oncoming vehicles appeared nearer than we thought and quickly they were upon us. We couldn't see what types they were, except the middle one of the three was a car. The first and last vehicles looked a little bigger than our 15 cwt. Morris Commercial Wireless trucks, which we'd had in the desert. They both had trailers attached and that was all we had time to see as they drove past. We gave them a little distance and then followed. It was certain that their speed would be governed by the slowest vehicle of the three, plus the road condition.

We didn't want to get too near them, in case the personnel in the rear vehicle would think that we were going to try an assassination of the VIP in the car. Of course we would have liked to do that if we had known for certain that the occupants were of such high rank as Martin Bormann.

Not long after leaving Toblach, the road became nasty with many hairpin bends and steep climbs, so we had to drop back for fear that our presence would start a shooting match. It was obvious that whoever was in that middle car had a strong bodyguard squad to afford protection, and I was not going to risk anything going wrong.

Brian was continually going into second, first, second gears as we rounded the tight steep gradients and the trailer kept reminding us that, in spite of its load, it was following under protest.

As we passed through Auronzo di Cadore, Guss ticked the village off on his piece of paper. We seemed to climb more and more before feeling any relief of a downward direction, then the road levelled out a little as we neared the three other Cadores.

Brian said, 'Skipper, I wonder, if those cars go straight on to Vittorio Veneto and Treviso, will they not be conspicuous and be stopped?'

'I find that the whole thing has been well planned by the Combined Allied Forces and the Governments of Austria and Italy and big politics is playing its hand,' I replied. 'I cannot see any other reason for this exercise, than to see where these guys are making for.'

The vehicles ahead were driving much faster now, which told us that the conditions were improving and that gradually we were leaving the high mountain area.

We had been motoring solidly for two hours and three quarters when we saw the three vehicles pull up in a square at Treviso. Our milometer read that we had covered 107.44 miles since we began the chase. From a safe distance, we stopped too and changed drivers. Guss took the wheel for this next leg. The street lights in Treviso were totally inadequate but thank goodness, the dawn was just up enough to give the slightest hint of light. We had left the snow behind, although the roads were still dangerous with the slush.

We watched the Germans as best we could from our distance and saw that they were all in civilian clothes. There might have been one or two still inside the vehicles who were in uniform but at this stage, we couldn't tell. Immediately their convoy stopped, we saw some figures scurrying from one vehicle to the other and Brian said that they were refuelling. In a flash, he unleashed a corner of the canvas covering the trailer, and heaved out a five gallon jerrycan. I held the can with him as his fingers were so cold. Just as we were only a few drops from being empty, Guss called out that the Germans were pulling away. We just managed to tie up the canvas and leap into the jeep before the last vehicle disappeared up the road towards Venice.

'Guss, did you make a note of the time when we left Dobbiaco?' I asked.

'We left at 0253 hours, Skipper,' replied Guss.

Brian remarked that it was no wonder he was cold, so to console him, we said that we were equally cold. We skirted Venice and followed a road beside the marshes to Chioggia.

Now we had a very strong wind to contend with, which blew in from the Adriatic.

Our ability to cope with the feeding arrangements whilst motoring was to be commended, although it was not without some misfortunes! It was clear now to me that this German group were intending to reach the south but I was still curious as to where they would end up. I warned the lads that at the next stop, I would try to get in contact with HQ.

Guss suddenly pulled up, for he had seen the convoy ahead had stopped. Several figures were darting about from one car to the other, in a sort of panic situation. We had just passed Mesola and the vehicles were stationary at a road junction off to the right. It looked as if it was a breakdown, or something like that, so I seized the opportunity and got Guss to turn the jeep around. Brian and I leaped out of the jeep and unhitched the trailer. Guss struggled with the wheel, having to take several moves forward and backwards, in order to turn the jeep around.

Facing the way we had come, Brian and I hitched the trailer up again and off we went to the little village of Mesola. All was extremely quiet except for some activity at the local bakery, which we were most fortunate to find. The bakers were shocked at suddenly seeing two men appear at their door, especially a British army officer and a civilian.

I showed them my ID booklet and told them that it was extremely urgent to make a phone call to my HQ at Padua. I told them that I was in a very great hurry and that I would recompense them for their trouble.

'Gee, Skipper, that bread smells good, doesn't it,' remarked Guss, who followed me inside.

The baker took us over to his phone which was hanging on the wall on a bracket and Guss immediately got to work on the phone, dialling the right number from his notebook.

Unfortunately, the phone didn't respond to the number Guss dialled, so he tried the operator at the exchange. The ringing out seemed to go on and on before there was a reply. Guss was now a little agitated and bawled down the phone that it was the police and an emergency!

On a surprisingly clear line, we managed to get through to HQ. By now it was daylight outside. The Corporal who was manning the office in Padua was trying to raise the duty officer, so more time was spent. Finally, Captain Manners came to the phone and Guss handed me the earpiece.

'I am following a convoy of Germans in three cars, and in one of them, I am sure it is Martin Bormann,' I said. 'The *Alpini* Army Intelligence alleged that Martin Bormann was holed up in the mountain redoubt with about fifteen hundred ruthless SS troops to guard him.'

I was cut short by Captain Manners, who replied, 'You are to follow him wherever he may go but do not apprehend. I repeat, *do not apprehend*! Keep—'

Then the phone went dead. I hung up the earpiece immediately and counted out some Italian money and gave it to the baker. He was more than pleased when he saw how much I had given him. Guss, meanwhile, had bought a couple of the newly baked loaves which were flat and round. I could hear the jeep's engine running, so losing no further time, we said our good-byes and fled to the jeep. Brian sped off as fast as we could making the main road with ease.

There was much more daylight now, so we could see quite a distance ahead and we didn't require the lights any more. Passing the junction where the Germans had stopped for whatever was their trouble, we noticed a wheel leaning against the stone boulder and quickly saw that it was deflated. What other troubles they might have had, was anyone's guess.

We drove on to the outskirts of Ravenna where we stopped for a minute for me to change over with Brian. We hadn't seen it when we had stopped, but further on we came across one of the street urinals, so we made good use of it. The 'oohs' expressed the relief each one of us felt.

With surprisingly little traffic about, we sped on through Pesaro and still the Germans were not to be seen. I was beginning to wonder if they had taken another route. Chatting with my crew, I suggested that perhaps they might think that we had given up the chase and that there was no further need for them to motor in such a hurry.

On a straight piece of road alongside the beautiful Adriatic, I was looking far ahead and saw a knot of vehicles stopped off the road beside the rocks. I stopped at what must have been about six hundred yards away. The Germans were clearly visible but still one could not pick out who was their leader.

Checking our position on our map, we saw we were four miles south of Fano. We found a spot where we could get across the road and put the jeep on firm ground, in a spot which also afforded us quite a lot of cover. I certainly didn't want to antagonise the Germans, for they easily outnumbered us. Apart from which, any scrap would defeat the object of the exercise.

Guss looked around our little area, sniffing the ozone which was very pungent as one faced across the water. Brian did his checks on the jeep and patted the bonnet as if to say, Good girl! The trailer was terrific, for there was no sway or lunging and it kept very dry inside. It was good to stretch our legs and after a little loosening of our muscles, we checked our food supply. We all took turns at every moment to keep watch on the activity of the German group, as we were not going to let them get away without us.

Almost at the same time, we saw the German party leave their vehicles and walk down to the water's edge. Their movement in a bunch caught each of our eyes, so we kept them under observation and were amazed at their nonchalance. We assumed that they'd peeled off their boots or shoes and socks, for they went into the water to refresh their feet.

It was obvious now that the party was not in any hurry – which was food for our thoughts – and again to our surprise, we saw they had smoke coming from something, which we could only assume must have been some kind of portable cooker. Brian and Guss wasted no more time and got our food out which was to serve as our breakfast. I kept watch. I wished it had been possible for me to have got a closer look at the party to assess who was who. There was always a tight circle of men around one person who looked to be their leader, but not a feature could be accepted for certain.

Cleverly, the lads got breakfast but at the same time, were ready to jump into the jeep at a moment's notice, should the Germans move off. Brian was a good lad and took his share of the 'domestic' side of our lives very well. One thing was for sure, he would have plenty of tales to tell his family, when he eventually got his demob. For instance, he learnt very quickly that on exercises such as ours, any inhibitions soon dissolved and matters concerning natural functions had to be attended to without becoming embarrassed.

All three of us had quite a stubble on our faces which made our skins itch. A good hot bath was merely a dream, but something glorious to look forward to. In typically German fashion, the party ahead had quickly and efficiently packed up and were moving off, a procedure which seemed to have taken only minutes. Thank goodness we had our things stashed away in readiness, so we moved off too.

The respite had taken up an hour and twenty minutes, which Guss noted down in his 'diary'. As we reached beyond the spot where the Germans had stopped, we got our first sight of the port of Ancona. Knowing it to be a port, I became anxious, fearing that the Germans might be making for a ship. I got Brian to speed up and to get closer to the convoy but to our relief, the vehicles turned off right and followed the road south, to Civitanova Marche. The further south we went, the more convinced I became that the Germans were making their escape by ship.

Keeping the vehicles well in sight, we saw them slowing down to a stop just outside a little village called Pineto. I was glad of this enforced stop, for I wanted to let Guss take the wheel, as Brian had been driving long enough and was getting tired.

The Germans were refuelling their vehicles, so we did the same. Guss and I had learnt to take advantage of any stops in order to keep the tank well loaded, for in no way were we going to be caught out by having run dry!

This time, we had stopped much nearer the convoy and were very surprised to see that the vehicles were larger than we had originally estimated. They had been painted almost the same colour green as our own army vehicles but the trucks with their trailers, were bigger than our 15 cwt. wireless truck. They appeared to be nearer the size of the American Personnel Carriers. The car, too, was bigger than our Humber Staff Car and it was fairly streamlined at the rear. It looked a powerful brute.

The Germans made sure that their VIP who they were guarding did not appear, which made me more resolved to get a look at him at the first opportunity. As the Germans moved on, so we followed and as we expected, the convoy drove straight through the centre of Pescara. When they came to the low bridge spanning the inlet from the sea to the docks, the tyres and the weight of the vehicles made a thunderous noise, startling the pedestrians at the side.

The coast road beyond the town was beautiful, and in spite of the heavy clouds which dulled the still waters, the Adriatic looked great. Relentlessly, the convoy drove on and on and we kept our distance. The sky was getting darker, partly because of the weather and partly because it was now late afternoon.

The road ahead became very twisty on a stretch before Vasto, and Brian and I had a job to prepare some food which would be manageable. However, we succeeded, for the three of us were becoming ravenous.

Just as we were entering the little town of Termoli, we saw the convoy had driven off the road around a small square and stopped at the far side facing the main road. There seemed to be quite a bit of activity around the vehicles, occupying everyone's attention, which allowed Guss to almost do an emergency stop and swing across the road down a little side street. We went down until we came to a street on our right, which seemed to me to run parallel to the main road, and then we were lucky to find that the next turn right took us up to the main road again. Brian remarked that we had been very lucky but Guss said that many towns and villages were built in blocks. We stopped short of the main road and out of sight of the Germans.

Leaving Brian to look after the jeep, Guss and I walked close in to the wall until we came to the main road, then we dashed across to the square where there was an electricity sub-station on one corner. The attention the Germans attracted allowed us to get fairly near without being spotted by the locals, near enough to faintly hear them talking.

Guss said, 'Skipper, they are speaking in French!'

Whispering to each other, we watched carefully and made our comments.

'Clever bastards, trying to make out that they are Frenchmen,' remarked Guss into my ear. Guss wanted to get nearer, as he was in civilian clothes, but I thought that it would be too dangerous.

Suddenly, a row developed amongst the Germans, and the French tongue alternated with the German by mistake, resulting in the door of the car opening. Then, out jumped a well-built, tallish man wearing a long heavy looking black leather coat. The row immediately stopped, with an exchange of words. Guss and I could see clearly but only for a brief moment, the man's face. It was Martin Bormann. We both said the same thing at the same time. We had carried the man's picture in our minds for long enough, as we had seen so many of him in the magazines in Austria. Short of hearing one of the Germans calling his name, we were prepared to swear that he was Hitler's deputy. The awe and respect the group had for this individual showed that he must have been of the highest rank. The man remonstrated with the offenders and ordered the convoy to move off as soon as possible.

We hurried back to the jeep and Brian, seeing us running, had the jeep already ticking over. It was getting quite dark now which helped us to get to our position without being noticed. We saw the Germans having a little difficulty in getting away because of the curious onlookers, but once free, they sped off in a southerly direction.

We followed and had to go like hell in order to catch up to our usual distance. It was understandable that within such a group, having sustained bombing and other harassments from the American and Italian forces up in the mountains for so long, and then this tremendous drive, nerves and tempers would be at breaking point.

In pursuit of the convoy, in order to keep their lights in view, Guss remarked that he wished he could gun the lot down. I agreed with his feelings and wondered what the politics were behind this escape. I said to myself, Well, Bell, yours is not to reason why. Yours is to do and die!

How often have we in the service said this to ourselves or to each other!

Guss remarked that it was a pity that I was in battledress, for if I had been in civvies, we could have got nearer to the group at Termoli. I admitted that I was too conspicuous in uniform and said that I would change next time we stopped if there was the chance.

Incredible as it seemed, we had gone only a matter of eight miles when we saw the convoy ahead had stopped. We pulled up immediately and switched off our lights. Brian edged the jeep and trailer just off the road. Guss volunteered to creep ahead to find out what the hold-up was about, for we could see some arc lights illuminating works of a kind. Brian helped me with the grips so that I could get to mine quickly. I grabbed my trousers, sweater and cap and flung my battledress blouse into the grip. Brian folded it a bit whilst I struggled with my trousers, for I hadn't taken my boots off and the legs were a bit tight to get them over the boots. Just as I was struggling and overbalancing, Guss came back and laughed his head off.

'Gee, Skipper! Caught with your trousers down!' I was too busy seeing the funny side of the situation to be embarrassed, but the changeover was darned cold! After making sure that I had not dropped anything on the ground as I transferred my wallet, keys and handkerchief, I zipped up the grip and made it safe in the back.

Meanwhile, as all that manoeuvring was going on, Guss told us the reason for the hold-up. There was a gang repairing a bridge which had been blown up during the battles and they were not expecting traffic at that time, apparently. We were quite used to seeing the results of the many battles which had been fought to reoccupy Italy, and now we realised that we had arrived in an area which once formed an incredibly strong line of defence which the Germans put up from this area across to Naples. Guss said that he could remember hearing the Forces Radio broadcasts announcing the news that the Germans were putting up fierce resistance along their line from Foggia to Benevento and Naples.

The battles had gone on for ages. Our forces were held down on this line for a long time and many many casualties were inflicted on both sides.

In the dark and near to the sea, we listened carefully in case anyone from the German group should wish to be nosey as to who we were. Guss felt a little uneasy and quietly reached for the sub-machine gun, slinging it over his shoulder in readiness. I kept my pistol ready in hand. The minutes turned into nearly an hour before there was movement ahead and we saw the convoy slowly negotiate the crossing which the engineers had temporarily made to let the traffic through.

As we drew near, we lost sight of the Germans for the arc lights blinded us, putting all beyond into pitch darkness.

'*Che succede?*' the workers called as we surprised them. Seeing a British army jeep following a convoy of strange looking vehicles made them very inquisitive. Guss yelled out that we were on military manoeuvres and told Brian not to stop.

'Phew, we got out of that one, Skipper!' said Brian. He raced through the gears and soon had the tyres whining loudly on the hard road surface. It didn't take us long to catch up with the German vehicles, as there were hold-ups after hold-ups because of the many bridges which had been severely damaged and were under repair.

We finally reached the outskirts of Foggia and the rain hammered down in a subtropical storm fashion. With the rain, the wind got up in strong gusts and where we were exposed to the sea, the wind caught us side on and made the jeep veer quite a lot.

Passing right through the centre, we negotiated a large piazza at the head of a big green park which looked dull and uninviting in the pouring rain. The street lights were dull too. Brian remarked that nearly everywhere along the coast we had passed through towns which had dull street lighting.

Beyond Foggia, we came across more bridges; some were rebuilt, some were half-finished and the majority were in a terrible state, causing long hold-ups for the traffic. We had to be very vigilant in order not to get too close to the Germans whenever they had to stop. The rain pelted down and made visibility difficult.

We passed through Cerignola and followed the road leading back to the coastline. In between the many hold-ups, one or other of the two passengers dozed, but we made sure that only one slept at a time, for fear of the driver falling off to sleep.

Midnight had passed and we calculated that if the convoy was going to Bari, we would have another sixty-five miles to go. I asked Brian to pull up and change over with myself. We did that in quick time and still had the rear lights of the vehicles ahead in view.

On reaching Trani, we found the rain abated to a nasty drizzle and that crosswind which had plagued us along the coast had now spent itself out.

It was getting on for three o'clock when we came to the outskirts of Bari and, moving up a little nearer now to the convoy, I was anxious not to lose them in the turnings of the many streets, for it was quite a large town. We couldn't see the docks yet for the darkness of the night, and it was only when we had driven well into the periphery of the town, were we able to see the harbour area. This was distinguishable by tall cranes which supported brilliant lights, and we finally realised that we had reached it when we saw them.

The German convoy drove straight through the gates off the long street which ran parallel to the sea, and passed huge sheds until it stopped alongside a passenger cargo ship. Gangways had been positioned near the aft deck housing. Before we had time to see more, we were challenged by the *Carabinieri*. I showed them my red booklet and they directed us to park the jeep near their cabin.

I was rooted to the spot with fascination, watching every move the Germans made, so Brian took the wheel and turned the jeep around and parked it where he was directed.

He quickly joined us and we found a place under cover where we could watch the whole procedure.

The moment the vehicles stopped on the quayside opposite the aft cargo holds, the Germans followed their master up the gangway and into the sanctuary of the ship. The cranes went to work with enormous steel nets attached to two steel channels, set apart. Each vehicle was driven on to the channel very carefully, so that the wheels would rest on the exact spot. The crane then lifted the vehicle high in the air and over the side of the vessel and into the cargo hold. This was repeated five times, for even the trailers were taken on board.

In our cold and exhausted state, we watched in incredulity at the happenings and remained baffled at the situation. The moment the last piece of equipment was on board, the lights went out on the dockside and the dockers slipped the mooring ropes off the bollards. Feverish activity on deck followed the slight movement of the ship away from the dock wall. We heard the clang-clang of the ship's instruments demanding response to the Captain's orders. A rush of churning water could be heard near to us, which meant that the screws were now turning. We couldn't see whether or not the vessel was being helped away by tugs, and we didn't really care.

'Skipper! Are you all right?'

I didn't know who asked but I couldn't answer. I was absolutely spent with fatigue, hunger, cold and anger.

My feelings were of burning frustration, and when I saw my two lads with red eyes and looking like scruffy tramps, my emotions got the better of me and I had to fight hard to prevent myself from breaking down.

I remember it was Brian who said, 'Never mind, Skipper, that bastard won't live for very long, wherever he may be going, for he won't have any friends.'

That was no comfort for me but the lad meant well. The navigation lights of the ship were now visible and some lights could be seen at the portholes. Activity was still going on aft over the hold, but by the time the vessel reached the end of the breakwater, the dock lights went out. The vessel was on its way but the destination was still unknown.

We turned away, thoroughly low in morale.

'What time is it, Guss?' I asked, just to say something.

'It's ten minutes past four, Skipper.'

We walked to the cabin of the *Carabinieri* and asked them where could we find a hotel. They recommended us to try the *Marina* in the Via Napoli. I then asked if they knew where the ship was bound for.

With a shrug of his shoulders, the sergeant replied, '*Non posso dire. Penso in Argentina.*' That's what we thought too.

Brian led Guss and me to where he had parked the jeep and we left to find the hotel. In our search, we passed the police station which would serve us later on in the day. The first priority was to get the lads and myself into the hotel, where we could have a hot bath and a comfortable bed. Beyond the police station, we found the hotel, and drawing right up outside, Brian switched off and we unloaded the gear.

I rang and rang the doorbell, and although there was a light in the hall, there was no response for a long time. I kept ringing, then the porter arrived and opened up. He got quite a shock when he saw us, for we looked a right mess. However, I put some money into his hand straight away and told him that we wanted two double rooms. When the porter saw how much I had given him, we were accepted without delay, and in return, I showed him my little red book. That was enough to put him into a panic situation, for he couldn't do enough for us after that!

I asked him to sell me a half-bottle of rum and he rummaged behind the hall desk and found the key to the bar. The four of us, for the porter had a swig too, drank the bottle dry. Grabbing our kit, we then made our way upstairs to our rooms. I gave strict instructions that we were not to be disturbed, and said goodnight to the lads.

It was 2.20 in the afternoon when I awakened and found myself still dressed but without boots on. The eiderdown was wrapped around me and two pillows were on the floor. My trench coat had been flung on to the chair and my grip was still fastened and dumped where I'd left it when I entered the room.

I wondered how the lads had fared and if they had slept as long as I. Gosh, I felt in such a mess and when I saw myself in the mirror, I didn't hesitate any longer in undressing, and grabbing my towel out of the grip and the bag of shaving tackle, I flung my trench coat over me and slipped out of the room, dashing for the bathroom. Thank goodness, it was free!

Whilst the bath water was running, I carried out my necessary functions and had a painful shave. That bath was one of the best I'd had for a long time. The water was soft and I was able to wallow in the big old fashioned cast-iron affair in comfort. It was surprising how quickly one regained the spirits after these basic comforts – almost necessities. I was just drying myself when a knock sounded on the door and Guss's voice calling, 'Is that you, Skipper?'

I hurried with my coat as cover and opened the door. There stood Guss just in his underpants and dashed in, passing me like a scared rabbit, making a straight line for the loo.

'Take your time, Guss, there's no hurry. The water is nice and hot. How did you sleep?'

As I was talking through the closed door, suddenly Brian appeared from a completely different room to the one I thought they both had. He too was clad only in his underpants and as he saw me, he dashed inside his room with embarrassment. I called through the closed door, asking if he was all right and if he slept well.

'After I got a room to myself, I slept like a log, Skipper,' he replied.

I told him to take his time and to meet downstairs, when ready.

It was late that afternoon by the time we collected together down in the hallway.

'What's happening now, Skipper?' asked Guss.

'We're going to get ourselves some food!' I said.

Brian nodded his approval, and feeling like quite different people, clean-shaven and far less tired, we walked to a trattoria, as directed by the hotel porter, which faced the castle in the old part of the town.

The folk at the trattoria couldn't understand the crazy Englishmen asking for food at such an early hour, but after we explained that we had been travelling all night and only went to bed at 4 a.m., they accommodated us and gave us a hot meal, starting with *zuppa di mare*. The owners were a peasant family but they knew how to cook and to look after their customers. They were so attentive and kind that I didn't have the heart to tell them that I had been a prisoner of war and held in a transit camp somewhere on the outskirts of the town. I was curious to know if it still existed but I thought better not to ask.

The questions the family asked us while we ate and drank were so numerous that by the time we had finished our meal, they knew our complete history, more or less.

They were such a happy family that we could have stayed longer chatting to them, but we had other things to do.

Passing by the police station on our way back to the hotel, we called in, and I introduced ourselves, to the officer in charge. Again, my red booklet came in handy as it put the officer more at ease. Our sudden appearance caused quite a stir. As soon as he recognised the rank on the epaulettes of my battledress blouse, he warmed to my requests and showed me to the telephone. I was anxious now to make a call to my HQ.

The Duty Corporal answered the phone and put me through to Captain Manners.

'Where are you now, Bell?' he asked.

'I am at Bari, Philip,' I replied. 'Now listen carefully, for the line is not all that good. We have seen Martin Bormann. There was a fleeting chance at a village called Termoli, which I will put in my report later, then we followed the convoy—'

I was interrupted. 'What convoy? What did it consist of?' he asked.

'There were two trucks and one car. To continue. We knew it was Martin Bormann himself, from the memories of the pictures we had seen of him in the magazines when we were in Austria hunting Reisler. We followed the convoy down to here at Bari and saw him again walking up the gangway on to a ship, which we were told was going to Argentina.'

'Are you sure, Ian, that it was him?' asked Captain Manners.

I got a nod from the *Carabiniere* officer, who had over-heard the conversation, agreeing with what I was saying.

'Philip, I couldn't do more than I did to verify if it was Martin Bormann or not, but we are as sure as we can be that it was him. Why has he been able to escape the country and go free?' I asked.

Captain Manners didn't reply to that question.

'What are my instructions now, Philip?' I asked.

'You'd better come back to HQ,' he told me, 'because you have an assignment to do for the Americans at Livorno. Brian Dixon has been granted Christmas leave, so he has to come back now. It looks like you and Guss will be spending Christmas with the Americans. Have a good trip!'

Captain Manners rang off. I gave the news to Brian about his Christmas leave and he was overjoyed.

'Guss, you and I are going to spend Christmas with the Americans at Livorno, so it seems.'

'Skipper, I couldn't wish for a better Christmas. It will be a lot of fun!'

We chatted a little while with the police officer, who told us that the ship had only docked a few hours ago. They didn't know where it came from, nor where it was bound for. Their guess was that it would be going to Argentina, as several ships had been going there in the last two years.

The police were told to expect a small convoy of vehi-cles carrying some VIPs, who were to be allowed through without any hold-ups, and that they would board the ship, with their vehicles. The vessel was to sail at 0330 hours.

'Did the vessel have a name or carry any national flag?' I asked.

'We didn't bother to see as it didn't concern us. Perhaps the Port Authorities would be more useful,' he replied.

It was obvious that we were not going to get much information out of the police, but the whole affair really baffled me. Question upon question ran through my mind and the more I thought of those bastards getting away, the more angry I became. Guss gripped me by the arm and pulling me towards the door, said, 'Come on, Skipper, let's go back to the hotel.'

Guss could now read me like a book and saw that I was becoming irritable and wanted to ease my feelings, so I gave way and, thanking the officer for his courtesy, we left for the hotel.

It had turned dark outside and after hours and hours of constant drizzle, it was finally abating. Back at the hotel, the porter took our coats to be dried and we went into the lounge to have a drink and to talk over our next move.

'Brian, would you please go and check up on the total mileage we have done so far since leaving Dobbiaco, before we forget and run up some more miles,' I said.

Brian dashed out and left Guss and me to comment on the lad's efforts so far. We both could not speak more highly of him, especially Guss, for he had more to do with him than I.

'We have clocked 633.4 miles exactly, Skipper,' Brian said as he came in.

'That's over one thousand kilometres,' remarked Guss. Guss always thought in kilometres, whereas I reckoned in miles.

'Thank God the jeep ran well and gave no trouble,' remarked Brian.

'I want to thank you two lads for putting up with that journey, for it wasn't one of the best for comfort,' I said. 'I very much appreciate your efforts. You will have a great deal to tell your family, when you return home, Brian.' We drank a toast to that. 'Now. Do you lads wish to stay here the night or move off and dig in somewhere on our way home? Somewhere where we can have some real comfort and the best of food?'

The two men went into a little huddle and then Guss spoke up.

'Skipper, we know your meaning of "early" so we would prefer to move off tonight and make our way north as far as we can.'

'Let's try to make Foggia for the night. It is only about eighty miles, what do you think, Brian?' I said.

Brian was all for spending a night in some luxury hotel and agreed willingly.

'How much petrol have we left?' I asked him.

'I'll go and make sure, Skipper.'

Off he went again and presently came back smiling, saying, 'We've got five full cans left, which is more than enough to see us to Padua.'

We decided there and then to leave. Up we went to our rooms to pack our things, whilst the porter had the bill prepared. I paid just a little over the odds and told the porter to keep the difference. Once the grips were down in the hallway, Brian went to get the jeep and the little beep on the horn, told us that Brian was ready.

The porter, poor soul, came to the door to see us off and his manner was so courteous but very servile, which made one wonder how they fared with their rich employers. It never took much to please them but once they were on your side, they would do anything for you.

We were soon on the coast road heading north to Barletta, and as I looked back and saw the lights of Bari receding in the distance, I thought of the last hours and felt my blood begin to boil again. I will never forget that dock scene at Bari, as long as I live.

'Don't stress yourself anymore, Skipper. There's nothing you can do about it. You did what you were ordered to do, so let the politicians sort it all out later on. They are far more expert at these high matters of politics, than us lesser mortals!' said Guss, and he spoke a great deal of sense.

'History will tell us if they were right or that we would have been right in capturing him.'

'Thanks, Guss. Remind me to promote you to the Senate when we get back,' I said jokingly.

'Okay Brian, put your foot down and let's get to Foggia,' I said.

We made Barletta in good time but then we had a few hold-ups again at the bridges which were being repaired. As we turned inland towards Cerignola, the drizzle had stopped completely and also the breeze. We wasted no time in passing through Cerignola, for we knew we still had some more bridges to cross which were being repaired and would, for sure, be held up.

Finally we came to Foggia and drove as far as the big piazza, which we'd noted on our way down. To the right was a wide street where we saw a couple of hotels with their illuminated signs. We stopped at the first one and Guss and I went in to see what they had to offer. Again, our presence was made most welcome. We were offered three single rooms with bath, all on the same floor. There was parking at the rear of the hotel and the porter directed Brian where to go. Brian came in from the back way, asking for our help as he couldn't unhitch the trailer by himself. He had to do this in order to park the jeep properly.

For a provincial town, the hotel was of high quality although it didn't have a restaurant. We didn't mind this, as the restaurants or trattorias were nearly always top grade. The three of us went up to our rooms to freshen up and to put out things we needed for the morning. It was a luxury not to have to dash out and along the corridor to the one and only loo!

As we got out into the street, the fresh air was invigorating, which aggravated the appetite. We walked up to the circular piazza and noticed a blue enamelled plaque with white letters, indicating it was the Piazza Cavour. I think that every town in Italy has a Piazza Cavour! To our right was a wide street which boasted shops and hotels and restaurants. We walked on a bit and came to a most attractive trattoria which appealed to us straight away. As soon as we were noticed by the staff, shrieks of joy were let loose. It was soon apparent that it was family owned and run and that the waiters were either sons and or cousins.

Our welcome was made more sincerely because of our ability to speak their language. I tried my best to speak Italian whenever I could, for I was making good progress and becoming fairly fluent, although I made many many mistakes. Guss was my tutor and constantly corrected me. We practically had two waiters to each of us by the time the á la carte folders were presented. The choice was enormous, so the lads took their time and ordered well.

Between the courses, we chatted to the waiters and heard their stories of the terrible times they had to endure under the German occupation. By the time the coffees had been served, we had heard the whole history of the war in their area.

Happily well dined and wined, we strolled back to the hotel and on the way, Guss teasingly asked Brian if he knew the name of the hotel.

'It is the Palace Sarti and it is in the Viale something Maggio?' came the reply.

'Good lad, the drinks are on me, next time!' said Guss, and patted him on the shoulder.

When we got into the hotel, we received the keys to our rooms and I told the lads that I would like to leave at nine o'clock in the morning.

It was a beautiful fresh morning when we left Foggia, and as we had anticipated, we were held up at the various bridges which were being remade. When some of the workers saw our jeep and trailer, they shouted remarks like, 'The War is over! The Enemy has gone home!'

It was all good-humoured banter and we gave back to them as much as they had flung at us.

As we came in sight of the sea again, we saw the island of Tremiti out in the distance. The sea was fairly calm, for there was only a gentle breeze. The coastline was beautiful. As we neared Termoli, Guss suggested that we stop in the square and have a look at the spot where we saw Martin Bormann.

'Perhaps one of that gang might have dropped something, which we could keep as proof,' he said.

We agreed to stop and have a look round. In any case, we wanted to have a coffee as it was already after eleven o'clock. Brian pulled into the familiar square, where we noticed a double urinal on one corner, which was directly opposite the electricity sub-station which we had hidden behind.

The German convoy had pulled up only yards from it, so we did the same, more or less in the exact position. Brian was the first to dash into the screened ironwork. His bladder was always weaker than ours. Guss and I waited until Brian came out so that the vehicle was guarded, then we went in. As we met outside, we had a look round in the gutter and on the sparse grass and well trodden soil, which formed the centre of the square. The ground was soggy after the rain and all sorts of small litter was strewn about, some half-trodden into the soil. We looked carefully but concentrated on the area where we saw the argument take place between the nervous Germans.

'What's that by your left foot, Guss?' shouted Brian.

Guss quickly looked down and saw something round, black and a bit shiny. Guss prised it out of the soil and wiped off the wet dirt. We gathered close to examine the find and it was a coat button with the German Eagle embossed in the centre in black paint on a white metal. It had a metal loop at the back, for sewing.

'I wonder if it came off Martin Bormann's coat as he got out of the car,' Guss remarked.

'That would be too much to expect, but it could be,' remarked Brian.

I suggested to them that from what we had seen of the group, they were in civvies but they could have been wearing coats too. Anyway, it was a great find and a wonderful souvenir. Clear evidence that they were Germans.

'Keep it safe, Guss,' I said as we got back into the jeep.

On the other side of the square on the main road, was a coffee bar, so we drove round and stopped outside. We went in and ordered three espressos.

'Wouldn't it have been interesting to have eavesdropped on their row, to know what they were arguing about?' said Guss, and brought out the button again to have another look. It was about the size of a halfpenny and quite strongly made. The German Eagle covered nearly the whole of the face and the black enamel was only partially scraped away, showing more of the white metal.

'I would love to keep this, Skipper,' pleaded Guss.

'Take care of it, for it may have a value in the future,' I remarked.

We arrived at Pescara in time for something to eat, so as we saw a trattoria on our road just beside the main railway station ahead, we stopped and enjoyed the break.

I took over the driving for the next leg which I intended to finish at Ancona. It was a very pleasant drive, for the road ran right along the water's edge for mile after mile. We reckoned it should take us about three hours and three quarters without hurrying, and it would be dark by the time we arrived at Ancona. The lads slept a bit, as the humming of the tyres on the road, plus the effects of the lunch, made them drop off to sleep. It was always a source of wonderment as to how much the body can or cannot stand, as the case may be.

After a very pleasant night spent at a good hotel, with good food at a nearby restaurant plus an early night, we were fresh to tackle the last part of our journey back to Headquarters.

Guss took over the driving for the first part and after sixty-eight miles, we stopped for our welcome break at Rimini. As there was only a further thirty-two miles to go before coming to Ravenna, Guss drove until we reached the town and then Brian took over for the last leg to Padua.

We arrived just before dusk and teatime. I said that I would be seeing the lads again soon, as they dumped my grip on the steps leading to the offices and they, greeting their friends, went off to their quarters and the garages, to return the jeep and trailer.

I was surprised to see new faces in the office. Even the Adjutant was new. I introduced myself and Captain Richard Hemmings responded with the usual courtesy salute to mine. With the niceties over, I replied to the usual questions like, 'Did you have a good trip?' and so on, and then asked if I may be taken to my hotel, so that I could get myself cleaned up.

I rang the office from my hotel to enquire if I was required to render my report straight away, verbally or written. There was no one who could give me an answer, so I skipped that question. I then left a message that I would see my two lads in the morning when I came over to the office.

I was collected from the hotel the following morning by the usual office 'buggy' and I reported in to the Adjutant. He was a very jovial type, young – about my age, twenty-six – and only recently had received his captaincy. He looked the epitome of an athlete but smoked like a chimney. I felt that he was endeavouring to show some respect for my experience but gave me the impression that he was too casual in his approach to his new duties as acting Adjutant.

However, we struck good mutual understanding right away, for I liked the man, he was pleasant and not stuffy. He could take a joke. He had a responsible job to do and I bowed to that authority and was ready to help where I could. He asked me into the enclosed office where we could chat over the events since my last departure, in our search for Colonel Bruno Zamboni.

Fighting hard to keep up with the questions, I replied to each one but began to change my mind about the fellow, for he was relentless with his demanding questions. Little did I know that everything we said had been recorded on tape through a small recorder on his desk. I gave my report verbally, exactly as I would have done if I had to provide a written one.

'Thank you, Ian,' he replied. 'Now you have two assignments for the Americans, with Christmas leave whenever you wish to work it in with your task. You will have Guss, of course, and a new driver, Driver George Titley of the RASC, from the pool. Corporal Jenkins will give you whatever you want for coupons, money and vouchers.

'When you get to Livorno, ask for a Lieutenant Michael Rod, he is an Aide to Colonel G. Villiers, who is in command of the CIC at the Headquarters of the American Forces of Occupation, Central Mediterranean Area. He will give you your brief and will obviously introduce you to his boss.'

'What on earth can the Americans want with me?' I asked.

'Ian, you know you gave them a lot of success by capturing Hans Vogle, and then you found that sod Bartinelli,' he said.

'I like the Americans and I am only too pleased to do something for them, but I hope there isn't a time schedule,' I said.

'You can have a week's leave over Christmas. Try and work in your investigations with more details about Zamboni, for we are not sure that he is dead. We have to have more proof. By the way, how did you find Brian Dixon?'

'I hope you will give him a good report for he behaved magnificently. He is a damn good fellow and no fool. He's tough and takes endurance well and he has a dry sense of humour. Yes, he is a good man,' I told him.

'Thanks, I'll make a note of that,' he replied.

As the meeting ended, I made my way across the yard towards the men's billets and the motor pool, when I saw Guss.

'Guss! How's it going,' I asked.

'Skipper! Who's going to be our driver for our next mission?'

'I don't know, Guss,' I replied, 'but come with me over to the Pedrocchi Club and we'll have a few frames of snooker.'

Just then, as we were about to arrange for the buggy to take us to the hotel, a soldier appeared leaving the office and approached us. With a smart salute, he stopped in front of me and asked, 'Sir, I believe you are Captain Bell. I have been assigned to you as your driver. Pleased to meet you, sir.'

'What's your name, driver?' I asked.

'Titley, sir. Driver George Titley of the RASC,' he replied.

'I gave him my hand to shake his and I was about to introduce Guss to him, when I was beaten to it by the two of them exchanging handshakes and names.

'We are just about to go over to the Pedrocchi Club to play snooker and to have a drink. Will you come too?' I said.

The lad looked a little perplexed with the informality but Guss soon put him at ease. Whilst we were waiting for the driver of the 'buggy' to come, I said to Driver Titley that working in our team, most of the time we would do many unorthodox things, such as what we were about to do.

'No one will ever challenge our actions, for the type of work we shall be doing demands complete unison of action and sometimes, the breaking of protocol. Where it is necessary to keep to rules and regulations, we shall. Otherwise, we shall get our job done as a friendly team. If you have any gripes or don't feel well, then it is up to you to tell me and I'll do my best to help you,' I told him.

The buggy arrived and we hopped in.

At the club, we sat out for a while in the lounge because the table was booked. Over drinks, we chatted and Guss answered many questions Driver Titley was asking. Apparently, Driver Titley had served with one other officer at the JAG Headquarters and knew some of the routine, but he seemed a little bit shy with me at first. I suppose he really didn't know what he was in for.

The snooker table became vacant, so we refilled our glasses and set the table up for the first frame. We tossed for who was playing who and the winner of three frames, would play the third person. I played with Guss first and lost out, so Guss took on Driver Titley. I had to remember to call him George but for the first hour I kept calling him Brian. I watched the two carefully as they played and knew that we were going to have a good team. George had an infectious chuckle and a wonderful sense of humour and soon had Guss on equal terms for leg-pulling.

'What do you have for transport, George?' I asked.

'Captain, you come and see my "Rolls" in the morning! She is the best in the fleet. No one dares to touch my vehicle.'

I promised to see the jeep first thing as soon as I got to HQ and told them, 'By the way lads, I'll give you one day to be ready and then we shall be off, okay?'

As I spoke between frames, I didn't put them off, and finally George won the match and took the fifty cigarettes.

I had received all my clean laundry and had selected what I needed for my next trip. This time, I had to take my dress uniform with me on account of spending Christmas with the Americans, so in my second grip, I also had my civvies and a couple of sweaters.

I was over at HQ at about eleven o'clock and went straight to the motor pool. George and Guss were standing in front of the most luxurious jeep. It had extra spotlights across the front and was painted a darker green than our usual Army green. There were twin wind tone horns on the front, similar to the one Nobby had on his jeep. Inside was very posh, with comfy seats. I am sure he had taken a leaf out of Nobby's book and benefited from it. I was only too pleased to see such a fine specimen of a vehicle, for after all, we were going to spend a great deal of time in that car.

George was ever so pleased that I gave him full marks for his initiative in turning a simple basic jeep into a really comfortable motor car. The trailer was alongside the jeep and again, there were ten five-gallon jerrycans full inside, all with a fresh coat of paint. The canvas that covered the trailer was new.

'Right, fellows, will you be all right to move off in the morning at 0800 hours?' I asked.

'We'll be round at the hotel at eight, Captain,' replied George.

Chapter Nine

The following morning, the lads arrived on time and we were soon off on our new assignment, heading for the American Forces Headquarters at Livorno.

During our journey, we made a diversion to Ariano so that Guss and I could show George the prison where Flight Sergeant Banks was tortured to death. Bologna was our first refreshment stop, then we proceeded to Florence. As we approached the city, the traffic became heavier with all types of American transport. I was becoming intrigued as to what the Yanks had in store for me, so I asked George to drive on to Livorno.

Knowing that we were going to be their guests gave rise to a curious speculation about our accommodation. We found the sprawling complex of buildings, with the American national flag flying high from a centre pole. The complex had been newly built for either the Naval Headquarters of the Italian Fleet or the Army's Central Command. At the main entrance, we were stopped by heavily armed soldiers, at the barrier. Our papers were demanded but my red booklet brought the desired attention and much more polite admission. A corporal politely gave us instructions as to where the offices of the CIC were located.

We passed several office blocks before finally reaching the building we required. An armed GI stood at the entrance and barred our way, even though I was in officer's uniform and showing three pips! Once more, I showed the soldier my ID booklet and as my identification was accepted, I was allowed into the building. Once inside the hallway, I was met by a corporal who escorted me to an office marked Lieutenant Michael Rod. The meeting was most cordial. His appearance was dapper and seemed extremely knowledgeable of my activities.

I found the man extremely alert and having a very active mind. During the preliminaries, the usual questions and answers about one's journey and so on, the intercom buzzer sounded on his desk and a real Yankee drawling voice said, 'Michael, will you bring Captain Bell in now.'

Colonel Gerald Villiers was about two inches taller than me but very slim. I gave him one of my best salutes and in return, I received the American equivalent, then an iron grip handshake. We went through many topics, including the report from Colonel Colacicco at Salzburg, and then I had the chance to ask him what has happened to Georgio Bartinelli. I was told that he was convicted and sentenced to death. He was hanged for his crime.

The Colonel went on to tell me about a case they have been trying to solve and to find the person responsible for the deaths of an entire crew of a Sherman tank during the battles around Viterbo. The tank had been disabled and the crew taken prisoner by the Germans and handed over to the Italians. It was not clear if it was the *Brigata Nera* into whose hands they were given, but their deaths were terrible. They were burnt alive in a small shed behind a farmhouse, near the village of Soriano nel Cimino. According to our information, some Germans witnessed this action, as they had demolished the farmhouse in the action that ensued.

According to the reports, one of the Germans, a crew member of the Panzer Corps, had tried to stop the Italians from carrying out the murder but was restrained by his colleagues.

'How many were killed?' I asked.

'There were five altogether. They were buried along with the couple from the farmhouse. We've had our guys out for nearly nineteen months looking for the culprits but have got nowhere.'

'Is there a time schedule on this case?' I asked.

'For heaven's sake no, man, you have your Christmas break first!' said the Colonel.

'Now, you and your crew can stay at the two hotels in the Piazza Ognissanti in Florence. One has been requisitioned for the officers and the other for the Warrant Officers, which your crew members will use. Lieutenant Rod will supply you with all the necessary passes for our PX stores and the various clubs in the city. Anything you wish to know or require, just ask Michael Rod.'

Whilst I thought the interview was most friendly, I still had the impression of an aura about the room and the personality sitting in the big swivel chair.

Once more back in Michael Rod's office, I was introduced to one of Michael Rod's friends, who was a doctor at the American Forces General Hospital. He was a black from Georgia. Michael gave me the various passes I required for the PX stores and the Clubs, for myself and for the lads, and said that the rooms at the hotels were ours until we told the hotel staff that we would not be wanting them again. I chatted quite a while with Michael and his friend and they invited me to join their party at the Club in Florence for Christmas Dinner and a dance afterwards. They said that there would be plenty of company, so I need not worry about not having a partner.

I could not have asked for better treatment. It was almost embarrassing to have such hospitality shown to me.

By the time I eventually got outside the offices and rejoined the lads, they thought that I had been kidnapped, for I was so long away. However, after I told them the whole story and when I revealed the details, especially about their luxury accommodation, they wanted to get there without any further delay, as it was already getting towards nightfall.

We arrived just as the street lights were coming on in the piazza. I went first to see the rooms for the lads, which I found to be quite luxurious. Both of them offloaded their grips and dumped them with the hall porter. I took both of mine to my hotel and the staff carried them up to my room, which was No. 19 on the first floor.

As arrangements to meet the lads in the foyer of my hotel had been made, when they were ready to go out, we met and went off into the city and had a meal at the restaurant where we had eaten once with Nobby, on our way down to Battipaglia. Guss remembered it well and gave George directions. As we arrived and George was parking the jeep, I realised that the trailer wasn't there, as I was so used to seeing it attached to the vehicle. George saw me looking and told me that it was well safe, locked up in the hotel's garage.

During the meal, we talked about our plans and I told them about our assignment.

'I say, Skipper, we've got something to do now, haven't we?' Guss remarked.

'Let's have your ideas, both of you,' I asked, giving them food for thought.

'Can we get Christmas over first and then have a go?' asked Guss.

'Yes, why not. We deserve to have a good time while we can,' I said. I was determined now to let the lads have as happy a time as they could, especially Guss. It was his seventh Christmas away from his family. Many times he had expressed the thought that he didn't want to go back to Czechoslovakia, as the Russians were in occupation, but he wished that he could see his family again as he loved and missed them so much.

The two men soon found plenty of friends amongst the GIs at the hotel and the men's PX Club. I was introduced to a horde of Michael's friends, who had their wives and girlfriends with them. Michael was engaged to the Cartographer at Headquarters, a lieutenant called Marion Renshaw, whose home was in Florida.

Christmas Day and Boxing Day were both celebrated with a large gathering at the Officers' Club in Florence, and we had a great time. When finally I met my crew, as I hadn't seen them for three days, they told me how they had spent their festivities and it seemed it was much in a similar way as I had, and they had no regrets. According to the lads, they had been taken all over the place by the Americans to meet nice young girls, both American and Italian. They had been to restaurants and dances, and other entertainments which I didn't delve into! The three of us were full of praise for the hospitality the Americans had shown, and somehow felt embarrassed that we could not have the opportunity to repay them.

Now that Christmas was over, we had to get down to our task ahead. We arranged to meet at the little coffee bar just around the corner to the piazza, where I heard their stories of the Christmas break.

'I think it would be a good idea to go to Soriano nel Cimino, where this crime is alleged to have taken place. We can begin our search of the area and hopefully meet some folk who can tell us the true story of what happened. I would like to leave in the morning at eight, is that okay?' I asked.

'That's okay, Captain, we'll be ready at eight!' was the reply. George and Guss were ready with the jeep and trailer attached outside the hotel and we loaded the grips, the large one in the trailer and the small overnight grip in the back, behind the bench seat. We drove off, following the road south through Greve, Siena and Aquapendente. Passing a beautiful lake, we arrived at Bolsena, which was such an attractive little town that we had to stop and have a break.

Reaching Viterbo in time for lunch, we found a trattoria and had a good meal. Throughout the journey so far, we were astonished to see the destruction to bridges and buildings. The Italians were so drained of finances and raw materials that they couldn't even to begin to think of a reasonable rebuilding programme. Any rebuilding we did see was mainly directed to bridges, electricity and gas supplies and the telephone lines.

According to our map, Soriano was only about ten kilometres away, so we reached there very quickly after our meal. Pulling up into the little square, we stopped beside a water pump. George stayed with the jeep whilst Guss and I went off to make some enquiries. It wasn't long before the local *Carabinieri* officers were in evidence, so we approached them first. Acknowledging their salutes, I gave them a package each of our cigarettes, which brought smiles and a willingness to answer our questions. The *Carabinieri* always walk about in pairs, in most places, and each like to be addressed as equals.

A very colourful picture of the battles in their area was given, with all the arm gestures, and also a rough direction of the area where the farmhouse had been located.

As soon as the villagers recognised us as being British and not American, they flocked around the jeep and stared at its unusual appearance. Guss told the two police officers why we had come to their village and they said to follow them and they would show us where the crime took place. We wandered down various paths which formed the boundaries to the vineyards, passing now and again great heaps of rubble which had once been a farmhouse. A retinue of inhabitants followed as they were curious to know what we were up to.

After a search around the area where the *Carabinieri* said the wooden hut had been, we saw nothing to interest us, so we returned to the square. The police officers introduced us to an aged farmer, who apparently, saw everything that was supposed to have happened. We thanked the two *Carabinieri,* who realised that they could not be of further help and devoted our attention to the farmer. After Guss introduced ourselves to him and gave him a couple of packets of cigarettes, he was very forthcoming with his knowledge of what took place with the American captives.

We took the old man over to a bar and sat him at a table inside whilst we got George to bring the jeep nearer and to join us. Four espresso coffees were ordered and when they came, we asked the farmer his name.

'Sergio Gimondi, *Signori,*' he replied.

Guss asked him to tell us all about the happenings to the American prisoners of war after they had been captured, during a tank battle near the village.

'*Dunque, Signori,*' said the *contadino*, and began his tale of the events, which Guss translated.

'The Germans along the line of defence were being heavily shelled by guns as well as the American tanks, and the Germans repeatedly counter-attacked. An American tank became disabled and the crew had to surrender to the Germans during one of their attacks and were taken prisoner. The Germans brought them away from the battle zone and handed them over to the Italians who were being used to supply their lines. The Italians looked a rough lot, though. They didn't seem to be regular army soldiers. The Italians locked the prisoners up in a wooden shed behind a farmhouse. That night, a carload of Germans, with some women, were returning from Viterbo. They were just coming into the village when a tank shell blew them to bits.

I was very near to this when it happened, that is why I have now to walk with a stick,' said the old man, and showed us his legs, which looked pretty ghastly, poor fellow.

'As a reprisal, the gang who were to look after the prisoners went over to the hut and poured petrol all over it and set it alight. *Mamma mia*, you could hear their screams from here! They were all burnt to death, *Signori.*'

'Signor Gimondi,' said Guss, addressing the old man to ask him many questions, 'You mentioned the word "gang". What did they look like? How were they dressed and were they often around this area?'

The *contadino* shuffled his sore foot and I thought it a good moment to provide him with a glass of wine.

'*Si, Signori,*' he replied, and then he went on to say that there were five or six of these soldiers, who were dressed in a grey uniform and who had bandoliers full of cartridges crossed over their shoulders. They carried sub-machine guns as well as rifles. They wore no hats, at least I never saw them wearing any. They used to date the girls here and in Viterbo, especially the leader, he was always after the daughter who used to live over there.' Signor Gimondi pointed out the house with his stick. 'Often the men would be with the Germans. They were up to no good, *Signori!* We all knew that but we were afraid of them. They were bullies, and if we didn't do what they wanted, they threatened us by saying they would get the Germans to come and shoot us.'

All this dialogue Guss translated, and George and I remained fascinated by the story.

Daylight was fading fast, so, thanking the poor old soul for all his help, we said that we had better go as we had to get accommodation at Viterbo, but we would be back in the morning and maybe we could meet again at the bar.

We found a small *pensione* in the Piazza del *Gèsu* at Viterbo, and managed to get ourselves rooms for the night. On the way, we discussed what we had heard.

'Somehow, fellows, we've got to find out what this "gang" was and who they were,' I said. 'It looks like this gang did the burning of the hut but we will have to be sure.'

'They may be a bunch of renegades, fortune hunters in the pay of the Germans,' George remarked.

'Somehow, I think you may be right, George,' Guss said, adding his weight.

That night while in bed, I lay thinking how were we going to establish who the killers were, and in particular, where would we be able to find them. If they were renegades, they would have no scruples with the local population while in the pay of the Germans, especially the SS Panzer Corps! They would also exercise their animal instincts on the local female population. That's it! I exclaimed to myself. We have to tackle the local prostitutes. I am sure we will be able to get something out of them which would be useful. I felt happier with my afterthought and dropped off to sleep.

Fierce banging on my door startled me out of my deep sleep. Guss was calling to ask if I was all right. I had overslept to an unusual hour and the lads were worried. I called to Guss that I would meet them in three-quarters of an hour.

I raced through my ablutions, dressed and packed and met the lads downstairs. Guss, meanwhile, had been talking to the wife of the owner of the *pensione* and had learnt a great deal about this so-called 'gang'. It seemed that they terrorised the area for quite some time, getting help from the Panzer troops in return for favours with the local girls. I told them what I had been thinking about before I went off to sleep and the lads said that they too had been thinking and wondered if their thoughts and mine had been the same.

'I know, Skipper, you want me to find out something from the local prostitutes!'

Guss didn't have time to finish what he was going to say when George piped up, 'Can I join you, Guss?'

'No, George, I want you with me as we'll go to Soriano,' I said. 'Guss will stay here. We will meet you for lunch at about one o'clock, Guss, over at the Mocca coffee bar.

Wasting no time, George and I raced off to Soriano and left Guss to make his investigations in Viterbo.

We parked the jeep in the square, which was very small, and the *contadino,* Gimondi, appeared from the bar to greet us. I asked him if he would point out to us again, where the girl he had mentioned lived. He was only too pleased. Knocking on the door of the house to where we had been directed, I waited for an answer. George stayed with the jeep because there were too many children showing an unhealthy interest in the jeep, trailer and contents, for us to leave it on its own.

With one more knock, the door opened to reveal a fairly well-dressed woman, perhaps in her early fifties. I immediately showed her my little red booklet and apologised for disturbing her. Looking somewhat perplexed, she invited me in and took me into her living room. In my best but inadequate Italian, I began to ask her the questions uppermost in my mind. I asked her to tell me all she knew about the events which led up to the deaths of the five American prisoners of war who were burnt to death in the village.

The woman firstly told me her name, Lilliana Banchetti. She said that two years before, her husband Paolo had died of cancer. She showed me a framed photograph of her eldest son, Pietro, and his family who lived in America. She then showed me another framed photograph of her second son Nino who was not married and worked at an hotel in

Innsbruck. I felt that as she was showing me the photos she was expressing both pride and sorrow. I saw on a side dresser a family photo showing a pretty young girl. I asked Signora Banchetti why didn't she have a photo of her daughter, as I knew she had one.

Trying her best to hold back her tears, she told me then the whole story of her daughter, the company and life she had led during the German occupation. As she related the events leading up to her death in early 1944, she rummaged in various drawers about the house, bringing out letters, scraps of handwritten notepaper and a hardback notebook which apparently her daughter Maria had used for a diary.

I felt very sorry for the woman and got the feeling that perhaps, I was the first foreign person to show a real interest and some sympathy for her tragic life. I asked her if I might come back in the afternoon with my official interpreter, for she had so much to show me and tell me of great interest to us. The *Signora* welcomed the idea and I asked her if she would kindly leave all the documents, photos and the diary out, so that we could look through everything properly. She was trying to be as helpful as she could, and agreed.

George hurried back to Viterbo where we met Guss as arranged. Between us, I don't know who was the more excited, Guss or myself. I allowed Guss to tell his story first.

'After touring around the town quite a lot, making a few enquiries here and there, I gathered that the best place to seek information of the events of those days was with a well known small group of prostitutes run by a woman called Bianca,' he said.

'I found her premises and was invited in, as I told her I wanted a "session". Plying her with plenty of money – but in doses – I got her to tell me that once, she and her girls were organised by a Maria Banchetti, and that they served the local Italians and the Germans who always wanted orgies, but paid extremely well. There was a gang of Italians who commanded the area ruthlessly and got what they wanted, when they wanted. The leader was Alfredo Giancarlo and his best friend was Luigi Franconi. She showed me their addresses and some of the gifts that they had been given. One or two of her girls were occupied in other rooms with their clients. Bianca was really a brazen hussy but, my God, Skipper, she knew how to give a bloke a good time!' he exclaimed.

'Gee, Captain, why didn't I stay with Guss?' said George, whose smile was bigger than ever.

I told Guss all about Signora Banchetti and at the very mention of the name, he showed astonishment. We had a quick meal and back we went to Soriano to the house of Signora Banchetti. I introduced Guss and immediately Signora Banchetti exclaimed, '*Come bello lui!*'

I hadn't seen Guss blush before.

Guss immediately began to ask all about the gang and how her daughter died. I excused myself for five minutes and went out across the square to the bar and bought some cigarettes and a big box of Perugina chocolates. I didn't know what they were like but I liked the box and they were expensive, so I knew they couldn't be bad.

Armed with these, I went again to the house and gave them to Signora Banchetti. She broke down with emotion, poor woman. By this time, Guss had managed to get all the information we wanted. He had the addresses of the two leading lights of the gang, although only one was complete. We had it confirmed that the killing was in reprisal for the death of his favourite prostitute, Maria.

Time was getting on, so we gratefully made our departure, telling the good woman that if ever we were her way again, we would most certainly come and see her. We were honoured with kisses on both cheeks each and then left.

On our way back to Viterbo, we discussed our good fortune and I was shocked to see that Guss was cuddling Maria's diary.

'It's all right, Skipper, Signora Banchetti gave it to me just as we were leaving,' he said.

'Now lads, we are coming up to New Year's Eve in a couple of days: where would you like us to be to see the New Year in?' I asked.

'Think about it and let me know later. I think we'll stop for tonight here at Viterbo again and set off early tomorrow morning, up north. What do you say about that?'

The lads agreed, so we booked in again at the *pensione*.

Up in my room, we chewed over the details and carefully went through the diary, page by page. It was most revealing.

There were references throughout the book to evenings spent with Nazi officers as well as with the lesser rankings. The details of her exploits would shock even the very hardest and seasoned perverts, with graphic details of each orgy from beginning to the end. She wrote paragraphs of her exploits with the 'gang'. Names appeared often in the narrative, such as Mario, Benito, Alfredo and Luigi. One page gave the addresses of Alfredo and Luigi, which matched the two from the list on Guss's piece of paper.

Alfredo and Luigi must have been her favourites out of the bunch. There was one passage where she wrote about the day both men came to her flat in Viterbo, with three German soldiers and watched an orgy involving three of her girls. She wrote of Alfredo's violent moods and how the men all laughed when one of the girls was beaten with a dog lead. Another time, according to her writings, Alfredo and Luigi came with four SS Panzer Corps officers, who demanded an orgy. There was an entry where she said that Alfredo loved Maria and that she was the best organiser of thrilling orgies for kilometres around.

At the back end of the book were a few blank pages, then came one page with the actual names and addresses: 'My best and most handsome friend, Alfredo Giancarlo, Via Goethe, Bressanone. My second best lover, Luigi Franconi. 22a, Via Milazzo, Cremona.'

It ended up with, 'They were the greatest young men I know and would do anything for us and they paid well.'

'So, lads! I'm sure we are on to the right men now, don't you think?' I asked.

'Yes, Captain, for my money, these are the guys all right,' quipped George.

'Have you decided where you would like to spend New Year's Eve and New Year's Day?' I asked.

'Yes, Skipper, I think we would like to spend it at Padua with the lads there, or if there is no one, we'll spend it with you at the Pedrocchi Club. Is that okay with you, Skipper?'

Anything was fine with me as long as the lads were happy, so I said, 'Right, we'll go and have a meal and a drink and then I'll turn in to have an early night. You two can do what you like but I would like to be away by nine in the morning.'

There had been a severe frost overnight and George had trouble with starting the jeep. However, with gentle persuasion and plenty of swear words, he managed to get the engine started and we were off. We had to drive even slower on account of the icy roads, but we didn't really mind as the countryside was so beautiful. It was a change to be on the road and not to feel that we had to dash, as we'd been used to. We reached Siena in time for lunch, but as the centre then is full of very narrow streets, we opted for a trattoria just outside the city.

The roads were once more dry, so we were able to make better progress. We arrived late that night at Headquarters, so after unloading our kit and parking the jeep away, the lads went off to their quarters and I was driven round to my hotel, in the buggy.

The following morning, I was picked up and driven round to the office where I was met by Corporal MacDonald, who informed me that Captain Hemmings was in. I knocked and went into the Adjutant's office.

'Hello Ian, I'm glad to see you,' he said. 'I thought you would be miles away from here and was a little bit worried how I was going to contact you, for unfortunately, you are going to lose Guss Pless. We have managed to get him his papers to return to Czechoslovakia.'

I was stunned, yet in a way at the back of my mind, I had known this day would come.

'We have an extremely good interpreter who will take the place of Guss. His name is Floris Dotto. You will still have Driver George Titley and his 'Rolls', which will give you good cover and warmth when driving.

'Does Guss know about his move, Richard?' I asked.

'No, Ian, not yet – but he soon will, as he is coming here at ten thirty.'

'When is he actually going off?'

'He is leaving here on the second, by train to Vienna,' he replied.

'Richard, I have been working on this case for the Americans,' I said, showing him some details on a sheet of paper, 'and I know where the criminals are. I don't want to lose much time in getting hold of them, so I propose to leave first thing Thursday morning, if that is all right with you.'

'Yes, that's okay. Have you got everything you require?' asked Richard.

'It's New Year's Eve today, isn't it,' I said, and with a nod from Richard, I went on, 'I don't know what celebrations there will be around here but I think I would like to celebrate the New Year in, with my crew.'

'Yes, why not. Major Williamson, Captain Reynolds and Captain Manners are all away and as yet, I don't know when they are expected back.'

'Thanks, Richard, I'll go and see if I can find my crew and fix something up. Anyway, I won't be leaving until about eight o'clock on Thursday morning,' I said.

'I'll be seeing you around before you leave anyway. Perhaps we'll see each other at the Pedrocchi and we'll have a drink together. And Ian, it may be a good idea if you are here at ten thirty, when I inform Guss of his move, and then you can meet Floris Dotto as well.'

'Good idea, Richard,' I replied, and with that, I left him alone to get on with his work and sauntered over to the garages hoping perhaps to find George. As he was not around, I went over to the Mess and looked at some magazines.

Ten thirty arrived, so I went over to the offices and joined Richard in his office, where he had Guss and Floris Dotto in conversation.

'Floris, I would like you to meet Captain Bell, with whom you will act as his interpreter,' said Richard. 'From now on, you will be with him until further notice.'

I told both Guss and Floris that I would see them later, after Captain Hemmings, and to come over to the hotel with George, when they were ready. I left Richard with the two lads to finish his business on his own. The office buggy ran me to the Leone Bianco where I waited for the three lads.

I didn't have long to wait before the three lads appeared.

'Guss, I am shattered to hear the news about you leaving us. We have been together a long time now and I feel it is like losing a friend,' I said.

I could see Guss was getting quite disturbed over the matter. 'Are you not happy to go back home, now that you have your papers?' I asked.

'Skipper, obviously I want to see my family so very much, but I am afraid of the outcome. I don't know what my family will do – try to keep me with them or to let me live in the West.'

I could see the dilemma the man was in, and said, 'You have been given permission to return, therefore, you must decide your own future and where that future should be. You have been a great asset to us and, to me, a friend as well as a bloody good interpreter. I shall miss your company, for we've had a damn good team, you, Nobby, then you and George here. Floris, you've to take Guss's place. I am sure you will do a good job. Welcome into the fold!'

We wandered over to the Pedrocchi Club and made ourselves comfortable in the lounge.

'Right, lads. It is New Year's Eve. What are your plans?' I asked. 'Skipper, we would like to have a bloody good meal together, partly because we are going to lose Guss and then with a bit of drink inside, we can celebrate the New Year in together. There's nothing much doing at the barracks as everyone has either gone home on leave or they have got fixed up with some locals, somewhere,' said George. He made a good suggestion, which after discussion, was unanimously agreed upon.

'Now, I suggest that we meet here at seven thirty and then we'll celebrate!' I told them.

I wanted to do some shopping and to get a wallet for Guss, similar to the one I gave Nobby. I made an enquiry at the Club, if there was going to be any party here tonight. They told me that lots of Service personnel were expected and that a dance had been organised. I knew then, more or less, the plan for what we would all do together.

The three young lads came together at the Club at seven thirty and I took them out to the best trattoria in the centre of Padua. I told them that I was giving a Going Away party for Guss. During the end of the last course, I presented

Guss with his present. While he was opening it, we drank his health and wished him a safe journey and a happy reunion with his family. It was an emotional moment and when he saw inside the wallet two white £5 notes, he was unable to speak for a few seconds. He gave a humorous but extremely friendly speech in return and we all hoped that one day, we might meet again.

As soon as the meal was over, we went back to the Pedrocchi Club and were surprised to see the place full of Service personnel of all ranks, thoroughly enjoying themselves with their lady friends. The dancing and drinking went on until midnight, when the church bells of the city rang in the New Year. The four of us drank to each other's health and to our respective families. Before we parted, I told Floris and George that we would be off at eight the following morning, and to pick me up at the hotel and we would go straight away. I also mentioned that I didn't need them for the rest of that day. Somehow, I felt that I wouldn't see Guss again, so I said my farewells, which was hard to do.

As it was New Year's Day, there was nothing doing at the office, so I took the opportunity to write some long overdue letters home and to reflect on the loss of Guss. He had been an exceptional interpreter. He never grumbled or seemed to baulk at any request to do something when asked. He had a sense of anticipation of what was required. He had a good sense of humour and knew his duties. I hoped that he would receive a similar citation. I wrote down my report to give to Major Williamson, as I thought that Guss well deserved every praise. I enjoyed the restful day and the preparation for my next trip up north. We were off to Bressanone.

Brian Dixon, Bell's relief driver.

Captain Bell and Sergeant Morgan flank the twenty-two year old war criminal, Emelio Cerati. He was a second lieutenant in the notorious *Brigata Nera,* and was in charge of the prison where Banks was tortured and denied medical treatment.

Gustav Pless and George Titley.

Captain Bell and George Titley beside the 'Rolls' on the main road
to Parma from Milan, 1947.

The partisan section leaders, photographed at the end of the war.

Sergeant Major Fernando Maroni and Sergeant Viglio Martinelli of the Italian partisans.

Twenty-two year old Floris Dotto, taken on the roof of his house in Monte San Savino, Italy.

Captain Bell with his own jeep outside Venice, April 1947.

Chapter Ten

George and Floris were punctual and after loading up my grips, we were off with our new crew member. George had the route all worked out, passing through Cittadella, Primolano and Trento. As we were entering Trento driving towards the centre, The Italian Military Police were stopping the traffic, as a column of *Bersaglieri* troops were coming towards us, on exercises. They looked very colourful with their long fluttering plumes trailing from their black hats, as they 'gaited' along. This type of very quick marching was a tradition with their regiment and we had to admit that, they looked very smart.

As they passed by, several gave a quick glance in our direction as they saw the jeep. This delighted George. One thing we both found out very quickly was that Floris couldn't drive.

We stopped the night at Bolzano after finding a hotel which had a convenient parking space for the jeep, without having to unhitch the trailer. There was no one else staying at the hotel, so we had first-class attention.

There had been a fall of snow overnight, which gave our surroundings a real winter's appearance. At our fresh croissant and coffee breakfast, we discussed our tactics for finding Alfredo Giancarlo.

'Floris, when we get to Bressanone, I want you to find out the number in Via Goethe where this man lives, where he works and who his friends are. Try to find out what he was doing during the build-up of the German Viterbo Line, in 1944. Here's some money for your drinks, food and any extras, should you need it. Make sure you are warm enough, and take care,' I told him. I mentioned that as he looked so young, yet I should have known that these youngsters were a tough breed, as I recalled my partisan days.

There didn't seem to be any more build-up of snow as we reached Bressanone and we stopped near to the park. 'Whatever you do or say, Floris, don't get too involved. Just ask cursory questions,' I said.

'Skipper, I have done quite a bit of work like this before with Captain Norman Downton. You can rely on me, okay.'

That confirmed my feelings that he would do a good job and we left him to go off on his own.

George and I got on to the main road again and made our way to the Brenner Pass and Innsbruck. The snow ploughs were very active and had cleared a reasonable track width, although the snow was getting hard packed. At the Brenner Pass summit, we stopped and we put the snow chains on the jeep. For the twenty-two miles to Innsbruck, the road was tricky but well negotiable. The scenery was fantastic, for the huge pines cupped the snow on their long branching arms, seeming to defy the law of gravity. The sky was not the usual bright blue as we had been used to seeing in Austrian skies, but dark grey and threatening.

George and I wanted to get to Innsbruck to find Nino, the son of Lilliana Banchetti, at Soriano. We both agreed that it would be a good gesture to surprise her with the latest news about her son. Of course, the main reason was to find out from Nino what he knew about the terrible gang that scourged the area around their village. He would have some knowledge of his sister's activities until her death with the Germans. It was necessary to get every bit of corroborative information, and although Nino had been in the navy at the time, he would have been at home a great deal because the Italian Navy had surrendered to the Allies, and he would perhaps have tried to avoid being taken by the Germans and used as forced labour, in Germany. Thousands of Italians were taken prisoner by the Germans, and hundreds were tortured to death for their activities against them behind their lines.

The town looked most beautiful nestling below the mountains and covered with snow. We carefully made our way through the streets until we came across the Goldener Adler Hotel, situated in the Herzog Friedrichstrasse. George pulled up outside and I dashed in. I asked at the reception desk if they could tell me which hotel was managed by a Herr Nino Banchetti. They rang through to another office and the reply came quickly. He is at the Grauer Bär Hotel in the Universitätstrasse. I was delighted with this information.

Back in the jeep, we moved off and after several enquiries for directions, we found the hotel. George parked the jeep at the roadside and came inside with me. With extreme courtesy, the receptionist asked if he could help, and when I mentioned that I had come with a message from Herr Banchetti's mother, the man looked very surprised and hurried away out of his office and disappeared.

As it was lunchtime, the rumbles in our stomachs could now be heard quite loudly, which was embarrassing. After a few minutes, Signor Nino Banchetti arrived looking very perplexed and somewhat wary. However, as soon as I introduced myself and mentioned that I had met his mother at her home, the man began to relax a little.

It had been such a surprise to him which I appreciated and we were ushered along a corridor into his private office. I now showed him my little red booklet, which drew still further expressions of bewilderment.

I related to him the reasons we met his mother and heard about the family troubles during the German occupation. I asked him to tell me everything he knew relating to this so-called 'gang' and the activities his sister played during the build-up of the German forces in that area.

'*Dunque, Capitano,*' he said.

'I can understand Italian if you speak it slowly,' I remarked.

'*Capitano*, I can speak some English but I think it is worse now because I do not get the practice.'

His effort was very commendable but I said that it would be better if we stuck to his own native tongue.

He confirmed the names of the 'gang' that his sister went with and felt very ashamed to tell me things about her. I felt very sorry for him but I egged him on to tell me everything. He and his brother Pietro had done so much to stop Maria from being such 'a disgrace to the family', as he put it.

George sat away from the desk, trying to understand the conversation, but couldn't.

'Nino, did you know your mother kept a pile of letters, documents and a hardback notebook, which Maria used as a diary?' I asked.

'No, *Capitano*. After my father died, I knew my mother fretted a great deal and wanted me and my brother to stay at home, but it was impossible. The Germans were rounding up all the men of military age and sending them into Germany, for forced labour,' he replied.

'*Mio fratello, Pietro...*' he began, and then went on at length, telling me how he escaped to the coast and managed to get to America. Nino told me how he had escaped the German 'net' and managed to get to the American lines. He was taken on as a cook at General Mark Clark's headquarters.

'Do you know who was responsible for that dreadful killing of the five crew members of the American Sherman tank?' I asked.

'We all felt that the gang took revenge on the prisoners after the car was blown up by a shell from the American lines, killing my sister and her friends, as well as the German officers,' he said.

'You see *Capitano*, my sister was a favourite of the leader, Alfredo Giancarlo. He was totally no good. He had such an influence over my sister. She revelled in the life she was leading, for apart from the sex fun she had, she received such wonderful gifts and money from the Germans and that gang. All her girls got wonderful presents and good living accommodation at Viterbo. It was probably better that my sister was killed, for she was bad. She broke my father's heart. I am sure it was that which really killed my father and not so much the cancer, poor man.'

I listened with compassion to his story and told him that, most likely, I would be going back to see his mother soon and would tell her about our meeting. Nino showed us around his hotel and I could see that he was very much liked by his staff. On reaching the foyer, we parted, promising that I would let his mother know how he was faring. She had not been up to Innsbruck.

When we stepped outside, we felt the cold very much so we were most glad to be roaring away back to the Brenner Pass. We had the same border guards to check our papers, which was really a farce, for the first time going to Innsbruck, both the Italian and the Austrian Customs merely waved us through when they saw the jeep. Now the Austrians did the same with a friendly wave, but the Italians, they stopped us. At first, I thought that they were going to be awkward and ask silly questions about the amount of petrol we had in the trailer or whatever, but instead they only stopped us to have a friendly chat.

I explained that we had to be at Bressanone for four o'clock, so they let us go with a shower of snowballs falling on to the jeep. George's driving was terrific but again, we seemed to be hampered a little by having the trailer, for it swung quite a lot.

As we drove into the forecourt at the station at 4.10, we couldn't see Floris waiting, so George stopped the jeep at the entrance and I went in search. I found him asleep on a bench in the little bar-cum-waiting room which was comfortably warm. He had the right idea but in the position I found him, I'm sure he must have been aching all over and glad to be awakened.

We got back into the jeep and moved off to Bolzano. Floris was full of his findings and excitedly told us snippets of what he had done. I told him that we would discuss all our findings when we were in a comfortable place for the night. At least he had eaten well and had kept himself warm. That was my main concern. We told him about our lunch which we had at Schönberg and the little 'flutter of worry' we had with the jeep. She began to play up again by not starting and we were anxious that we were not going to be on time at the station.

We found a good-looking hotel although it appeared partly closed. However, we were able to get fixed up with accommodation. The management was only too pleased to see us and opened up the small lounge bar and lit a wood burning fire in the corner fireplace. It soon sent out its heat in all directions, and this coupled with large drinks of whisky, soon made us comfortable.

'Now, Floris, tell us all you know about this man,' I said.

'He lives with his parents at No. 47, Via Goethe, which is a small house in a row. It is about two-thirds of the way up the narrow street towards the church. He works in Innsbruck at the railway depot and travels by train each morning at 0750 hours, and returns at 1820 hours. He spends his weekends at Innsbruck, because he has an extra job as a ski instructor. He hasn't had that job for long and is going to move to Innsbruck to be closer at hand for his work. He is also glad to get away from his parents, as he doesn't get on with them at all. He is not married, but has quite a female following. There is one special girl prostitute who is willing to move to Innsbruck too, if he should move. He is prone to bragging and when he has too much to drink, he gets abusive and sometimes violent. So far, though, he has not been put "inside" as far as I can gather, but has come very close to it. He supplies the girls with very expensive presents, which the girls believe they are stolen because his wages are not enough to pay for them. Of course the girls don't ask any questions, as they are only too happy to receive such gifts and to live well.'

George and I were fascinated by the story. George piped up, 'How did you find all this out, Floris?'

'Here in Italy, if a bloke wants to find out things about men, especially young men, then you go to a brothel or to a well-known prostitute and have yourself a good time by paying over the odds! If the girl is reluctant to give you the information you want, then you frighten her into submission. We know how to deal with them and they always give in, in the end!'

George looked at me and said, 'Next time, Captain, you can go alone to Innsbruck!'

We had another round of drinks.

'Right,' I said, 'tomorrow, we will go to the station at Bressanone and hide the jeep somewhere. Then we will take up inconspicuous positions in different parts of the station where we can get a good look at this man, as he comes in. 'Do you know what he looks like, Floris?' I asked.

'Not at all, Captain. I know he has darkish blond hair and is about five feet ten inches tall. I would presume he would be dressed in working clothes, perhaps an overall under a heavy coat, maybe a ski jacket,' Floris replied.

The following morning, the three of us, dressed in civvies, were out early and up at Bressanone station well before the train from Verona to Innsbruck was due. We looked around nonchalantly for the best positions to have a good look at our man, without drawing any attention from the station staff or passers by. Just casually mingling with whoever was there was the best policy. I found a seat and sat down in order to conceal my height and hid behind a blackboard standing on an easel, which was used for chalking train time alterations and so on.

As the time of the train's arrival became due, we heard in the distance, the hooter of the locomotive heralding its approach.

There was no horde of commuters, but enough for us to get confused as to who might be our man as they passed through the ticket gate and on to the platform. As the enormous steam engine slowly passed pulling the long train of coaches, we carefully watched but as the train stopped, clouds of steam exuded from various pipes under the coaches and momentarily blocked out our view.

I thought that I had got a good sighting of a person who seemed to fit the description of our man, so I slowly wandered away from the building and over to where we had parked the jeep. I was soon joined by Floris, and a little later George arrived. We returned to the hotel. We concluded that the person each one of us had thought most likely to be our man tallied by description.

We had the best part of the day to lose before going back to the station, for the return train at six thirty. It was boring at the hotel, so we went out into the centre of the town and had a look at the shops. We didn't want to use the jeep unnecessarily, for the fewer number of times the people saw the jeep going backwards and forwards in the direction of Bressanone, the better. We were lucky to have the trailer stowed in one of their lock-up garages behind the hotel.

The shops were lacking merchandise and attractive displays of goods in their windows. The pâtisseries and meat shops were the brightest and the bars were always an attraction for an espresso for a quick warm-up.

We were back at the station with the jeep parked well out of sight. As we had given ourselves plenty of time to pick out the best vantage points, we split up and left each other to go where we preferred. It was dark, so we were able to keep in the shadows mainly and away from the not so brilliant lights of the station.

The train rumbled in a few minutes late in clouds of steam from the central heating systems on the coaches. That hissing sound, plus the vocal announcement over the speakers that the station was Bressanone, created an atmosphere, especially as we were trying to identify a criminal. I hoped that Floris and George were watching the commuters alighting from the coaches and making their way to the exit ticket barrier, like myself. I watched and saw a man walk out on to the illuminated forecourt and go across the main road which ran parallel to the railway. He then cut across a grass verge and walked down the Viale Mozart. Then I spotted Floris quite some distance behind the man, following him.

I went back to the jeep. A few minutes later George arrived and then Floris appeared. We three agreed that the person we had seen and followed would most likely be our man. Wasting no more time, we returned to the warmth and comfort of our hotel at Bolzano.

Having decided that we would give it another run to make more certain, we went once more to Bressanone station. We changed around our positions and watched.

More or less, the travellers were the same crowd and we were able to pick out our man. Now that we had got him fixed in our minds, he became more conspicuous, somehow. We watched him board the train, carrying a metal container rather like a small toolbox.

Back we went to Bolzano, for the last time we hoped, and discussed our plan for the arrest. Floris had drawn up a plan of the station forecourt, the main road and the Viale Mozart. At the corner of that street and the main road, was a garden wall, in front of which was a line of trees. This line would afford good cover for me.

George would have the jeep and trailer ready facing Bolzano. My young interpreter would come up behind the man and I would time the meeting just as Alfredo would be beside the jeep. The lad had one of our service revolvers with him and I had mine and George had the handcuffs in the jeep. We went over our plan again to make sure that it was fairly workable and rested for the few remaining hours, before having to make our journey back to Bressanone.

George had checked over the jeep and topped up the petrol tank. Our kit had been stored away in the back of the bench seat and in the trailer. We even checked that we had the handcuffs handy. Floris checked the chamber of his revolver to make sure it was full, then we both helped George to pull the trailer out of the lock-up garage and hitched it on to the tow bar. I settled the hotel account. Now we were ready.

Although we were itching to be off, there was no point in going too early as we would only get cold waiting out in the open.

'Floris, I'll leave it to you to time your approach from behind, just as Giancarlo is near to the jeep,' I said. 'Most likely he will be curious to have a closer look at George's "Rolls". I will also time my approach from the forward direction and we will nab him. The element of surprise will succeed. George, you be ready to snap on those handcuffs before he has time to sneeze.'

'Where are we going with him afterwards, Captain?' asked George.

'We'll get him to the prison at Verona and then we'll go after Franconi,' I replied.

The moment arrived for us to leave the hotel and make our way back to Bressanone. On arrival, George positioned the jeep facing the way back to Bolzano. Floris left me to take up his position somewhere in the station, so that he could follow our man without him noticing anything amiss. I walked across the main road and hid behind the last tree at the corner of Viale Mozart. It was eerie standing there in the shadows. I hoped no one would come along and for a long time, no one did.

Again the train was late by twenty minutes this time, so to our advantage, the people made their way out of the station fairly quickly and were far enough away not to see Floris follow our man as he made his way over towards the jeep. As was anticipated, Alfredo was curious to see the jeep and just as he got up to it, Floris plunged the revolver into his back and told him to keep quiet. I was right by him with my revolver pointing at him and George snapped the handcuffs on in a flash.

In his fright, the man dropped his metal box and we had him inside the jeep before he was able to do anything. Floris picked up the box and George had the vehicle moving off even before I had time to shut my nearside door. We drove down the road a short way, then stopped so that we could get the man's hands handcuffed behind him. We couldn't tell if anyone had seen us. We were too interested making our criminal safe and getting away from Bressanone as fast as we could.

'Are you all right, George?' I asked.

'Okay, Captain,' came the reply.

Now our man knew who we were but couldn't make out why we had one of his countrymen with us and why we were in civilian clothes. Floris asked the man his name immediately after we had made him safe with the handcuffs.

'*Mi chiamo Alfredo Giancarlo. Cosa vuole con me?*' he asked.

Floris told him that no harm would come to him provided he behaved himself and did exactly what we told him to do. One step out of line and he'd get shot.

'George, drive us to the hotel and if possible drive into the yard at the back. Can you do that?' I asked.

'I think I can just about get the jeep and trailer in but I will have to do a fair bit of manoeuvring.'

'Then just swing round and draw up alongside the wall,' I said. 'Now, when we get there, I'll go in with my grip and change to my battledress uniform, and you two guard this brute with all your alertness. If you have the slightest trouble, knock him over the head. If anyone comes to disturb you, chase them away. You, George, will have my revolver, so you both will have him covered. I'll be as quick as I can changing. When I am back, you, George, go and change into your uniform. The toilets are just inside the back door on the left, okay?'

Our captive was now beginning to realise the situation he was in and started to bawl out abuse. Floris quickly threatened him if he didn't shut up, by gagging him. That kept him quiet for a while. I was more anxious about what he would do when we got to the hotel.

George drew up alongside the wall of the yard and switched off the engine and the lights and got out. I grabbed my grip, gave my revolver to George and told him to use the butt on Alfredo's head if necessary, or shoot the bastard. I dashed inside and quickly changed into my uniform. I was already dressed in my khaki shirt and tie, so I just had to swop my civvy trousers, sweater and jacket for my battledress blouse and trousers, and added my webbing belt and holster. I quickly saw the manager and told him that I and my driver were making a quick change as we were going south.

He wondered why I didn't have a bedroom to go and change in, but I explained that the changeover was only going to take a few minutes and it wasn't worth while opening up a bedroom. I tipped him, which kept him happy and dashed out to the lads.

'Everything okay?' I asked.

'Thank God you're back, Captain, for I am dying to have a pee and I know this bastard is too,' remarked George.

'Right, give me my revolver and hurry up changing.'

George dashed off with his grip. Having our captive well covered, Floris struggled to get him out from the rear seat and undoing one hand, slipped the loose handcuff on to the handle on the side of the jeep. With his free hand, he was able to relieve himself beside the jeep and against the wall.

As soon as he had finished, Floris forced his arm behind him and snapped the handcuff back on. Once more he was safe inside the jeep and Floris had his turn to relieve himself.

George had only taken a few minutes and flung his grip into the trailer. Standing a little away from the jeep out of Giancarlo's hearing, I told George that I had decided to go all the way to Livorno, or Leghorn as he called it, and get the bastard into the hands of the Yanks.

'It is about 275 miles, which will take us at least nine hours, maybe ten. That will get us in at around seven in the morning. We will take it in turns to drive; are you fit?' I asked.

George put his thumb up and got into his seat behind the wheel. On a piece of paper out of my pocket notebook, I wrote down one or two names of towns, ending with Livorno and handed it to Floris.

'It's all right with me, the best idea, Captain,' he said.

Thank heavens, the jeep started straight away and we were off on our way south as quickly as we could. For one thing, driving at night gave us some form of cover and the roads would be still more free of traffic.

I was most relieved, to see the back of Bolzano. It was beginning to snow again so we had to drive with extra caution. I wondered what the conditions would be like now at Bressanone. Perhaps the snow would be really thick there. I counted our blessings and now I was determined to get to Livorno without any hitches.

I changed over with George just before Rovereto and drove to the outskirts of Verona. There we made a swop around. George took the wheel again and I changed seats with Floris. Now I was next to this 'inhuman' being! George took the opportunity of our stop to fill up the tank, as we had covered ninety-eight miles already.

As we had to go through the centre of Verona, we kept our eyes open for some establishment where we could get some food, hoping that at nearly midnight, some place would be open. Floris said that in Italy, lots of places would still be open for the Italians like to eat late as they sleep most afternoons until five!

'Seeing is believing,' quipped George.

It had stopped snowing, leaving just slush.

We followed the wide river round to the south side, and on the embankment road near to a bridge crossing we saw a trattoria well illuminated, so George stopped. I said to Floris to get anything he could, which I knew was not going to be easy. Ten minutes had gone by when the lad came out carrying a brown paper bag. After settling himself, he produced food out of the bag, like a magician pulling a rabbit out of a hat! There was salami, bread rolls and cheese.

By the time we arrived at Reggio nell 'Emilia, George was ready for a break, so I took over again and told him to try to have a kip. It wasn't the distance which made one tired, so much as the drone of the engine and the whine of the tyres on the road surface.

It was good to know we had reached over halfway and were making reasonable time, in spite of the necessary stops to relieve our bladders. It was amazing that once we were over the Passo del Cerreto, we could feel the slight difference in temperature.

Our captive had been given food and a cigarette during one of our stops but later, when he tried to butt Floris in the face, screaming suddenly to distract George's driving as well as giving Floris a nasty bang, we got some rope from the trailer and trussed him up and gagged him tight.

This he didn't like one bit but we were determined to punish him without resorting to other means of force. There was many occasion when I felt like thrashing him, as did the other two, but we couldn't do that. We left our captive unable to move even his feet for two hours, until at one of our stops, we untied the rope and freed his legs and the gag. He had had enough, and as we allowed him to get out of the jeep for a brief break, he cried with pain as he was so stiff. However, we had succeeded in controlling him and had him most submissive right to the end.

We stopped at Sarzana outside La Spézia, where we saw the first coffee bar open. The sky was becoming just a little bit lighter with the dawn. A man was cleaning the front of the bar, and inside we could see the chairs turned upside down on top of the tables so the floor could be cleaned. I asked the man outside if could have a hot coffee and in doing so, led him as far away from the jeep as was possible. Luckily, he came with me into the bar and began to operate the espresso machine. He told me that it would take just a little while before it became hot enough to make the steam.

I got into conversation with him in order to distract him from looking inside the jeep, for he was most curious at the sight of the vehicle, as it was so unlike a normal jeep.

To our great relief, the coffee machine became active and we had the most welcome cup of coffee each, including our captive, as Floris went for a second cup, telling the man that his coffee was that good he wanted more. He paid for the coffees and for a handful of chocolate biscuit bars.

We jumped back into the jeep and then it happened: the jeep would not start. George tried and tried and just as the barman was coming out to help and offer his advice, the engine started, puffing out volumes of bluish grey smoke from the exhaust pipe. George warmed the air with his comments and slammed it into first gear and drove off. We prayed that we would make Livorno before the jeep packed up altogether.

However, George nursed the vehicle and we made Livorno without any further engine trouble. We drove straight to the main entrance to the CIC Office buildings and pulled up at the barrier. A Military policeman with his automatic weapon stood to block our way until we actually stopped and then approached to my side. Several of his colleagues came out of the cabin and then a corporal showed his training and saluted upon seeing an officer.

I was glad to get out of the vehicle and stand upright, for my legs were beginning to ache. I returned the salute and showed the Corporal my red book as my ID card. Handing it back, he gave orders for the barrier to be lifted and for the outfit to be driven inside the compound. The Corporal indicated to George just where to park.

I told the American that I had a prisoner inside and wanted him to be locked up. With a brisk turn, he went into his cabin and took up the phone.

In a matter of a few minutes, a jeepload of Military Police arrived with a sergeant in charge. The usual courtesies were exchanged and his men surrounded the jeep out of curiosity. I told the Sergeant about the captive I had inside the jeep and he asked me then to hand him over into their care. I gave him the key for the handcuffs and stressed that I wanted them back afterwards.

Floris and George tugged the man out from the back and the Sergeant ordered his men to take 'the sonofabitch' away. I told them to watch him carefully. There and then, the Sergeant wanted to know the story but I briefly told him that, he was wanted for a crime against the Sergeant's fellow men. The Sergeant gave the prisoner a big kick up his backside and bawled to his men, 'Lock him up!'

That was a moment of great relief and more so, when I saw Lieutenant Rod appear.

'Good morning, Michael,' I called, 'I've brought you a real bastard. He is the leader of the gang who burnt to death your tank crew.'

Lieutenant Rod gave instructions for the Sergeant to look after my two lads and then we went together to their club building. I took my overnight grip with me.

'You've done well!' he told me.

Michael showed me to the locker room and the ablutions and said that he would go and arrange a breakfast. To be under that hot shower was heaven and it was while I was washing down that I remembered I had left my clean clothes in the grip, in the trailer. I was just drying when Michael came to ask me how long would I be, so I was able to ask him if someone would be good enough to fetch the grip for me.

All spruced up once more, I met Michael in the Mess dining room. Over a really good breakfast, I told him briefly of the events and said that more details would emerge when I got to see Colonel Villiers.

'There is one thing you can do for us, Michael,' I said. 'We are having trouble with the engine of our jeep. Could your garage look at it and repair it for us, please? We had some awkward moments on our trip when it wouldn't start, and then ultimately it gave out blue smoke from the exhaust.'

'Sure thing, I'll get that seen to straight away,' he replied.

Michael called the Mess waiter over and asked for a phone.

'I'll just get on to the workshops. Where is the jeep at the moment, Ian?'

'We left it near the Guardroom but perhaps it may have been moved,' I told him.

Just then, Colonel Villiers came in with some other officers, and on seeing me with Michael, the Colonel came over and asked if he might join us. The other officers made their way to the tables that they normally sat at. I was only too pleased to have the Colonel with us as it was far less formal there than his office.

He was most keen to hear all about our venture and I had to relate in great detail all the events leading up to the capture. I told him that I was now anxious to get the other criminal, Luigi Franconi. I felt very pleased that I could name him, for the first time, to the Colonel. It was interesting to see the pleasure on the Colonel's face, for I was sure that he must be thinking that at long last, justice could be done.

I promised him that I would be back within a week, with the other main criminal of the gang. He asked me if there was anything he could do for us and I mentioned that I had already asked Michael if the workshops could look at our jeep engine, as it was playing up. With his delightful accent, he asked Michael to make sure the garage workshops were looking after the vehicle.

The hospitality was extremely generous and the atmosphere was very friendly. One felt at home with them – at least, I did.

I was a little concerned as to my tactics in arresting the criminal but the Colonel assured me that I did the right thing and any questions would be answered by him later, if there should be any.

The breakfast and the meeting with Colonel Villiers was over and I was thankful really because I couldn't have taken another cup of coffee!

Michael led me over to the workshops and there we found George and Floris. George gave him a very smart salute and got his deserved recognition in return.

'Look what they are doing, Captain,' remarked George. 'They have taken the engine out and the gearbox and have replaced it with a new one!' George's voice sounded incredulous.

I peered closer to the vehicle without interfering with the mechanics and saw the new engine. I was assured that it had been run in, too, so that we could drive normally without fear. George was over the moon with joy. Not only did we have a new engine and gearbox, but a set of new tyres as well. The attention we received was tremendous.

As we had been at the Headquarters for almost three hours, the time was beginning to tell, as we had not slept for nearly twenty-four hours. Michael could see how tired we were and suggested that the lads go to the Men's Club and have a sleep. I would be able to kip down in one of the bedrooms at the Officers' Club.

'Right, lads, you take the opportunity, and meet me at the main office entrance at four o'clock. Have a good sleep,' I told them.

I left the lads with the mechanics, as one was going to show them where to go and I walked over to the Club with Michael. Chatting about the mission on the way over, Michael remarked how well we had done and commented that it would make their outfit look silly. At the Club,

Michael gave instructions to the GI Orderly and then said that he must get to his office and would see me later.

The soldier was immaculately dressed in his uniform, with not a crease out of place. There were just one or two bedrooms. I was shown into the first one. It was extremely masculine in decor but most warm and comfortable. It even had its own bathroom. The GI asked me what time I wished to be awakened and I told him, three forty-five. I flipped off my shoes, flung my jacket on the chair and flopped on to the bed.

Precisely at a quarter to four, I was awakened. Although the sleep had been short, it had been profound and I realised that we needed much more to recoup the loss we had inflicted upon ourselves.

I met the lads who were just returning with the chief mechanic after a trial run with the jeep and George seemed extremely happy now with his 'Rolls'.

Checking that the lads had packed away their kit and that they had received back the pair of handcuffs and key, I packed my grips away and then went up to Michael Rod's office, to give him my salaams and to thank him for all that he had done for us. I received two sticks of American cigarettes, which was more than enough to keep us going for a long time. The CIC Office apparently could not do enough for us in return for what we had done and were still doing for them. They were truly a great outfit and I was looking forward to returning with the second criminal to the crime.

Chapter Eleven

We moved off and got as far as La Spézia, where we stayed the night. We all felt that to have one early night in a comfortable hotel would be more than beneficial and we asked a man in a *giornalaio*, to recommend us to one. He told us to go to the Hotel Mary, in the Via Fiume. It was the easiest town to follow directions, for it is built in block formation with everything at right angles to the two harbours. The parking facilities were very good as long as we could unhitch the trailer. Both units were locked up for the night.

The lads had to share a room with twin beds and I had a single. We were too tired to worry about the finer details but it was adequate and the proprietor did his best to make us as comfortable as he could. We ate out, so that was no problem. The very name scared me a bit, for it sounded as if we were going to stay in a brothel.

Having bribed the proprietor in giving us a good 'English' breakfast, we met at nine o'clock as arranged, to have the meal together. One by one, the lads appeared, still bleary-eyed.

'Morning, Captain. Did we have to wake up?' asked Floris.

'When you see what you are going to have to eat, you will open your eyes wider,' I said.

George was more awake and began to rub his hands in recognition of the smell of cooking bacon coming from the kitchen. The tea was strong and hot, which was such a change to what we'd had in the past in Italy. Both the lads had slept well and were now getting themselves back to normal.

'Now lads, I suggest that we make for my *contadini* friends at Fontanellato, which is about eighty miles from here. We can get to the trattoria in the little town at about one o'clock and have something to eat before going to the farmhouse at Parroletta. I think we tuck the trailer away there and use the Ferraris' house as a base. I know they would like to have us stay with them, and it would only be for a couple of days and nights,' I said.

The lads thought it to be a very good idea and looked forward to meeting the farmers who I had told them so much about.

George went out to the jeep and got the map and we plotted our route. I told them, 'I know part of this road well, especially around Berceto, because we had skirmishes there with the Germans when I was with the partisans. At Fornovo di Taro, we'll take the left fork and make our way through Noceto and turning left on to the main Parma road to Piacenza, we should see the signposts to Fontanellato.'

'How far do you say it is, Captain?' asked George.

'It is about seventy-one miles to Noceto and then about ten or twelve miles to Fontanellato,' I answered.

'I can show you the place where we were imprisoned and we escaped from, when the Armistice was signed in 1943. By the way, Floris, how is your head now? It still shows some bruising.'

'It hurt for a while as you know and if you hadn't put that cold wet hankie on it, I'm sure I would have had a big lump there. Now I don't feel it at all, thanks,' he replied. He was a tough lad in spite of his fairly lean figure.

With all our gear loaded up, Floris and I helped George to hitch the trailer on to the tow bar, as George drove the vehicle out of the garage. The engine sounded most sweet. I don't know why, but I felt very happy being on the move again. I was also looking forward to meeting old man Mari and the Ferrari family again.

As we had planned, we arrived at Fontanellato in time for a meal at the trattoria under the arches, where I once ate with Guss and Nobby Morgan. It was a beautiful day and both the lads were awestruck at the architecture of the extremely old castle.

Inevitably our arrival caused great interest with the locals, and soon we were besieged by them, asking all sorts of questions. Some had remembered my last visit with Guss and Nobby, and from the crowd, a young man barged his way to our table and introduced himself.

'I am Giuseppe Fattori,' he said. 'I am an English teacher here in the town. I can remember you four years ago when you escaped from the camp. You were with a colonel and two other officers and I was one who came out to you all when you were hiding under the vines. I then knew you were staying at the Ferraris' farmhouse. I also saw you when you came with two other men recently, yes, last year now.'

I gripped his hand and made him welcome to drink with us.

'What memories, *Signor*! I have some friends in another village who want to meet you, for I told them that I had seen an English officer in my town, the last time you came. They wondered whether you might be the officer who led them up in the Appenines. Were you with the partisans?' he asked.

'Yes, I was their leader and helped to train them and we did some very good work in harassing the German lines of communication,' I replied.

'They want to meet you, Captain! I will go and phone them to make a meeting.'

'Floris,' I said, 'will you go with him and arrange something for us?'

It was now getting quite exciting at the thought of our mission, coupled with the reunion with the *contadini* friends and now the possible reunion with a couple of my old partisan comrades.

Floris and Giuseppe came back and told me that we are going to meet the day after tomorrow at the dance hall in their village.

'It is at Soragna, not very far from here. If you pick me up here at seven o'clock, I will show you the way and also introduce you to some nice young girls,' he told us.

That was arranged, and I bought 100 cigarettes for Mari, and 100 for Ferrari. I went out to the *Farmacia* and bought a bottle of perfume for the two women. On coming back to the trattoria, I found the crowd were still gathered round, listening to all the conversations between us.

Floris and Giuseppe were getting along like as if they had known each other for years. After we had had our disrupted meal, we took Giuseppe with us to show the lads the orphanage, which was our prison camp in early 1943. It gave me a strange feeling to see the place once more, especially the area at the back of the building, where we had our small field for recreation and tunnelling activities! There was no trace of barbed wire anymore and the building was still unoccupied. It seemed a shame that the authorities were not putting the fine building to good use.

We dropped Giuseppe off in the centre of Fontanellato and made our way out to Mari's house at Parroletta. We got a great welcome as usual and they were pleased to meet George and Floris. The presents delighted them, but seeing them in their humble surroundings made one feel that whatever one gave was totally inadequate to recompense their kindness. We showed the lads the cowshed where the Colonel and I hid from the searching Germans and their

Fascist sycophants. There were no cows there anymore, as the dear old souls were too old and infirm to look after animals. Even the path which led to the maize field, where we also hid when the cowshed was getting too much attention by the enemy, was a feature in our memories. Mari would risk coming out to tell us that it was safe to return to the house or the cowshed, when the searchers had gone. I was glad to have photographs, for they tell so much.

Time didn't allow us to linger any longer. The parting was very emotional, for perhaps we were the only people who had brought a little sparkle into their lives for a long time. The Ferraris had heard the commotion at Mari's house and seen the jeep and trailer standing on the road, so they were waiting for us, as we drove down their long winding grassy path from the road. They both stood outside their front door, tears rolling down their faces for emotion and arms outspread in welcome.

Floris now understood the 'bond' between myself and this endearing couple. Both of them gave George and Floris a heartfelt welcome and we gathered in their only living room which combined their kitchen. The big wooden table was still there for us to sit around, as we had done in the past, and Signor Ferrari brought out several bottles of his best vintage wine.

I gave the presents, which more than delighted them. We sat talking and talking about all topics which concerned them and their now grown-up children. Both Aldo and Alda were living away from home. Signora Ferrari insisted that we stayed with them for as long as we were in the area and began to busy herself in preparing the bedrooms upstairs. Signor Ferrari and Floris got on fine together, for they both had the same type of humour and already were leg-pulling each other.

I told them that we had met a Giuseppe Fattori who lived between Parroletta and Fontanellato and who had arranged for us to go to a village dance the day after tomorrow. Both the Ferraris knew the Fattori family and spoke highly of Giuseppe. Apparently, he had done much good work on behalf of the British officers who escaped, so that they were not recaptured by the Germans.

Signor Ferrari assured me that I could trust Giuseppe implicitly. It came out in the conversations that Giuseppe was trying to get one or two ex-partisan comrades to meet us at his favourite dance hall. Surprisingly, Ferrari knew something about this and encouraged me to meet them. This made me more anxious and curious for the meeting to come, for if they were part of my group, it would be a tremendous reunion.

That evening, we ate polenta and cheese and drank more wine. Even Signora Ferrari drank with us, which was most unusual as she rarely drank wine. I gave her enough money to buy food for her enlarged 'family' and told her that we would take her into the town to buy what she required.

The Ferraris had given up their bedroom for the two lads, as they had two single beds, and I had Aldo's room. I wouldn't have minded sleeping in their cowshed that night, for I was so tired and very much feeling the effects of Ferrari's potent wine. The morning was frosty, clear skies but cold, and the room was like the north pole when I stirred out of the cosy warm bed.

Signora had an enormous kettle simmering on the hot plate of her kitchen range and supplied a pot for me to shave with. They had no bathroom, so we had to use the kitchen sink. The loo was well outside, just beyond the yard, and most primitive. In stages, the lads appeared and likewise carried out their ablutions in more or less the same way as I had done. The yells that came from George as he applied the cold water to his body equalled mine when I stripped off to the waist. This caused great amusement with our hosts.

Breakfast was just bread, butter and cheese and coffee, made from roasted sunflower seeds. Signora Ferrari made this specially to bring back memories for me, for that is what we drank when we were 'on the run'. It made very good coffee when one got used to the taste!

Signora had soon completed all her chores and was ready to be taken into Fontanellato for her shopping spree. We asked Signor Ferrari to come with us but he declined, saying that he had too much to do around the farm. We didn't think the poor woman had received a day out like it for a long time, as she revelled in being treated to coffee and cakes at our favourite bar.

At the grocer's, Floris kept saying, 'Why don't you take half a dozen instead of one, and why not a larger packet?'

The poor woman ended up quite confused. When it came to the more luxurious items of food, like chocolate biscuits, she protested loudly until she realised that I was paying out of my own pocket, as a way of saying thank you for all they had done for me.

We returned absolutely loaded with stuff. We even surprised them by giving them a gift of a 25-kilo sack of flour, to last them throughout the rest of the winter and spring. We even had a sack for the Maris, which we dropped off at their house. At least, it would give them a change from the maize flour, which made their polenta.

Signor Ferrari looked dazed when he saw the jeep being emptied. For the rest of the day, George cleaned up the jeep and trailer, whilst Floris helped Signor Ferrari around the farm, mending certain items which had long awaited an extra pair of hands to carry out the repairs; then we had our siesta as we became tired.

It is strange how one doesn't always feel tired when one keeps going but as soon as one relaxes and rests, then one feels like dropping off into a deep sleep.

The following day, we went to Cremona to seek the help of the Security Police, known as the *Guardia di Pubblica Sicurezza,* and had no difficulty in finding their Headquarters. On my showing them my little ID booklet, we were immediately welcomed inside and shown into the office of their chief. By the various insignia, I understood him to be a Captain, so we were on level terms.

I immediately told him what I was in Cremona for – to arrest a war criminal by the name of Luigi Franconi of 22a, Via Milazzo. The officer swung his chair around and looked at his big wall map, which was studded with tens of multi-coloured pins.

'*Ah, si. Lui abita là,*' he said, pointing to a spot on the map. Floris asked him what sort of place is it and was told that it was a flat in a large block, part of the *Comune.*

'In other words, Floris, is it a council flat?' I asked.

'Yes, Captain, and it is on the second floor too!' came the reply.

The Captain asked to see my 'interesting' red book, as he put it, for he had only a cursory look the first time. He seemed most impressed and read it carefully. With great respect, he handed it back to me saying that anything he can do for us, he was willing to do. He said, 'I will have the flat put under surveillance immediately,' and he picked up a phone and gave his orders.

The Captain wanted to know the details of the crime, where it took place and when approximately. He wanted to know if we had the right man who was alleged to have committed the crime. I told him that I don't go vast distances on assumptions, but on facts, and with this case I know it to be a fact that the man I was after, was one of those responsible. The other of the two leaders of the so-called gang was now in custody, with the Americans.

'*Capitano*, when do you wish to arrest Franconi?' he asked in his language.

'I want to arrest him tomorrow night and at about 23.45 hours,' I replied.

'*Dunque, lei deve essere qua alle undici e mezzo,*' he said.

Floris wanted to translate that for me, but I understood it.

We had to be at his office at eleven thirty, was that right? I asked. The lad nodded. Now, it all depended on whether or not Franconi would be home. I told him that we would have to be with his men in making the arrest, to which he agreed, and he said that it would be better if we left the jeep and trailer at their Headquarters and we could go in one of their cars. We would do the transfer over of him into our jeep back in the yard, afterwards.

The arrangements seemed simple enough for me and again, I was banking on the element of surprise. After all, no one had bothered him for over four years – except his own conscience – so he had nothing to suspect that some-one was after him.

Getting back into the jeep after our meeting with the *Guardia,* George asked me if I could trust the Captain.

'I just have to do that, George, for I'm not able to make an arrest in a building without the Italian authorities being in company. Arresting a person out in the open is quite a different matter under these military circumstances, for no other civilian is involved,' I told him.

We hurried back to Parroletta and our temporary home. We told our hosts what the plans were for the following night and that we would have to leave early enough to get us there for eleven thirty.

The time arrived for us to set off on our evening of pleasure, with Giuseppe leading the way. Following Giuseppe's clear directions, George was able to follow the route to Soragna without any difficulty. The hall where the dance was held had once been part of a church which had been almost completely destroyed during the last stages of the Italian campaign.

George made sure that the safety switch, similar to the one Nobby had on his jeep, had been activated. Giuseppe led the way in and we three followed. The lights inside were remarkably bright in contrast to the darkness of the night and for a moment, we were taken by surprise by the festive decorations as well as the coloured lights.

The astonishing thing was to see the amount of people. We must have entered just as a dance had finished, for we were confronted with the incredible sight of a solid line of chairs, backed against each wall. Every chair was occupied by an elderly chaperone with her young female charge sitting tightly next to her. Looking from left to right, it was one old woman, one young girl, one elderly woman, one young girl all the way round. The young men stood in a group in a corner. It was rather embarrassing when we entered, for there was a sudden hush and everyone's eyes began to stare in our direction.

Everyone seemed to know Giuseppe, especially the group of young men. He quickly realised we were becoming very self-conscious before the preponderance of women and drew us over to meet his friends. That broke the ice quite a bit. The small band struck up a typical Latin dance tune, which signalled the men to circulate and take a partner. It was most amusing when we gazed around, to see the chaperones hold tighter their wards, as if to say, 'Hands off soldier!'

Out of sight of anyone, Floris quickly slipped his revolver to George to look after, while he asked a young girl for a dance. Many of the women watched carefully how Floris danced and seemed highly delighted with his style. As soon as the dance was over, they tried to eye Floris in order to 'claim' him for their charge, for the next dance. This was most amusing to watch. George began to take up the idea and approached one woman, who quickly shook her head in a negative response. George returned to my side and whispered would I look after Floris's revolver, which was becoming a nuisance tucked into his battledress blouse.

I chatted to some of the men with my best Italian, as they couldn't speak one word of English, and I found out that some of them were not just farmers but artisans as well.

Whilst talking with the group, four men came in of more or less my age, and were immediately hailed by Giuseppe from the dance floor. He immediately returned his partner to her chaperone and came over to introduce them to me.

'Captain, these two men here are great friends of mine, who were up in the mountains with you as part of your partisan group. This man is called Emilio Scholatti and this one is Bruno Tambroni,' he said.

I gripped the hands of both men, for I was so pleased to know them, although I could not recognise them at all.

'This is a great surprise, Giuseppe. How did you organise this?' I asked.

'As soon as I heard through the grapevine that you were back in the area, I contacted them, for they wanted to see you again. Do you recognise them?' he asked.

'No, unfortunately I don't, but then there were so many in the group and the sections were never in the main camp all at one time,' I replied. I asked the two many questions, to which their replies gave me the confidence that they had been part of my lot and that they were not just making stories up for bravado's sake.

They gave me a photo of Fernando Maroni and Vigilio Martinelli together, who were my two commanders, and a photo of the Leaders of the sections.

I asked them if they knew where they were now but unfortunately, they hadn't seen or heard of them since they disbanded, immediately after the Allied troops arrived in the area. We forgot all about the dancing and chatted about the good and difficult times we had together. I only wished I could remember them, but we had so many men ultimately.

They told me that they lost quite a lot of men during the last stages of the Allied advances, for the Germans were more ruthless than ever and shot anyone whom they suspected of aiding the Allies. They remarked on the day I left them, that they vowed to carry on as they had been organised to fight. They remembered the time when we blew up the trains in the cutting and closed that line of communication for the Germans. Giuseppe listened in very intently and one could see that he was very proud of his two friends. The other two men who came with my ex-partisan lads were just friends of theirs who worked with them at a cheese factory.

George had danced enough, although he didn't have many willing partners only because the chaperones wouldn't allow their wards to dance with a stranger in uniform. He came over to join the men and tried to listen to what was being discussed. He thought it was great for me to meet two of my old partisan comrades and had a good look at the photos. I gave him Floris's revolver but he said for me to keep it for a while, as he wanted to play a joke on him.

As the dance session was coming to an end, so was our meeting, and reluctantly we had to part company. I took their names and addresses and said that I would write to them both and should they hear of anyone else from our great crowd, they were to let me know.

Driving back to Parroletta, Floris asked George to let him have his revolver back. George said that he didn't have it. Floris immediately got himself into a flap, for he thought that he had left it somewhere back at the dance hall. He pleaded with George to turn the jeep round and to go back to look for it. I told Floris to look under the seat, which he did and at that moment, I slipped the gun over to George and popped it into the inside of his blouse. George played his pal up just a little bit more and then produced it, putting the poor lad out of his misery.

The bars were still open in Fontanellato on our return, so we were able to get a toasted cheese sandwich apiece and an espresso. I wrote down Giuseppe's address on the same piece of paper that I had the two ex-partisans' names and tucked it into my jacket pocket.

I was really lost for words, enough to convey my feelings of gratitude for what Giuseppe had done for me and in return, I bought him an expensive cigarette lighter from the tobacco counter. Luckily in Italy, all bars have such a *tabaccaio*. We dropped him off near his home and made straight for our farmhouse. The two good folk were waiting up for us, to hear how we had fared.

They were delighted that I had met two of my ex-partisans. They wanted to know how George and Floris fared with the girls. They roared laughing when they were told about the chaperones who hung on to their charges, in case they got raped by the invading English soldiers! Floris was the only one who had success with them.

'Of course the boy would, as he is the youngest, and very handsome!' remarked Signora Ferrari.

We discussed our plans for the next day and agreed to take our prisoner straight down to Livorno, after the swop over at the *Guardia* headquarters.

'It will be about 155 miles to Livorno from Cremona and we can reach the main Piacenza – Parma road at Fiorenzuola. Don't leave anything behind here as we won't be coming back,' I told the lads.

Signor Ferrari brought out a bottle of Asti Spumante and five glasses. There were tears in his eyes as he offered a toast to our welfare, bless him. We reciprocated by toasting their health and thanking them for all they had done for us. It was now past midnight, so we turned in, as we needed all the sleep we could get before our forthcoming night's work.

It began to rain, which made me recall the days in 1943. It was nearly lunchtime when finally we disturbed. It was pouring down with rain and the thought of having to dash out to the bog was not a happy one! *Signora* had the hot water ready for shaving and as she had noticed that I had a loose button on my battledress jacket, she had resewn that on. Just the sort of thing a real mother would do, I thought.

I had dressed by the time the lads appeared and was a glass or two up on them of Ferrari's best red wine. It was good rich full bodied wine and one didn't need too much before one felt a little bit woozy. *Signora* had made a super lunch of chicken done in a casserole. This time, the coffee was real and percolated and tasted wonderful.

The household slept again in the afternoon, after we helped George to hitch up the trailer. The unit was made ready for our departure at about 10.15 p.m. The rain never stopped and I reminded Signor Ferrari the night that the Colonel and I left him, to escape, for it also was a very wet night. He remembered all right.

It was very hard to say goodbye to these extremely good folk. They were the salt of the earth and asked for nothing in return. I vowed that some day I would be back to see them.

We had difficulty at first in finding our way, until we were about seven kilometres from Parroletta, when we picked up the signs to Busseto and then Cremona was indicated. We were in good time at the headquarters and George was shown where to park the unit. Several cars were in the forecourt and a couple of jeeps of Italian make.

We bided our time by being shown around the headquarters' building and the canteen, where we had a coffee. The Captain indicated to his men that it was time we moved out and we made our way to the front entrance. There the Captain pointed out to us the car which we would travel in. It seemed to rain even harder and I hoped that the block of flats that we were going to would not be all that far from the road. I didn't relish the idea of the possibility of travelling south in wet clothes!

The Captain had received a message from his men who had been watching the flat that Franconi was inside. When we got there, one of his overalled policemen went to the door and rang the bell. A light came on just above the door and it was opened by a youngish man. I heard the policeman say that there was a gas leak somewhere in the block of flats and they had to check up. Then, a second policeman in overalls joined the first man and entered the flat. With the door being open, the Captain motioned me to join him and we both went in and found the young man, his father and mother and a young lady sitting there, wanting to know where the gas leak was.

The moment the young man saw me, he wanted to bolt out of the flat but I grabbed him and held him back. Pandemonium broke out, as the young woman tried to wrestle with me, but the Captain restrained her and warned that she would be charged if she didn't calm down. The screaming persisted and Luigi fought on until the policeman in the overalls was able to get his handcuffs on him. By now, some of the furniture had been broken and the father and mother had been led away into another room.

The Captain formally read the riot act and told Luigi Franconi what he was being arrested for. Of course he protested his innocence and cried like a baby, I suppose the girl was his fiancée, but I was in no mood to care. The police gave Luigi no free hand to get his gear together. He was told that all he would need for now was a sweater, shoes and a raincoat. The Captain told his men to bring back the father and mother into the room and then told them that, within a few days, they would be informed when the trial would take place and where. They were informed of the charges against their son and that he could have the best lawyer available. They remained incredulous and begged and begged us to let their son go free. Floris and George had arrived in the room too, and it was only then that Luigi began to cease his fighting.

His mother was allowed to get a sweater, shoes and a raincoat as extra clothing to what he was already wearing. It was explained that any toiletries would be supplied by the authorities at the prison. When the woman was told that her beloved son was being taken to Livorno, to be handed over to the Americans, she fainted and was caught from hitting the floor by the policeman who entered the flat first. She was carried into a bedroom to recover. The father sat absolutely bewildered, with a look on his face that could kill!

I was glad at the easy way the arrest had gone but now I was anxious to get away, back to headquarters of the *Guardia*. The Captain left orders to his men to finish off the details and to return as soon as possible. We took Luigi Franconi out. George held him on one side and Floris gripped his arm on the other side, and frogmarched him down the stairs. I followed close behind and when we reached the car, we pushed the prisoner inside, positioning him between the two lads. I sat in the front with the police driver. It seemed only minutes until we arrived, followed by the rest of the policemen. The Captain beckoned us to follow him with our prisoner and guided us to their canteen.

The civilian staff offered us a selection of sandwiches and coffee, which was more than welcome. The prisoner was offered the same food but refused in a bad temper. One couldn't blame him really, for we had given him a hell of a shock. Luigi, under close supervision, had his arms positioned behind his back and handcuffed, as it was a better way for safety. We knew what strength he had, so we didn't want any trouble on our journey. The police helped us to get Franconi inside the jeep in the back, and I sat beside him for the first leg. Floris had instructions to look after George and George had instructions to look after Floris! As comfortable as we could be, we moved off.

It was still pouring with rain. George found the signpost to Fiorenzuola, although it was bent and very rusty. Soon we reached the main Piacenza – Parma road and coming to the place which I recognised was where Colonel Peddie and I crossed several years ago, I recalled that it was raining then! Such memories came flooding back and I wondered where the Colonel would be now. In the meantime, I reflected it was no wonder George called his jeep his 'Rolls', for it sounded most sweet.

At Noceto, we stopped for a change about and the inevitable quick pee – as it was raining that hard, to linger longer would soak us right through. Our prisoner wanted to have a piss too which was most awkward, for we had to remove one hand at least. He was firmly threatened that if he tried any tricks at all, he would get shot. I was ready to really bash him one if he didn't do what he was told. We managed to get one manacle off and snapped it on to the carrying handle of the jeep's bodywork, thus freeing one of his hands to allow him to relieve himself. Floris covered him with his revolver. The moment Franconi had finished and had made himself somewhat decent, we got him back into his original position and shoved him back into the jeep. By this time, we were thoroughly wet. Franconi protested time and time again at his innocence, only to be bawled at by Floris.

'You bastard, did you make it comfortable for those Yanks in the shed at Soriano?'

At every opportunity, Floris rammed the name of the village down his throat. Only on one occasion, when we were nearing the halfway mark, did the prisoner ask what was going to happen.

We told him that he would be put on trial and for sure he would be found guilty and would be hanged. He screamed that he was innocent, totally innocent. Floris said that sometimes in court, if one confessed, then one was spared the hanging. There was sudden silence from the man.

Slowly but surely, little mutterings came from him, which helped us to prove our conviction that he was the No. 2 in the gang. I pretended not to take any notice. Floris goaded him on in a subtle way. He wanted to sleep but we prodded him to keep him awake. We wanted him to feel that he was in for something really nasty when he got to Livorno: 'The Americans are not so kind as we are and have a very different judicial system,' we told him.

As we were reaching La Spézia, we could just see the sky turning bluish. The very heavy rain was now turning to fine light rain but the water splashes at the side of the roads were still fairly deep, causing the steering wheel to veer a little, as we couldn't help ploughing into them.

As I had been driving from Noceto to Aulla, I stopped to let George take the wheel. I went in the back again beside our prisoner.

George said, 'Captain, that really was a piece of cake taking this man, what do you say?'

'Yes, George, it was,' I replied. 'You see a person who has been involved in a crime and has never been approached by the law at any time over such a long period, begins to think that he will never have to answer for his misdeeds. Especially as it happened to the Yanks, and during the battles. He probably thought to himself, Oh they don't know who did it, for it could have been a shell like the one that blew up the car with the prostitutes and the German officers. He was totally taken by surprise and it is that element which scores. Yes, we were lucky that he was at home when we wanted him, for he had been out with that girl, earlier in the evening, according to the police.'

Our captive never heard a word spoken, whether it was in his native tongue or in English, for he was almost in a stupor. The journey, plus having to sit in a most uncomfortable position for the entire length and the late hours, didn't agree with him one bit.

I was determined that he should not have the chance to escape, for I wanted to deliver him alive to the Americans. We purposely never mentioned that we had his friend and accomplice already in custody. I would like to see his reaction when he was led to his cell and then saw Alfredo Giancarlo locked up too. That would be more of a shock, and might even get a confession out of him. He would be frightened that Alfredo might have told the whole story to save his skin.

When we reached the red and white painted barrier across the entrance beside the Guardroom, the GI sentry momentarily blocked the way. Then he recognised a similar outfit to the one he'd seen once before, and approaching the jeep said, 'Gee, you guys, not another one! Come inside and be our guests!'

The barrier was quickly lifted and George drove round to where he had parked the jeep before.

It was such a relief to dismount and to be able to stretch the legs. In a few minutes, a jeepload of smart looking Military Police arrived. This time, they were commanded by a corporal.

'Good morning, sir,' came the quick welcome with a smart salute.

'Morning Corporal! There,' I said pointing to the inside of the jeep, 'you will find the other half of the "terrible twins". Watch him carefully and don't take any risks! You better keep his handcuffs on until you get him well and truly locked up. Those handcuffs are mine, so when you have finished, I would like them back; here's the key.'

'Yes sir!' came the smart reply, with an equally smart salute as he turned to give his orders to his men.

Franconi must have fully recovered, for he was trying to give the police a hard time getting him out from the back seat.

I could hear the GIs saying, 'You sonofabitch! Ouch! You bastard!' When they finally pulled him out, he almost collapsed for I think he had been thumped in the stomach by one of the men.

Now that Franconi was well in their care, I didn't want anything more to do with him. It was all up to the Americans what they would do with him and Alfredo Giancarlo. I told the lads to grab their grips and to go off to where they went before and to get themselves a good breakfast. I would see them at the jeep at ten o'clock.

Grabbing my grip, I sauntered over to the Officers' Mess quarters and received a welcome recognition from the staff. The usual courtesies were extended and I was shown to the ablution and locker rooms and while I was changing, my uniform was taken away to be pressed.

It was a real treat to be able to luxuriate under the hot shower. All the aches of the journey were disappearing and I soon felt exhilarated. I took my time drying and then shaving, and noticed that it was high time that I had a haircut! All spruced up once again, I dumped my bag in a locker and went off to the dining room for breakfast. Some officers were having their meal but were engrossed in reading some sort of magazine.

I was enjoying my grapefruit, when Michael Rod came in and joined me. He was very excited at our conquest and couldn't ask enough questions. He told me that he had heard he was going to receive promotion soon, so we drank to that with a cup of coffee!

I was very pleased for him because I knew how hard he worked for the Corps, as Colonel Villiers once told me in our conversations.

'I believe you are going to hear some very good news too, Ian, but please don't ask me what it is. Colonel Villiers will tell you when you see him at nine,' Michael told me.

The breakfast was superb, with all the trimmings. I told Michael about our easy arrest and the gamble we took beforehand, which had worked.

Michael came to meet me in the reading room just before nine, so that we had time to be at Colonel Villiers' office for nine o'clock.

The atmosphere was most cordial and I was made to relax from military protocol. The Colonel asked me to relate the events and showed wonderment at the exercise being so simple in the end. I remarked that often, situations appear to be most difficult then they turn out to be just the contrary. What helped us really in this case was the fact that there had been such a time lapse and he was taken completely by surprise. The chasing after Luigi Franconi immediately after the arrest of Alfredo Giancarlo didn't allow anyone to warn Luigi before I got there. That was my only fear but I had to try working on my hunches.

The Colonel then handed me a set of keys and said that, in gratitude for what I had done for them, they were presenting me with a new jeep. I was greatly surprised and naturally thrilled, for I had an enormous affection for their rugged vehicle. The Colonel said that it could stay in their garage until I wished to pick it up.

It was now my turn to thank them and a thousand thoughts flooded my mind as to how I was going to register it with my military authorities. However, I would cross that bridge when I get back to Padua. I was expecting Colonel Villiers to give me a new assignment but instead, he said that my HQ had sanctioned a few days off, and to return there after the weekend.

I could easily work with Colonel Villiers, for he was a type I would very pleasantly get on with. He, like me, knew when to use military protocol and when to ease off and be 'human'. He had a good sense of humour, which I liked. He was also very astute and good to his staff.

'Captain Bell, perhaps there might be another assignment for you on our behalf at a later date, so until then, my best wishes and good hunting!'

We shook hands and I gave him a salute before leaving his office.

I was alone out in the corridor, so for a moment, I looked at the keys I had been given by the Americans and thought that they were a thoroughly generous lot.

I met the lads at the jeep and told them the news about my own jeep which had just been given to me. They were very pleased and we went off to the garages and workshop, to have a look at it. It looked very perky standing on its own, all without a mark to show.

'You're a lucky man, Captain! What are you going to do now with it?' George asked.

'I really don't know yet, George, for I cannot run it on the roads without it being registered or licensed in some way. I think I'd better leave it here until we have been back to Padua and then I'll ask Major Williamson what I should do.' I replied.

'Now, you two lads, apparently we have been given a few days off, so what would you like to do?' I asked.

A broad smile came over Floris's face and he asked, 'May I take George to my home at Monte San Savino, for the few days, Captain?'

I was only too pleased for George to have a break and certainly for the lad to see his family. It was kind of him to want to take George.

I didn't require the jeep, for if I needed one specially, I could use mine now, but I believed that if I needed to go anywhere, I would have a vehicle put at my disposal, with driver.

'Let me see, lads. What day are we at, yes, Thursday. Okay then, I would like you both back here by ten on Sunday night. You can take the jeep, George, but you'd better look after it.'

'Thanks, Captain,' he replied.

'George, one thing you'd better do before you go off: put the trailer in the compound and find something to put under the tow bar, to keep the trailer level. Now go off and enjoy yourselves. If you stick a couple more cans of petrol in the back, you should have plenty of petrol to take you anywhere you want.'

'Thanks again, Captain, and you have a good time too,' said Floris, with a cheeky smile.

My big grip was left in the trailer, which I was not requiring straight away unless I was going to a function of sorts with my American friends. I was just contemplating what to do next, when Michael came out of the main building and said that whenever I needed a vehicle to take me anywhere, just to ask at the Guardroom and one would pick me up there. What wonderful treatment I was being given, I thought to myself. I thanked Michael as he returned into the offices.

I decided that I would turn my jeep into a 'station wagon', the type that I had seen the Americans having with their Ford cars. It would look great. I couldn't possibly drive around in a vehicle in army green. I thought then of finding an Italian coachbuilder in Livorno. That's it, I said to myself. I then went to the Guardroom and asked if I might have a vehicle to take me into the town.

I didn't have long to wait when a Chevrolet Staff Car arrived and the driver got out to open the door for me. I felt like a rich potentate, but of course I had to show my lookers-on that I was used to such treatment! I asked the driver to take me to the local *Carabinieri* police station, as they would be able to tell me where I would find a good, yet reasonable coachbuilder. An address was given, so off we went. The premises were not all that big and I soon found the owner. He was as grubby as his assistants; at this I was glad, because he would be working on the project, making sure that it was built properly.

I explained what I wanted and between us, we drew a picture. He then gave me a price and told me that he could not begin to do it for several weeks. I haggled with him to make it earlier, as I didn't know how soon I would be able to come back to Livorno to pick the car up. I told him that my Headquarters was at Padua.

He moaned and groaned, telling me that he had so much work on, then I just happened to have some large lire notes in my hand and he just happened to see them, quite by accident on purpose, which quickly changed his mind. He then said that I better get the vehicle down to him.

I found that to hesitate would be disastrous, so I hurried back to the HQ garages and drove my jeep to the coachbuilder. The Staff Car followed and brought me back to the Club. There was no sign of my lads nor the jeep, so I assumed that they had moved off as quickly as they could. I informed the Guardroom that I had given permission for our jeep to be used by my driver.

I rested in the Club for the remainder of the daylight hours, until Michael came and joined me. He told me that he had booked me in at the Excelsior Hotel in Florence until Monday and that on Saturday night, he wanted me to join him and his fiancée at the American Army Officers' Club in the city at eight o'clock, for dinner.

A Staff Car was waiting to take me to Florence but first, I had to retrieve my big grip from the trailer, as it had my dress uniform inside. Lord knows in what state it would be in by now!

I felt like a four-star general receiving this treatment but I hoped it would last, as I was enjoying every minute of it.

I had stayed at the hotel before and even the hall porter was beginning to recognise me, which was not really difficult, because I was the only British army officer staying there.

The short stay was not enough to see even a fraction of the wonderful sights. I walked and walked through myriads of narrow streets, each one displaying a gem of an art treasure. I was pleasantly surprised to see how many American Servicemen were also interested in the beautiful architecture.

By the time I got back to the hotel, I was feeling ready for my hot bath, to ease the aching feet. Michael and his fiancée were to pick me up at seven thirty, so for once in a long time, I was able to dress in my best uniform. The valet service polished up my Sam Browne belt and the brass buttons and pressed the jacket and trousers, so they were worthy of a brigadier's inspection! Once dressed, I checked that I had everything with me that I needed and went down to the hall to meet my hosts.

Michael's car arrived on time and the driver came in for me. Once inside, Michael introduced me to his fiancée.

'Ian, I would like you to meet Marion Renshaw. Marion, this is Ian Bell, who I have spoken to you about.'

Marion was a lieutenant and she looked stunning in her immaculately tailored uniform. We chatted in the car on our way to the Club. She was a cartographer and enjoyed her work very much.

The Club still had all the Christmas decorations up, making the place looking very festive. Colonel Villiers was there with his wife at a table surrounded by three couples, who looked to be his favourite friends. The dance floor was crowded, making it difficult for the waiters to negotiate a brief space to deliver or take an order from a diner.

The whole atmosphere was wonderfully friendly, as many colleagues who passed our table had a quick cheery word with Michael and Marion. Some couples would stop their dancing, in order for Michael to introduce me to them.

Everything about that evening was most memorable and I had an extremely good night. It was evident that Michael and his fiancée were very well liked, apart from the acknowledgement of the position they held at Headquarters. It was in the early hours of Sunday morning when I was delivered to the hotel and I was more than ready to get some sleep.

It had passed midday when I got up and luxuriated in my ablutions. After the many days of dashing from one end of the country to the other and sitting for hours on end in the jeep, it was most pleasant to be able to take one's time with the procedure of dressing.

I wasn't a bit hungry, so I went along the embankment road beside the River Arno as far as the Ponte Vecchio. The Germans had wanted to blow this bridge up but were foiled in their attempt by General Mark Clark's troops. It would have been a tremendous crime if they had succeeded.

As arranged with Michael, a car came to fetch me the following morning at eight o'clock. At HQ, I was asked to pop up to Lieutenant Rod's office, which I did. Michael seemed loaded down with paperwork and the various phones around the office were ringing away, making the two clerks go from one to the other. Michael motioned for me to take a seat.

'Ian, working in conjunction with your Advocate General's Department, we have to amass evidence of war crimes perpetrated by the Nazis, under the Command of Field Marshal Albert Kesselring, during the occupation of Italy. Your office wishes you to return in order to brief you on your next assignment. Obviously, we shall be seeing you from time to time and any help we can give you, don't be afraid to ask,' he told me.

I said my farewells, as the office was a hive of activity and I had finished my business with them.

I went to the garages and met George and Floris packing up the jeep. The two of them had found my grips and were stowing them in the right places, along with theirs.

'Well done, fellows, all ready to go? How did you get on George?' I asked.

'We had a super time Captain and Floris's mum is a great cook. I've been able to take some photos. It was really great,' he replied.

'I introduced George to many of my pals who I have not seen for a long time and also to some of the girls I know well,' said Floris, looking quickly over to George with a big grin.

'Gee, Captain, I don't know how Floris does it, for they are all beauties and judging by their clamour, they must miss him a lot!' said George.

I was glad for both of them that they had a good time and a memorable one.

'Are you ready, lads?' I said. 'Then let's be off! But first, George, I would like to go round to the coachbuilder, to see what progress has been made to my jeep.'

The GI guards gave us a friendly wave as we drove out of the main gate and we headed towards the docks. The coachbuilder had started on my 'car' and was pleased that I had called, for there were several points he wanted to clear up with me about the bodywork. I told him that I would be back sometime within a fortnight and left him to it, quite happy.

Leaving Livorno well behind, we were on our way back to Padua to get our new instructions. The following morning, I was at the office at nine o'clock, after having had a good sleep. The journey back had been uneventful but tiring, as we were feeling the after effects of our wonderful break. Major Williamson and Captain Reynolds were in the office, so we had a long chat about all the various happenings. Major Williamson showed me a document which had come from the American Counter-Intelligence Corps. It was a proper printed document with my full title and name, written in copperplate. I took it from the Major and read it. It was a document asking me to join the Corps. According to Major Williamson, everything had been approved by the American authorities and the War Office. All I had to do was to put my signature in the appropriate place near the bottom. Then I read carefully the small print section beneath where I would have to sign, and was shocked to see that I would have to give up my nationality and become an American citizen. In no way was I going to do that and I emphatically told Major Williamson my feelings.

He informed me that I would have to talk it over with Colonel Villiers, adding, 'He has told me that they have presented you with a jeep, for all the work you have done for them. What are you going to do with that? How are you ever going to get it on the road?'

I could see the difficulty so I asked my superior as to how I would get it registered. The Italian authorities didn't want to know, as it was a military vehicle and not an ordinary motor car.

Major Williamson then got on to the War Office in London by phone and asked their advice. The answer was that they too didn't know what to do, as this was without a precedent. The person on the phone in London said to Major Williamson, why not ask the owner of the vehicle what to do about it, and the phone was put down.

I suggested to register it in my own personal private number – 232219. It was agreed as being a good idea and that was how it remained. The Italian authorities were informed and so was the War Office. I asked the Major if I might have a 'clearance' letter which would act as registration certificate, stating my details and that the vehicle was registered with my own army number, and that it was a present to me. I was a little bit concerned that people might think that I had stolen it or kept it as 'war booty'. However, everything had been sorted out and the vehicle was legitimately mine. I was delighted and felt rather proud to have created something unique with the War Office.

Chapter Twelve

My new assignments were to investigate and if possible to apprehend the criminals responsible for crimes committed against Allied personnel during the occupation of Italy, by the German forces. I was given a list. Amongst the list, was one item which attracted my attention straight away. It was the shooting of an English officer, Lieutenant Llewellyn of the Royal Tank Regiment, after he had escaped from the POW camp at Fontanellato in 1943. I'm sure I'd known this young officer and the last time I saw him was in the *bund* under the vines when we had just escaped from the camp and were sheltering until it was all clear to go our own ways to freedom.

I was asked to gather as much evidence as I could for the forthcoming trial of Field Marshal Albert Kesselring. He was the German Commander-in-Chief of the Nazi forces in Italy. I thought to myself, he was some general but a real bastard.

'Ian, you have been doing a great job for us and we hope that you will have some success with that list,' Major Williamson said, and pointed to the sheet of paper I held in my hands. 'You have complete freedom, and we will see you when we see you, okay?'

I felt honoured to be asked to 'take charge' of this list of about six cases concerning British personnel and two more cases of American personnel.

During that day, I had a long meeting with George and Floris and we went through the list, beginning with Lieutenant Kenneth Llewellyn.

I told both lads to sort their clothes out for a long haul and to prepare the jeep and trailer for a morning start at about nine. Back in my room at the Hotel Leone Bianco, I prepared all my gear for a lengthy trip away, leaving nothing in my room this time. When I was satisfied that I had completed my domestic chores, I went over to the Pedrocchi Club and met Major Williamson, Captain Reynolds and Captain Philip Manners, having a 'Bar Conference'.

I asked my chief what should I do with the prisoners when I'd caught them. He instructed me to hand them over to the Italian authorities at the nearest big town. 'They will inform us, as well as yourself, and we will arrange to have them brought to the prison here at Padua,' he said. 'The moment you have arrested someone, get him inside somewhere, let us know and then carry on to the next case.'

I was now satisfied that I had all my thoughts clear on what was my procedure, and joined them in a drinking session. They asked me what I thought of my crew. I told them that they were a great couple and that Floris was doing a fine job, although he couldn't fully take the place of Gustav Pless. I wondered if there was any news of him but unfortunately, no word had been received up to now. I told them that I couldn't do without George. He was fantastic, a great credit to his regiment.

That evening, I arranged to meet the lads in order to have a meal together. We went to our favourite trattoria in the centre. Over our meal, we pondered on the list we were given and the inadequacy of relevant details to each one.

'Where the hell are we supposed to find these sods?' demanded Floris.

'I think we will have to begin our investigations around Darfo at the top end of Lake Iseo. Llewellyn was supposed to have been shot at Brescia. Anyway, we shall head for that direction tomorrow and we'll meet at my hotel at nine, okay, fellows?' I said.

'When was he supposed to have been shot?' asked George.

'He was on the run for only about a fortnight when he was caught. He was making for Switzerland apparently, like a great many of them tried to do,' I replied.

The jeep arrived punctually and once my kit had been loaded, we were off on our way to Verona, then Brescia.

Our road took us along the edge of the bottom part of Lake Garda, which looked most beautiful and in our search for an attractive spot to have lunch, we came across Sirmione, which lay on a promontory. A small but a clean trattoria fed us well and after a quick look round the most scenic village, we made our way out of the tiny streets on to the main road again.

We reached Darfo just before nightfall and were sur-prised to see that it was a spa town, along with its neighbour, Boario. We chose the most convenient hotel in sight, one which also looked like being open. There were many hotels in and around the town but they were not all open. We picked out the San Martino, as it showed more lights on inside than the others.

We took our own luggage inside and sensed an atmos-phere of eerie hollowness. The smell was a mixture of chlorine and pinewood polish. Our footsteps echoed across the wooden floor, from the door to the old reception desk, and signalled our presence. Our voices echoed too, which rather scared the boys. Two mirror-panelled doors were opened to reveal a grey-haired man, dressed in light grey striped trousers and white shirt with bow tie, covered with a green velvet waistcoat, but striped with yellow braid on the front. It was the uniform for the 'lesser ranks' of the hotel. As he shuffled across the hall towards us, this man appeared to have severe trouble with his legs, for he wore soft carpet slippers which covered enormous bandages under his socks.

'You can only have two double rooms,' he said, even before he arrived at his desk. Seeming to be in a world of his own, he muttered on that most of the hotel was closed, as were all the other hotels in the town. The restaurant was closed, so we would have to eat out. Floris asked him how long had he been at the hotel and his reply was, 'Longer than your age, *giovanotto!*'

He took the keys from the key board, and we followed 'old shuffler' up the wide carpeted stairs to the first floor. Our rooms were en suite and next to each other. Dumping our grips, we wandered down with the old man to the hall. George asked Floris to ask where we might park the jeep for the night. The old boy gave Floris a key with a numbered tag and pointed to a building opposite.

Keeping our keys, we went outside and saw a courtyard surrounded by a high wall with an arched entrance. George fetched the jeep and drove in through the arch and swung round near to lock-up number six. The length of the lock-up was not enough for both units, so we unhitched the trailer and pushed it inside. The jeep we left outside because we had the safety switch to make it safe.

'Floris, will you pop over and ask the old man what time the hotel closes, please,' I asked.

With a big grin on his face, he returned, telling us that it would remain open until we got back and that the old boy would be waiting to have a drink with us.

Sure enough, when we got back after our meal at the little restaurant just near the centre, the man had brought in several gas heaters, to warm up the lounge bar. His favourite drink was grappa, a very potent Brandy made from dried grape seeds. As the room was still very cold, the three of us decided to have a drink of the same brandy. That was a good starter to a very interesting – but somewhat creepy evening.

The more we drank, choosing a variety of drinks, the more the old boy mellowed to our questioning and we heard rather sad tales of his war experiences. Of course as the evening lengthened, we had to be wary of what we were told, whether it be true or false or slightly 'tinted'.

The old boy told us stories of the days when King Victor Emmanuel III used to visit Darfo for health treatment and later, Mussolini used to come and he stayed here at this hotel. There was turmoil in the town when the King dismissed Mussolini in July, 1943, for around here, Mussolini was very popular.

'Were you a Fascist?' asked Floris.

'*Si*,' came the quick reply. He told us that everyone of working age had to join the Fascist Party, or they were arrested and put in prison: 'Your family would be without money for food, even accommodation was taken away from you. Of course, there were many forged papers to be got on the black market but they were very costly. If you were caught by the *Questura*, then you were summarily shot,' he told us.

'When the Germans came, they took over everything and the Fascists, who still thought that the Germans were going to win the war, turned against their own people.'

He told us of the day several small groups of English prisoners of war were reported to be in the area, trying to make their way to Switzerland. Some had already been caught and taken into custody at Brescia and Bergamo. This was in August and September, 1943.

'*Signori*. You must imagine this hotel. It was fully occupied by the Germans and if anyone was taken prisoner in the area, they were brought before the Nazi officers and interrogated, down in the wine cellars. 'Those were terrible days, *Signori*! You see the landing there,' he said, and pointed up the stairs to a landing, partly open to the hall and the rest closed by a wall. The balustrade joined the banisters to the staircase. He continued, 'It was just before lunchtime one day, when some Fascists came in with an Englishman in civilian clothes, whom they had caught near Capo di Ponte. They took him upstairs to the balcony and tied a rope around his neck. I was up there doing some rooms, when I heard the commotion and came to see what it was all about. Then I saw how young the man was and that he was putting up a really good fight. I yelled to the soldiers to stop and they picked me up and threw me over the edge. I didn't see what happened after that, to the young man nor to myself, but you can see my feet now – and look at my legs, too!'

Now we knew why he wore the soft slippers. Although the rooms were comfortable, neither of us slept well on account of the eerie atmosphere which permeated the whole building. I said to the lads to get their grips as we wouldn't stay there another night. Slipping a little bit of money into the old boy's hand, I paid for the rooms and we were off to 'sniff around' elsewhere.

We were looking for somewhere to eat, as the hotel didn't have anything to offer, although as we were leaving, several other people who looked like hotel staff, were arriving.

We 'smelt' our way to the local *panetteria*, where Floris bought some hot cobs of bread and croissants. They were delicious as we ate them with an espresso at the bar nearby. This is quite common in the mountain areas, for the locals to dunk their bread in their coffee, and eat that way.

The local *Carabinieri* calmly walked on to the scene, for they had seen the jeep and trailer slowly touring around the little streets. They obviously had their curiosity glands titillated and were eager to know what was going on. As soon as they recognised my rank, they jumped to fling a salute and I returned the compliment, bidding them a good morning in their own language.

They asked us where we had stayed for the night and when Floris told them, they exclaimed in unison, '*Mio Dio!*' and crossed themselves.

I was intrigued, so I asked Floris to ask them why were they so shocked. Between them, they gave us a story about the whole town; how it was run by the Fascists, the *Brigata Nera*, then the German High Command and the Gestapo. 'Mussolini used to come here, well then *Signori*, you can imagine what went on then!'

Each one was getting his words out a little quicker to the other as the story developed. By this time, quite a gathering of locals joined our small group and as word was spread about, '*Gli Inglesi sono qui!*' and we had half the small square filled with jabbering people.

'Floris, will you ask them how long they have been in Darfo,' I asked.

He put the question to them and they seemed proud to announce that they had been there since the days of Mussolini, *Il Duce!* They clasped their hands, but we were not sure if it signified a throttling action or one of lament. They told us about the hotel we had just vacated and said that it was once occupied by the German High Command. *Contadini* who refused to work for the Germans were imprisoned down in the cellars and never saw daylight again. Floris translated the woeful tale they were saying about our hotel and two others, which they thought were now haunted.

Some of the bystanders heard bits of that conversation and crossed themselves, nodding to each other in agreement with what the *Carabinieri* soldiers were saying.

'Floris, ask them if we can go to their office so that we can talk more peacefully,' I told him.

The lad put the question to them but they declined. I then showed them my red booklet. They stared at each other and motioned us to follow them. Floris and I walked with them, whilst George brought the jeep round with difficulty, as the youngsters hung on to the sides of both units, to get some sort of a ride.

As we arrived at their local prison-cum-offices, they had to organise a guard to see that the youngsters didn't steal anything from the jeep or trailer. Floris supplied the two police officers with a couple of packets of cigarettes each, which they accepted with great enthusiasm. In the warmth of their office, we felt easier about asking them further questions, and I let Floris have his head. He had developed a very good technique and I liked the way he used his brain to trip up his 'adversary'. I waited for some sign which would give me hope that we could narrow our search for the culprits involved in young Llewellyn's death.

I asked my interpreter to get them to tell us the whole story of the events after the collapse of the Fascist Regime in September 1943.

'*Capitano*,' they then told us, 'we were just taking orders from our superiors but what we saw, we disapproved of. There was a *Tenente* in charge and a *Sergente*, called Dino Ruggero. We were just soldiers then. They remembered well how the Fascists helped the German troops in rounding up many ex-prisoners of war, and the *contadini* who harboured them, and brought them to Darfo and Boario. They were herded into that yard opposite the hotel where you stayed. They slept in the garages. You see, they were handy for the interrogations by the Germans when they wanted them. They were only there for a few nights and then they were taken away to the railhead at Brescia, for transportation to Germany. Some people never came out of the hotel or were not seen again, so we don't know what happened to them.

There was one young man, who was easily recognised as an Englishman, for he was tall and slim and aggressive. He looked as if he could be an officer and he was picked out from the bunch of prisoners by the German guards. He was taken to the hotel where he was interrogated and from what one heard, he was used as a 'toy' by the German Officers and was nearly killed, as they tried to hang him. He was then returned to the yard, for transportation by rail to Germany.

'Can you give us the names of those who were in charge of the prisoners,' I asked.

'There was a *Tenente Simoni* and a *Sergente Dino Ruggero*,' came the reply.

'What regiments were they in?' Floris asked.

'They were both in the *Carabinieri, Signori*.'

'Where would your General High Command be situated?' I said, asking Floris to translate.

'It is in Rome, *Capitano*, not far from the Villa Ada, in Via Salaria. *Tenente Simoni* was killed in a car crash in the September of 1943 as he and some Germans were coming back from Brescia. Their car went off the road between here and Pisogne and skidded across the road and over the precipice into the valley below. That left *Sergente Ruggero* in charge then and he was no good. He used to bully the poor prisoners. We didn't think there was any need to terrorise them as they were very submissive after being caught, with the exception of the young Englishman. He was always trying to escape, *poverello!*'

'Do you know by chance where this Sergeant Ruggero might be stationed now, or even if he is still in the service?' I asked.

'No, *Capitano*. The only way would be to look up the records at the Headquarters, for they would have all the information there,' I was told, and I thought that made good sense.

'What we do know is, that the young man was shot. It was recorded that he was shot whilst trying to escape.'

'Where are your records kept of prisoners who pass through your hands at this station,' I asked.

'This is the Register, *Capitano*. It is a big one. We just rule off when we come to the end of a year, like so,' said the Corporal, and showed us.

The Register went as far back as January, 1943, so Floris and I scrutinised each page after September 1st, 1943.

There was one page which had many names written down, which included Italian and English names. Against the English, it was difficult to know if the person concerned had given his real name, as often a false name was given. We looked for a Llewellyn but could only see a 'Lieut. "Tiger" Marrowbone'. Floris had a giggle when he saw this entry but I remarked I was convinced that it would be typical of young Llewellyn.

'Would you think the English ex-prisoners were making for Switzerland or was it just to bypass the big towns that they were here?' I asked.

'*Signori*, we are so close to the border at Tirano and Campocologno which is just inside Switzerland. Certainly they were trying to get over the border. Do you think this entry here is the same as that of the young officer?' the policeman asked.

'I would think it is just the sort of name this person would give in order to annoy the authorities,' I replied.

I said to Floris, 'I think we have exhausted our questions here, as I don't think we are going to get anything else out of these two jerks, so let's say our farewells and go.'

Floris thanked the two officers of the law and we joined patient George out in the jeep. At least he had his time taken up with trying to see the kids didn't steal anything. They were so quick and crafty.

'George, turn the jeep round. We're off out of this dump, and head down to Iseo,' I said. 'We'll stop there if we find a place to eat something and discuss what we should do next.'

On the way down, we had to admit that the area was most attractive, especially when we caught sight of the lake. The road between Darfo and Pisogne was most scenic and we could imagine what happened to the car that Lieutenant Simoni was killed in. The road was certainly very precipitous and one wouldn't stand a chance if the vehicle went over the edge, as it was a great distance down to the valley and river.

George took the road very easy as it was narrow and in some parts, quite twisty. Iseo looked to be the sort of place one could imagine being a beauty spot for tourists under normal times. For once, here was a little town which had not been destroyed in any way by war. We found a trattoria right on the lakeside and it was open, much to our delight.

It was too cold to sit out, although the morning so far had been really beautiful. The mountain air was very fresh and invigorating, giving one a good appetite. According to the Italian custom, we were early to have lunch, but we had a drink first while we chatted over our next move. The indoor dining room looked right out on to the lake. A big glass window provided our view. Floris said that it looked a good lake to do some water-skiing.

'Now lads, choose what you would like, so the kitchen can begin to satisfy our moaning stomachs,' I said.

As soon as the lads had chosen their food, I began telling George what we talked about at the police station in Darfo. I told him that it seemed inevitable that we would have to go to Rome, as a result of what we now know. By the look on his face, he was keen on the idea.

'I'll just go and get the map from the jeep,' he said. He was back in a flash and we opened it out fully on the table next to ours.

'That looks like the route, George: Brescia; Cremona; Parma; Bologna; Florence; Siena; Viterbo again, then Rome,' I said, and Floris suggested that we could possibly break the journey at Florence, which looked like being halfway, more or less.

'Yes, we could do that. If everything goes well, we could make the hotels for about nine o'clock. Are you game for a hard drive, you two?' I asked.

The young stalwarts were game, for they knew they would get a good comfortable bed at their hotel, where they stayed once before.

'How far do you reckon it is, Captain, to Florence?' George asked.

'I would say it is about 211 miles, which will take us about nine hours,' I said.

'That means we should get into Florence at about the time you said, Captain,' George replied.

With minds made up in complete accord, we relished our food and once again feeling refreshed, we set off to Brescia. When we arrived at Fidenza, I took over the driving and gave George a rest, until we reached Bologna. We had a short break with hot coffee and toasted cheese sandwiches from the first bar we came to, and then George took the wheel again, to Florence.

'Captain, you were right, we have made Florence for nine o'clock!

Shall I drive straight to the hotels and get our rooms? Then we can go and eat somewhere,' said George.

I took a look at Floris whose head was nodding away frantically.

'Go on, George, get there quickly, as I am starving!' said Floris. Poor boy! He always seemed to be hungry and ate like a horse, yet he was quite slim.

The porters at both hotels recognised us and gave the lads a good double room *en suite*. I had a single room again. George managed to stash the trailer away in one of the lock-ups at the Grande Hotel, so we were free of that encumbrance, enabling us to search for a different restaurant.

As soon as I got back, I rang my HQ at Padua and gave them a brief as to my movements and asked them to let me know the name of the hotel in Rome which is used as an Allied officers' hotel. There were two to which I could go, the Eden or the Continentale in the Via Nationale.

The following morning, it seemed both parties had slept well, although I gathered that Floris had kept George awake for a while, with his snores!

I took the wheel first and we moved off towards Siena. Having had experience of that town, we managed to get through without much difficulty. We got as far as Aquapendente before George took over the driving, and then he took us the rest of the way to Rome. Several times we had to ask the way into the centre, especially the direction to the Via Nationale. We found out where the barracks were for the lads and then we came across the Hotel Continentale, which was situated at the top end of the long wide street.

After the lads had dropped my grips off, I told them to go off and to enjoy themselves until they heard from me. I suggested to George to keep the jeep fully loaded with petrol and to put the trailer away somewhere but handy, in case we want it with us. They were only too happy to be 'free' of duty and quickly drove off. I grabbed my grips and went into the hotel. It was about four o'clock. I dumped the grips in readiness to sign in and looked around the hall for the hall porter or the receptionist to sign me in, when I noticed the bar was open to my left. One person was leaning against the bar, chatting to the barman. I'm sure I know that man, I said to myself, and my curiosity got the better of me. I approached the man and then I yelled out, 'Jan Halstaar!' He swung round and, raising his arms, recognised me straight away and replied, 'Ian! What a pleasant surprise!'

The reunion was terrific and we immediately celebrated with a good chilled beer.

'Where have you come from and what are you doing here in Rome?' asked Jan. A barrage of questions came at me, not giving me time to answer even one properly. 'Listen,' he said, 'Go and give yourself a rest. Have yourself the three S's. Change to your dress uniform. I will pick you up here at seven o'clock and then I will introduce you to some friends of mine from the Dutch Embassy, who will be at the Eden Hotel, where there is a dance tonight.'

'Right, Jan! What are you doing here now?' I asked, while walking out to the reception desk.

'I am attached to the Embassy and am having a very interesting time,' he said.

'Good for you! We'll talk all about that later. See you at seven!' I replied.

Jan left me and I was shown up to my room. I felt great meeting up with Jan again. We had so much to talk about and now the expectation of meeting people from the Embassy, was quite a new venture. I had a big room, with bath and plenty of wardrobes to hang out my crushed things.

I rang for service and soon a housemaid came. I asked if my clothes could be ironed and my uniform pressed. I met with a willingness which was so pleasant; anything I wanted doing, was never too much trouble. I rested and must have slept for a while, then I bathed, shaved and when my uniform arrived, dressed. I checked myself over in the long mirror on the wardrobe door, and using my heavy raincoat, which was lined with the lambskins, I wandered down to the hall to meet Jan.

A taxi drew up and Jan emerged, so I joined him. In the cab, Jan went on the offensive again, asking me thousands of questions, and I tried my best to get a question in between his. The directions he gave the cabbie was to go to a certain place in Piazza Ungheria.

It was dark, although the dim street lights of the piazza just illuminated the building which the taxi driver stopped at. He sounded the car horn, and the concierge opened the solid gates to allow a young lady to meet the car. The driver opened the door and as she got inside, Jan greeted her most civilly. She was so elegantly dressed. Jan said, 'Andrée, this is Ian. Ian, may I introduce you to Andrée. Ian is the officer I have spoken to you and Kitty about, whom I met at Klagenfurt.'

With the formal introductions over, Jan said that we were now going to pick up another Dutch friend of his, who was the daughter of the Dutch Consul. We pulled up outside a villa and again, the driver sounded the car horn. Responding to the call, another young most elegantly dressed lady appeared and joined the party.

Jan introduced me. 'Kitty, this is Ian Bell whom I have spoken to you about and Ian, this is Kitty... both these young ladies do some secretarial work at the Dutch Embassy, to while the time away,' he explained.

I was very pleased to meet them and was struck by their youth, elegance and slimness. Both looked like they had just come out of a fashion magazine.

It didn't take long to reach the place where Jan said that we were going to have a dance and dine. It was the Eden Hotel, one of the official Allied officers' hotels in the city.

Now that we were sitting at a table, I could appreciate the two young ladies much better than when we were in the taxi. Andrée had the most beautiful auburn hair, cut long. Kitty had long hair too, but hers was almost jet-black and smooth. Part of her hair she wore coming over one side of her face, which I took to be a fashion. Between the meal, we danced alternately. Jan danced with Andrée and I danced with Kitty, then we would change about. Both girls were so light and their waists were that slim, I could almost get my hands around to touch the fingers at the back!

I soon found out that neither of the young ladies could speak English but they were fluent in German, French and Italian. Their own language, I heard, was very close to the German and some words I could just about understand. I felt inadequate not being able to communicate in a language that I could be fluent with. Italian seemed to be mutually acceptable and as I was not able to be grammatically correct, my mistakes were courteously accepted, causing many an amusing moment. Jan of course was most fluent and, like the young ladies, could speak in many tongues.

Jan and I saw the young ladies home. I thanked them for their company and for providing such a pleasant evening. However, I did say that I was unable to arrange a further date for a similar evening, as I had special work to do. I would let Jan know when next I returned to Rome and he could arrange with each one the time and place for the next meeting. Jan knew what my work was and understood my desire to be free of any commitments. They were two such charming and well-educated young ladies that I had a great desire to see them again and to get to know them further.

The following morning, I called the barracks where the lads were staying and left a message to say that I would like to see the two members of my crew at the Hotel Continentale at ten o'clock. The lads arrived on time and we went óff to the Headquarters of the *Carabinieri*, to enquire about *Sergente* Dino Ruggero.

The police were very co-operative and after a search through their records, we found an entry; *Sergente* Dino Ruggiero. *Nato*, 25.6.1918. *Servizio Militare*: 16.1.40.–4.2.44. *Posti di Servizio*: Benghasi, Lybia. Catanzaro. Grosseto. La Spézia. Verona. Darfo. Roma.

As soon as Floris and I saw the name Darfo on the list, we knew we had the right man, but his name was spelt differently from what we'd thought. We checked this but the correct spelling was Ruggiero. Now we had to find out what sort of work he was doing and where he could possibly be.

The police wanted to know the reason we were after this man, so we told the Captain, who seemed to be the most senior man around, and I also showed him my red ID booklet. I told him it was alleged that this Sergeant Dino Ruggiero was involved in the murder of the British Army lieutenant.

We said that he was one of many British prisoners of war, who were escaping after their release from their camps by the Italian authorities when the Armistice was signed in 1943. The officers and men went many different ways in order to evade the incoming German troops, and of course most of them tried to reach the Swiss border and seek sanctuary in that neutral country. Floris gave all this information in his own language.

'Do you have any information as to his present whereabouts?' asked Floris.

'As far as our records show, his last known address was with a Cattinale Maria, 82, Via San Luca, Genoa. It seems to be a lodging house or something like it,' said the Captain. He offered to phone the *Questura* in Genoa to ask them to verify if Ruggiero was still living, at that address. He said that it may take a little while to make this verification and suggested that we be taken by one of his staff to their canteen.

This seemed a very good suggestion, so Floris went off to fetch George in order for him to share the pleasure of a break. I was escorted by another policeman through a maze of corridors, past offices which showed a great deal of activity, by male staff. Once we were together in the canteen, we discussed what we had been able to find out so far, and it was agreed that if Ruggiero was still living in Genoa, we would have to go and interview him.

'I wonder what sort of work he is doing, Captain,' said George.

'I wouldn't be surprised if he was connected with the shipbuilding in some way, as the docks there are very extensive with quite a lot of building too,' I ventured.

We had eaten some sandwiches and had drank several cups of coffee, when after about forty minutes, we were recalled to the Captain's office.

'You are in luck, *Capitano* Ruggiero Dino is still living at the house of Signora Cattinale Maria,' he told us.

I was always confused when the Italians used the surnames first when referring to people. We left the *Capitano* in no doubt as to our gratitude for his assistance and made our way back to the Continentale Hotel.

'Have you lads got all your things together in the jeep and have not left anything at the barracks?' I asked.

'We've got everything with us and we can go off anytime to suit you, Captain,' George replied.

'Give me ten minutes then and I'll be with you. You can wait here.'

I took the lift to my floor and soon had all my gear stuffed into my grips. I phoned the Dutch Embassy to let Jan know that I had to go away and would let him know when I would be back. I asked him to pay my respects to the two young ladies.

On the way up the west coast, we stopped at Livorno and I took the lads to see how my own jeep was getting on. The coachbuilder was doing a tremendous job on the bodywork and promised to have the vehicle ready in two weeks' time. The lads were most interested and were surprised to see that a normal jeep could be completely transformed by making a wooden body and furnishing the inside like a car.

Having stayed the night at Livorno, we were off early the following morning which allowed us time to look around the famous cathedral in Pisa and the Leaning Tower. It was truly an amazing sight. The whole area was teeming with American troops of all ranks and colour, taking snapshots one after the other, in order to send them back to their families in the US. Out on the road again, we headed north past many picturesque villages, some partly concealed by tall pine trees, which appeared to grow in a wide belt right along the coastal road for miles.

I had to admit, with some pleasure, that this part of our journey was the most scenic and beautiful of all our journeys in Italy so far. It was interesting and it looked as if it had escaped the ravages of war completely.

The town of Viareggio appeared to us to be calling out for the baking hot sun to dry its many puddled streets and promenades. It wanted to parade a host of scantily clad sunbathers, and to project their happy voices to a mammoth hum. It wanted to be dressed once again in all its coats of many colours and to attract its multinational guests, so that they could frolic in the beautiful warm waters and then recline peacefully on the baking sand.

We had to stop at the only bar we could see which was open for business. To be able to walk even some paces on that hallowed promenade was like walking on millions of fantasy footprints, beckoning us to walk on until they faded away. It was a town which, although dressed in its sombre winter clothing, made us make a jotting in the notebooks of our minds.

George remarked how strange it was that we had never seen Viareggio like this before. We had covered that road with one of our criminals, and as it were, just ignored it. What he didn't realise was that we were then driving south and far too preoccupied with our captive. Driving northwards, we had a much better aspect of the town and besides, we were free of trouble!

Floris suggested that we try and stay the night at Portofino or Santa Margherita, as they were a paradise for artists. We slowly made our way along the coast road, eyeing the villas, the plantations and the sea with its rich blue hue. We passed through Sestri Levante, Chiavari, Rapallo and Santa Margherita, with our eyes popping out of their sockets, for there were wonders to be seen everywhere. We were not used to the tranquillity nor the complete absence of the slightest war damage. We were enthralled with what we saw, yet we had to explore even the remotest corner, and drove round the narrow road to Portofino. What a little gem of a place it was. Unfortunately, there was nowhere suitable for us to stay because of having the jeep and trailer. It was too risky leaving it out in the piazza all night, as the cans of petrol would certainly be taken for the much rationed fishermen's boats. Petrol demanded an extremely high price on the black market and the slightest smell of petrol escaping from under our canvas would create a riot from greedy hands.

We returned to Santa Margherita and toured around for a while, seeking a convenient place to stay. Most places were closed, for there were no tourists. We finally found one place, which luckily had a garage, called the Minerva in Via Maragliano. By now, the evening was getting darkish, just allowing us to see enough to get our gear and to park the trailer away safely. The lads were well accommodated and I had myself quite a good room. After we had settled into our rooms, we went for a stroll on the seafront. The weather was dry but crisp air made us glad that we had worn our topcoats.

Leaving the trailer in the garage, we left for Genoa the following morning and sought the address of Signora Maria Cattinale at 82, Via San Luca. We parked the jeep in the little square outside the church at the top end of Via San Luca and walked to the address. It was very old property and not surprisingly, there was quite a bit of evidence of war damage. We found No. 82, which was tucked on the side of a tiny alleyway, and disturbed a huge cat which was in the process of devouring a rat.

We had to climb some stairs and reached the wooden door which had a peephole in its frame. The doorbell rang several times before we heard a shuffle inside and as it opened, we saw a woman who looked just as if she had finished her circus act, heavily gowned and heavily made up. Her hair was died strawberry and her gown showed her leg right up to her thigh as she moved. The mascara on her eyes were thickly painted, which spoilt her vision, as she was eternally blinking. She was ready to slam the door shut in our faces but Floris had his foot inside the hallway and I showed her my red booklet. Frightened now out of her wits, she stammered words of acceptance to her home and Floris answered as calmly as he could, as we followed her into her living room.

There was no doubt that we had come to a queen of the local area's ring of prostitution. George stood by the door, awestruck by all, the paraphernalia around the room. Floris sat nearby on a settee and I took up a chair.

'*Signora*, does Dino Ruggiero live here?' Floris asked.

'*Si, Signori,*' she said. She looked at us from one to the other.

'What does he do, and where could we find him?' Floris said, looking straight at the woman, who was now trying to reveal her chest a little. A big black Spanish-type comb lay on a small table beside her and every now and again, her hands would grab it and with a nervous flick, she would run the comb through her thick matted hair.

We were now becoming aware of a sickly sweet aroma which was permeating the whole house.

'What do you want of him?' she asked. Floris slowly related the story. At first, the woman sat motionless as the story was told, then she began to protest as she was certain that her Dino would never have been so bad, *cattivo* as she said.

Slowly, the mascara mixed in with her tears and in the act, she tried to disguise her 'light' sorrow by revealing more of her body. Floris became stern and told her that we had not come to have a session with her but to ask simple questions only. She got up and approached Floris, running her hands through his hair, which infuriated him. He let out the most fierce rebuke and told her in no uncertain terms that if she didn't stop her play-acting, she would be charged with obstructing the course of justice. She retook her seat and purposely left her leg showing as before.

'Now, *Signora*. Where does Dino Ruggiero work and what does he do?' asked Floris.

He was now raising his voice, showing firmness.

'He is a ship's carpenter and works for the Adriatic Line, *Signori*,' she replied.

Floris said that she had nothing to fear for telling us and that we would not send the *Questura* after her, as a lot of Italians thought, whenever they were questioned about one thing or another.

We didn't wish to disturb the woman longer than was necessary, so we left her, knowing that we had sufficient information. Winding our way through the narrow streets and down to the shipyards, we found the docks belonging to the *Linea Adriatica*. Approaching the guard control point at the main gate, I showed the guard my little red booklet and was allowed through, following the directions given, for us to drive to the administration buildings. It was a bigger place than we first thought, for seeing it from the road, it looked much smaller. There was a fair amount of activity outside the big sheds but one could not see what was going on inside. I was sure the shipping line would be building or repairing as many ships as they could, for there was virtually no shipping during the war.

We were pleasantly welcomed and shown to the office of the Personnel Manager. Floris made the introductions on my behalf and told him the reason for our visit. A junior staff member was summoned to produce the record card of Ruggiero Dino. We chatted about the rebuilding programme and the number of employees they had. A knock on the door signalled the return of the junior clerk.

'*Ecco, Signori,*' he said. Together, we looked over the man's record card and saw that he was a good time keeper and worked well. There was no entry of his past. The Personnel Manager spoke very well of his employee.

Floris asked if we could have a talk with the man, which was agreed, and it was arranged that we should talk to him in the Personnel Office.

The summons was made, and as the man entered the office and saw me in my military uniform; he suddenly tried to dash out but was stopped by George. The Personnel Manager bawled at the man to behave himself and to sit down. After Dino Ruggiero had calmed himself down, we began our interrogation.

Lieutenant 'Tiger' Llewellyn was recaptured just outside the village of Schilpario. He was trying to disguise himself as a *contadino*. He tried to resist arrest by local Fascist youths but was restrained until the *Carabinieri* arrived. He was then taken to the temporary prison compound at Darfo by the *Carabinieri*, who had to hand him over to the German troops. Apparently, he had given the Germans a hard time while they 'questioned' him and he was sent, along with many other prisoners, down to Brescia, in order to be transported to Germany by rail. Seizing an opportunity to escape again, the young lieutenant flung himself over the side of the truck between Darfo and Pisogne, injuring himself quite considerably. The truck turned around and took the injured officer back to Darfo. The Germans shot the officer for trying to escape.

This was the statement given on oath by Ruggiero, which I believed.

'Can you remember if the troops were ordinary *Wehrmacht* Infantrymen or were they special units of the SS Panzer Corps?' I asked.

'They were a mixture, *Capitano*. We just did what we were told, for you know, *Signori*, they were taking us Italians away for labour over in Germany, even if we did nothing against them. They were so *suscettibile* to the slightest thing,' said Ruggiero.

Floris turned to me with a shrug of the shoulders, indicating that he was more or less satisfied with the man's explanations.

Warning the Personnel Manager that it might be necessary to revisit at a later date to ask Ruggiero further questions, if necessary, we left the yard and made our way over to the headquarters of the *Questura*. Informing them of what we had done, we returned to our Hotel Minerva at Santa Margherita and picked up the trailer.

Chapter Thirteen

With a cocky whistle and smile, George said as he mounted the jeep in the driver's seat, 'Some you gets and some you lose!'

Both Floris and I had a feeling that George was pleased that for once the Italian was not to be blamed for anything.

'I'll tell you what, George,' I said, 'I would still like to get my hands on the bastards who shot Lieutenant Llewellyn, for they couldn't have given him much help for his injuries.'

'Captain, perhaps his injuries were so bad that it might have been a mercy killing,' remarked Floris. 'Remember, it was alleged that he was used as a "toy" for the Germans' amusements at the hotel at Darfo.'

Recalling that made my blood boil, and I said, 'I'll tell you what, fellows. We'll try to find the sods. Most likely they think that they can get away with this crime, but we'll show them!'

'What do we do now, Captain?' asked Floris.

'We'll go back to Padua and give them our report about Ruggiero and then we will try to get as much information as possible about the German troops who were in that area at that time. I am sure that our Military Headquarters must have some records for us to work on. Let's get on the road George and head for La Spézia.'

Floris reminded me that our General Military Headquarters had moved to Rome, and that we should be able to get much more information from both the British and the Italian Military Authorities in the capital, rather than a provincial headquarters.

'I like your idea, Floris, you're so right, and then, if we want to involve the Americans in this, we can do, as they do not have a branch of their headquarters at Padua. Okay, we go to Rome. Drive as far as we can go before dusk, George, and then we'll stop the night somewhere,' I said.

Taking turn and turn about between George and myself, we managed to get as far as Piombino where we found a delightful *albergo* in the piazza. We had the most superb view of the Island of Elba from the little harbour. It seemed so near that one could even swim out to it to touch its flickering lights, which bade a welcome. The atmosphere created this nearness although the island was about twelve miles away.

We settled into our rooms and then strolled out into the little town. We had a seafood meal at the only trattoria open and watched the locals enjoying their wine as much as we were.

The following morning, we were off fairly early as we had more or less a six-hour journey still to do before arriving in Rome. George had refilled the jeep up and had checked the tyre pressure of one of the tyres on the trailer, as it looked somewhat suspect; but we were too early for the little garage to be open, so we drove on, hoping the tyre would not let us down until we got to a garage which was ready for business.

The lads dumped me with my luggage at the Continentale and they went off to their barracks, having made arrangements to meet the following morning at nine o'clock at the hotel.

When I had completed my soaking in the bath, shaved and dressed in my better uniform, I felt great and ready to tackle the evening's fun with my new found friends at the Dutch Embassy. When I phoned, I spoke with Jan first, then he put me through to the room where the two young ladies worked. It was agreed that we should go dancing again at the Eden Hotel, so Jan arranged to meet me at my hotel, as he was now living in a small flat of his own, and then we would go round to each of the young ladies' houses, to escort them to the Eden.

Each time we went to the Eden Hotel, we seemed to be lucky in getting the same table quite near to the small dance floor. Between dances and drinks, we chatted about the secretarial work the ladies were doing and their social life. Kitty, the daughter of the Dutch Consul in Rome, enjoyed her social life with the Diplomatic circle; and Andrée, her best friend, was the only child in her family, apparently and she too enjoyed the benefits of a high social life. At this stage, I didn't want to ask too many questions about the two ladies, for I felt that Kitty was developing a crush on me, as she was pushing herself more often to have a dance with me, rather than her friend. I didn't wish to get involved with any girl at that time, as my work was more important to me, and I felt it my duty to keep romance from interfering with it.

My responses to their overtures were very friendly, but evasive and intentionally cool, which allowed them to begin to understand that I was not interested in getting 'hitched up'. In spite of my feelings, we always passed extremely pleasant evenings together and it was unanimously agreed to have a similar evening whenever I was again back in the city.

The following morning at nine o'clock, Floris, George and the jeep minus trailer were at the front door. We went off firstly to the General Headquarters of the British Military Command and sought out the office most suitable for our enquiries. The Guardroom indicated us to drive to the main Administration Offices, where there was a good car park.

Floris and I wandered from office to office until finally we came to a room marked 'Records'. A sergeant was busy with rolls of maps, trying to keep them from rolling up into a tight roll, as they had been kept for quite a while. Seeing his predicament, we dispensed with the usual protocol and greeted each other with a handshake, which created a good relationship straight away.

'Sergeant, do you have any information at all about the German army which occupied the Northern Sector of Italy, after their invasion in 1943?' I asked.

'Just a minute, sir, I'll put these away and I'll have a look,' he replied. The Sergeant expertly handled the rolling up of the graphically designed maps, which I was tempted to look at, for they fascinated me as all maps did. The shelving of the Maps Division had been carefully designed to accommodate the largest map, for there was one which measured three feet by four feet six inches! The Sergeant selected a map and brought it to the table. It was a relief map of the north-western side of Italy, from the Bernese Alps to the Dolomites.

Unfortunately, it didn't show the part we wanted, so that one was put away and another one was brought out.

'Ah! This is better, Sergeant,' I said, as the much hair-greased man laid out the map. 'I can get a good idea now as to why the Germans liked this part of Italy for their rests, during the campaigns down south. Their General Hospitals were established way up in the mountain regions too, to be as far away from the battle zones as they could be.'

While Floris and I were scanning this map, Sergeant Neville Willys was getting some Operational Maps from the archives. As soon as I saw the rolls unfurl, I couldn't keep my eyes off them. They were fascinating and so full of detail of the German defences and our Allied positions of advance. Several maps we passed over as they bore no useful purpose. With careful selection and scrutiny, we found one map which helped us to discover what sort of German troops would have been in the area during the months of September to November 1943.

Field Marshal Albert Kesselring was Commander-in-Chief of the German 10th Army, for the entire operations in Italy. The Nazis had eight Divisions of their crack troops under the command of General Vietinghoff, including the 16th Panzers of the hated Hermann Goering Division and the 26th & 29th Panzer Grenadiers. It was the units of the 26th & 29th Panzer Grenadiers, which were actually in that area of Milan, before moving down south to reinforce their front lines. There was not much between the Panzer Divisions as to which was the most brutal, as both had gained a terrible reputation whilst in Russia, and then Poland.

Now we felt we had the first step secure in our minds, that the Nazi troops who were up in the area of Bergamo and Brescia, were Panzer troops and most likely, those from the 26th or 29th Grenadiers.

'Captain, how the bloody hell are we going to find the bastards who were responsible for the Lieutenant's death?' asked Floris. He showed his concern with a sign of slight frustration, which was understandable, as he was as keen as I to get hold of the perpetrators.

'We'll find them,' I remarked, trying to appease his volatile nature. The Italian character was so loveable that one couldn't ever be angry or unable to understand them. By now, I had plenty of experience of the delightful Italian nature. Their moments of being down one moment, then up the next and always bearing no grudges, endeared one to them. I had felt for several years now, that they were my 'brothers'. Young Floris was one of the best ambassadors for his country and family.

'Sergeant, I think we have something now to work on. Before we go, do you have any records at all which would indicate the troop dispersements, as the German forces invaded Italy?' I asked hopefully.

'No, Sir, he replied. 'There are only the Campaign Maps which would not give the details you require. You would probably get that information from the Italian General Army Command.'

Armed with that useful advice from Sergeant Willys, we left him with our gratitude for his help and made our way over to the Ministry of Defence. My little red book was so much in demand that I had no time at all to put it away, for we had to pass many checkpoints before we were able to get inside the enormous building. A guard of the *Pubblica Sicurezza* approached us, to act as our guide and to help us to get to the office most suitable for our quests.

As we walked down the terrazzo tiled corridors, I whispered to Floris, 'We're stepping where angels fear to tread!'

He smiled surreptitiously. The guard stopped us at a door marked, *Maggiore A. Ugolini*, and knocked. A civilian opened the door and for a moment, I expected to be met by military personnel and was surprised. No one inside the office was in uniform. The civilian bade us to enter and immediately introduced us to Major Ugolini. He was a short man with greying hair and a face full of wrinkles, brought on perhaps by years of service in sunnier climates. His disposition was friendly, especially so after he had a look at my red booklet. As he spoke fluent English, we were both able to ask the Major questions without the disturbance of translations.

We must have been in his office a good two hours, which resulted in discovering the actual unit which was stationed at Darfo to service the Recreation and Rehabilitation Centres for the German officers and men. We were given a list of the units occupying the area to maintain control of all communications and law-enforcement. We even had a list of the German officers who had been temporarily 'hospitalised' at Boario and Darfo. We had discussed with the Major, more or less the exact dates when the crime against Lieutenant Llewellyn was committed and who of the German officers were resting at that hotel at that time. The Major's patience was endless in helping us to discover the German criminals. He showed no love for the Nazis, which was not surprising when he told us that he had been nearly shot by them before he went into hiding to avoid being coerced into serving the German troops. As an opponent of what the Nazis stood for, he would have been stripped of his rank and forced into slave labour in Germany, as many of them were.

A Company of the Panzer Grenadier troops, commanded by Major A. Kauffmann, were in control of the area right up to the Swiss border, until lesser infantry troops had been drafted in to relieve the Panzer troops for the bitter fighting which had begun on the mainland of Italy. We were elated with all the wealth of information provided by the genial Major Ugolini, and feeling quite exhausted, we courteously gave our salutations and left.

George was more than pleased to see us, for the poor man had thought we had completely forgotten about him.

'Come on, George,' I said, 'drive us down to Trastevere where we can have a really good slap-up meal at very little cost!'

We bundled into the jeep and headed for the old quarter of Rome. As time went, it was nearly teatime instead of lunchtime. However, the Italians are always very accommodating and provided us with enough to satisfy our aching stomachs.

During the meal, we related to George the events that took place in the Major's office. Floris told George about the many phone calls, the despatching of the Major's office clerk to various offices and the gradual build-up of information from different branches of the Ministry.

'Captain, I have to hand it to the officer, for he certainly knew which department to phone and how to get what he wanted,' remarked Floris.

'We'll have to inform our HQ about what we now know and see what they would like us to do. Most likely, they will want us to go to Germany and to continue the search there!' I said.

'Gosh, Captain! You don't think they want us to go there, do you?' asked George.

'Would you not like to go to Germany, George?' I asked, hoping that he would say no.

'I'm ready to go anywhere you say, Captain. How about you Floris?' George put the quick question over to his pal.

'Let's see what happens when I get in contact with Major Williamson. We'll go now back to my hotel and I'll give HQ a ring,' I told them.

Back at the Continentale, I got the two lads into the corner of the lounge at a table, where we would be out of the way and arranged for a phone to be connected nearby. The HQ switchboard put me through to Captain Reynolds and he asked me to tell him all I knew about the case of Lieutenant 'Tiger' Llewellyn so far. While I was talking, George and Floris were sitting on the edge of their seats in expectation of our next move.

'...Yes, I have that too. It is the 26th Panzer Grenadier Division. No, Peter, they came later. Apparently, a Company out of the 26th Division, commanded by a Major A. Kauffmann, who was once in the Hermann Goering Division of the Panzers as a lieutenant, had control of the area right up to the Swiss border. Yes, they were there at the time 'Tiger' Llewellyn was shot. No Peter, I don't know where their base was or would be in Germany, perhaps the Americans would know or our High Command in Berlin. Do you wish me to find out for you, Peter?' I asked.

Captain Reynolds suggested that I return to Padua and to discuss the case with Major Williamson. He left the decision whether or not we should seek further information by going into Germany until we returned to HQ.

'Gosh, Captain, that was a long phone call. Does HQ pay the bill?' Floris asked.

'Of course, lad, my expenses here are paid by Headquarters,' I said.

'So it looks like we have to set off tomorrow for Padua. Can we go via Leghorn?' asked George.

'Yes, George, for I'm sure I can get to know where the 26th Panzers' Depot is in Germany from them. This would be a help. The Americans have so much gen on the German army. I have a hunch that they are stationed at Lamsdorf, for when we were in the POW Transit Camp, we saw plenty of Panzer units continually on manoeuvres. I am only guessing, but it was a hell of a place, teeming with troops, including Cavalry,' I said.

'When we get to Livorno, I'll phone the Adjutant again before we set off for Padua. Anyway, meet me in the morning at nine, at the hotel, with everything, including the trailer, and we'll go to Livorno first, okay?'

The lads went off to pass the rest of the day as they wished. I phoned the Dutch Embassy and made arrangements to meet the young ladies with Jan at the Eden Hotel.

Another, splendid evening was spent in the company of the two young ladies and my friend Jan van Halstaar. It was getting very obvious that Kitty was realising that I was not going to get tied down to a love affair. She was a great girl, pretty, intelligent and exquisitely presented, but I had to withhold my feelings, as I didn't know where I would be sent to next and for how long. I didn't know then what my plans were for my future, whether or not to stay in the army or to seek a civilian post somewhere. I even thought of joining the Diplomatic Corps, for the life was very appealing. I enjoyed meeting people of any race or creed. To learn a little of their ways of life was fascinating to me.

The other, young lady, Andrée was demure but brimming with intelligence and kindness. She appeared to be more genuine in her responses and less pushy. My main concern was for my present job and how best I could carry it out. So my thoughts went back to Llewellyn's case.

At nine o'clock, the lads were outside the hotel, waiting to load my grips into the jeep and the big one, inside the trailer, then we were off. It was near four o'clock when we arrived at the American Army Headquarters, as we had several stops, including lunch and surprising our old landlady, Signora Vergone, in Viale Italia.

The lads waited for me outside the offices of the CIC, whilst I went up to Michael Rod's office. As we greeted each other, I could see that he was now Captain Michael Rod. I was so pleased for him, as much as he was for himself. I told Michael why we were back and what it was that we were after.

'Phew, Ian! You do give us tall orders! Of course we'll try to get you that information. When do you want it for?' he asked.

'Tomorrow morning, please. Certainly by midday, if it is at all possible.'

Michael rose up from behind his desk, came over to me and said, 'Now, if you want all that stuff, get to hell out of here and leave me in peace!'

His broad smile, and almost a kick up the backside, were his way of saying, 'Okay, I'll help.'

Walking down the stairs away from Michael's office, I thought to myself that if anyone could get the information I wanted, he would be the man.

'Now lads, let's go and see what my jeep looks like at the body shop. To our pleasant surprise, the jeep was nearly ready. There was only one more coat of varnish to be put on the woodwork of the body. It really looked great. The doors opened almost silently and the windows were extremely well made, in fact, it looked most professional and worthy to be taken anywhere. I told Cesere Rossi that I would be back within the next fortnight and to have everything ready, including the bill.

'*Si, Capitano. Non pensa piu. Abbia confidenza,*' he said.

With that satisfaction, we left to go to our landlady, where we had arranged to stay the night.

We booked in to the same rooms as I had before with Guss and Nobby. Signora Vergone was very surprised to see George and Floris and made the all familiar remark whenever the women set eyes on Floris, '*Come il giovane è bello!*'

Our landlady had been fairly busy considering the time of the year and had done better business than she had expected. Of course she complained that she was not busy enough but was well satisfied and said that our last visit had brought her luck.

The following morning, I was around at Michael's office at nine, ready to lend a hand or to answer any questions which might arise from the various phone calls. His office was bustling with two clerks manning telephones and another ready to run errands for him. I kept myself to a corner as much out of the way as I could. I offered to go but Michael bade me stay to help.

'Gerry, is that you? Are you there, Gerry?' he said, and put his hand over the mouthpiece and whispered, 'The lines to Germany are terrible today. I'm trying to get my friend at HQ in Berlin. 'Hello! Hello! Are you there, Gerry?'

A horrible crackle could be heard in the phone, even from where I was standing. Michael put the phone down and began dialling another number, saying, 'I'll try our HQ at Salzburg.'

We waited patiently until we could hear the ringing out tone.

'Hello! I want to speak to Ziggy MacNair of Records, please. It's Captain Michael Rod, speaking from Livorno.'

Holding his hand again over the mouthpiece, Michael said that if anyone could give us the information we want, then Ziggy was the guy.

'Is Ziggy a man or a woman?' I asked.

'Definitely a man! Hello. Hello Ziggy! Help again. Can you look up the details of the 26th German Panzer Grenadiers who fought in Italy, from the date they entered the country round about the September, or a little earlier, in '43. Where were they dispersed, if possible. Okay. I'll wait your call. Will it be before lunch? Okay, I'll wait for it. So long, Ziggy.'

The phone was replaced and immediately, it began ringing again.

'Hello, who's speaking, please,' asked Michael. 'Ian, it's for you. It's Captain Peter Reynolds, Padua Headquarters.'

'Peter, good morning!' I said, and then listened. 'Okay, Peter, I'll carry on with Llewellyn's case. I've got pretty close now to narrowing the investigations and will keep you informed. How are things going about the mass murder of the civilians in the quarry outside Rome? Right. Yes, I'll keep you informed. Cheers, Peter!'

'I'll have to meet your gang up in Padua, one day,' Michael remarked as I replaced the phone. 'You'd like them. They are a good crowd but there are several on the payroll who I have not met yet and I don't suppose I ever will.'

As we were not expecting the phone call before about midday, I left Michael in peace to carry on his work. Rejoining the lads, we went off to the coachbuilder to see my jeep again, but the doors were closed and no one could be seen, so we went over to the harbour to see the fishing boats. As we came into the open spaces of the harbour walls, we could see further on the main docks which contained fairly large American naval vessels.

We were more interested in the local fishing fleet and the characters who sailed them. The deep-sea trawlers were eye-catching, for they had quite neat lines, not so bulbous in shape as our ships. The smell of diesel fuel and old fish didn't exactly invite one to make a closer inspection. The boats with sails were more to our liking so we lingered longer until George suggested we go and have a drink at the bar, which was just behind the lighthouse next to the police station.

As we had been interested in the boats and some beautiful yachts, we didn't realise how the time had passed. Reaching Michael's office once more, I had the best welcome, for Michael had managed to get the information I wanted. Fortune was with me that day! Michael handed me a sheet of paper with the details written down and we discussed them together.

'Major Alexis Kauffmann, commanded 'C' Company of the 26th Panzer Grenadier Division. The Division was moved in from the Eastern Front along with the 29th Division and the Hermann Goering Panzer Division, which Rommel passed over to Kesselring to bolster up his defences in the south of Italy. 'C' Company was halted for a while to police the area around the Como, Bergamo and Brescia districts, in order to stop the exodus of Allied prisoners of war who had escaped from their prison camps, when the Armistice had been signed. Many Italians, who saw the danger of being trapped, as their allegiance to the Nazis was nil, were also endeavouring to get to Switzerland by the shortest routes. Meanwhile the Germans commandeered the hotels and turned them into rest centres and hospitals for their troops,' Michael told me.

'Major Kauffmann assigned *Feldwebel Hans Kraiss* to oversee the detainees, and to supervise the shipment by road and rail of all prisoners to the Reich.'

I had to interrupt Michael then, 'So it was that bastard Sergeant Kraiss who was responsible for Llewellyn's death,' I said.

'It looks like it, Ian,' he replied.

'I don't know how to thank you, Michael, for getting all this gen for me. Now I have to find him, if he is still alive!'

Absolutely elated with this finding, I couldn't get out of Michael's office quick enough, to tell the lads. 'Now where shall I find him, where, where?' I repeated to myself as I walked out to the jeep.

The lads were eager to learn what I had managed to find out, so I was trying to tell them in my excitement as we slipped out of the compound and away up the road to the bar behind the lighthouse. There we would discuss between us our plans for further searching, as well as a little fortification for our eager stomachs.

'We've to find a *Feldwebel Hans Kraiss* of 'C' Company of the 26th Panzer Grenadier Division,' I announced.

'That was one of the Divisions which were down on the Viterbo Line facing General Mark Clark's army, wasn't it, Captain?' remarked George.

'Yes, I think you're right, George. Further than that, I think they were down at Anzio,' I answered.

Several avenues of investigation were opening up in my mind, stimulated by the delicious cheese sandwiches, which were toasted to perfection by the barman. Strange that they never tasted as good with wine as they did with coffee.

'If we begin by finding out if he is still alive by enquiring at the War Cemeteries first, we will be sure then that he is still alive!'

George stunned us with that piece of thinking.

'Floris, what do you suggest would be our first line of attack?' I asked.

'I think it's not a bad idea at all to ask at the various War Graves Sites, as they have lists of all who have been interred, including the enemy soldiers,' he said.

'They would have copies of the lists from each site at Military Headquarters in Rome. Most likely, the Americans would also have records of their Sites and the German sections, so we can ask them first whilst we're here,' I remarked.

Nicely refreshed, we drove back to the American army complex and completely on the opposite side of the establishment, we found the Documentary Office.

The Sergeant at the enquiry desk, which was policed by a Lance-Corporal of the American Military Police, gruffly asked what I was wanting. It was the first time that I had come across insubordination from the Americans, and when I demanded that he respected an officer, the MP Lance-Corporal came to the Sergeant's aid and he then demanded to see my credentials. I held my temper and showed the two cocky GIs my little red book. I was even intimidated by the sight of the MP's drawn revolver! I was told to wait where I stood, and that I did until I was relieved by the approach of a lieutenant.

'Will you please follow me, sir,' he said.

I didn't utter a word until I was way out of earshot of the two men in the entrance hall.

'Lieutenant! Who is in charge of those two servicemen?' I asked in a demanding tone.

'Have you had trouble with them, sir?'

'Yes, I have had a nasty meeting and I would like to put in a complaint.'

'Sir, we have that kiosk bugged and we heard every word that was said as you came in. We've had many complaints about those very two. For some time now, we have had suspicions that the two are receiving drugs from the outside and so we have been listening and watching. Purposely, we have put them on duty together, so that we can catch them. A courier came just ten minutes before you came and passed over a parcel to the Sergeant. He has not had time to dispose of it yet. Now we can arrest the two and break up the little ring they both have formed.'

'That's a sad story, Lieutenant. I hope you will throw the book at them,' I commented.

'They'll get more than that, sir. They will be flown back to the US and charged there. I wouldn't like to be in their shoes!' he said.

Now that we were away from the hall, the Lieutenant kindly asked me what it was I wanted. I asked to be shown to the office which controls the War Graves Sites and Rolls of Honour.

The Lieutenant couldn't have been kinder and more helpful, after my bad experience. He led me into a fairly large room which had to be illuminated and then showed me some black bound books. Within each book was a section at the back, which was reserved for the German War Dead. I scanned each book, for they not only held the names of the dead German soldiers but each book represented one site. Such slaughter, I thought, needless bloody slaughter, as I saw names after names – and to cap it all, many entries were just numbers. So far, there was no *Feldwebel Hans Kraiss*.

I asked the Lieutenant if I might phone my Headquarters and when he realised where I was from, he pleaded with me not to take the matter of the two receptionists in report. He assured me that they were not now even on duty but placed under arrest. The whole exercise had been carried out that swiftly.

Headquarters in Padua were going to make enquiries with all the British Headquarters in Germany, including

Berlin. I was to carry on making my enquiries here in Italy. If the man was to be found in Germany, then war crimes investigators responsible for Germany would seek the man. I wanted to retrace the gradual retreat of the German Forces, specifically where the 26th Panzers were involved, and found that they were kept on the western side of the country, facing General Mark Clark's onslaught.

'Lieutenant,' I asked, 'are these books kept up to date?'

'We try to, sir, but unfortunately, the Italians keep finding bodies in the most unlikely places. Perhaps they had been found and taken for burial by the local population to avoid disease, and later, when the War Graves Commission had ventured into their area, they had surrendered the corpse to them, for, proper burial,' he told me.

I had reached the final book and the final name of the German sector, and I failed to find an entry marked *Feldwebel Hans Kraiss*. I was quite happy to leave that office, in spite of the efforts of the Lieutenant trying to make amends for my inhospitable reception in the hall.

I went over to Michael's office, taking Floris with me this time. The welcome was as usual, and far different to the one I had at the Admin. Block, and when Michael saw me, he lamented on what had happened to me earlier.

'Good morning, Michael, news travels fast!' I said.

Seats were offered for myself and Floris after I had introduced him to Michael. As I was, so Floris was cordially received.

'Ian, I'm glad you called in, because I had a long chat on the phone with a colleague of ours at Salzburg, Captain Cartwright. Do you know him?' he asked.

'Oh yes, he was so helpful to me and my crew when we handed over Hans Vogle to them,' I said.

'He has been making enquiries on our behalf about Llewellyn's case. Now, when the threat of an Allied invasion of the Italian mainland was a reality, the Germans moved three of their best Panzer Divisions from the Eastern Front into Italy, as soon as the collapse of Mussolini was known,' Michael continued.

'In order to stop the exodus of Allied prisoners of war escaping into Switzerland, Kesselring diverted a Company of troops from the 26th Panzer Grenadier Division to police the area from Como to Brescia. At the end of October – the actual date is not known – 'C' Company were relieved by the Infantry, and ordered to rejoin their Division down south. Whilst in transit by rail from Brescia, the troop train was blown up in a cutting by saboteurs or partisans, somewhere up in the Appenines. It must have been a hell of an explosion, for it completely blocked the line! The whole cutting came down on top of the train and the line was useless until well after hostilities ceased.'

'Gosh, Michael!' I exclaimed.

'I was responsible for that! I'm sure that there couldn't be a similar case.'

'You'll have to tell me about it sometime, Ian, for it sounds a tremendous story,' said Michael, who seemed genuinely interested. 'How come that you were involved with the partisans?'

'Michael, it is a story much too long to go into details now, but I hope that one day, you will read my story when I can get it to a publisher, when I get back home,' I told him.

'What's the story called,' Michael asked.

'I have named it ...*And Strength Was Given*. It is absolutely true throughout and I hope that the publishers will keep it that way,' I said.

Floris spoke up and told Michael that recently we had a reunion with two of Captain Bell's ex-partisan friends, at a dance hall at the village of Soragna. Michael was getting more and more intrigued.

'Going back to this tremendous news,' I said. 'I just cannot believe this twist of fate, after all this time. It means that Major Kauffmann and Kraiss were killed in that cutting.' I was almost stunned by the information Michael had given me and I asked his permission to phone my HQ at Padua.

The Adjutant at HQ was just as surprised and relieved that we could wrap up the case of Lieutenant 'Tiger' Llewellyn, as I was, and suggested that I return as convenient.

We gave Michael our salutations and left the building to join George. On the way out, Floris remarked, 'It's some building this, Captain. What do they do to occupy all these offices?'

'Floris,' I said, 'this is the central Headquarters of the American Armed Forces, serving the whole of South-Western and South-Eastern European Areas, which requires a hell of a lot of administration. There is also the Naval and Air Force included too.'

'Now, George, we've discovered that the Nazis responsible for Lieutenant Llewellyn's death are dead, and therefore we have no further need to make any more enquiries about that case. So, we have to return to Padua. It is too late to make it now in one day, so we will stay the night at Florence where we know we will get a good night's sleep in comfort and also have a good meal.'

We were soon out on the road to Florence, where we arrived just before eight o'clock, after a fairly successful drive in spite of the heavy American transport on the road. George had put the trailer away in one of the lock-up garages behind his hotel and we had all checked in, to secure a room. Once we had refreshed ourselves, we were ready to explore more of the beautiful city, even though it was night-time.

George drove us for a short while to parts of the city we had not seen before, until our stomachs forced us to curtail the sightseeing and to seek the nearest restaurant or trattoria.

We saw the coloured lights of one establishment on the other side of the Arno River which looked inviting, so George drove over a bridge after the Ponte Vecchio and turned back to the place. As we approached, we saw that the car park appeared to be full of cars and American military vehicles. Some cars were even parked on the pavement at the foot of the wall to the embankment.

Inside, it was packed with civilians and GIs of all ranks. The atmosphere was alive with chatter and smoke, mainly from cheroots and the strong American cigarette tobacco. There was a small dance floor which was packed with dancers, so much so that each couple hardly moved to the jazz music.

The waiters did a fine job scurrying in and out of the crowd to serve the tables and soon found a table for us. George and Floris found a couple of young Italian ladies to dance with after our meal, and although their style of dancing was different, it was nevertheless entertaining to watch.

The moment we got out of the place, we felt the effects of the smoky atmosphere as well as the wine, which always was good, but it made one very sleepy. As we had a journey to do the following morning, we didn't stay as late as the rest of the crowd. Knowing the Americans, they stayed sometimes until the early hours of the morning. We always found that wherever their troops were, there was very little trouble with drunks. They liked their wine and beer and their women, but all in good humour, and they invariably treated the girls chivalrously.

Somehow I had mixed feelings going back to Padua this time. I didn't know if my next assignment would allow me to be near to Rome or Florence or whether it would take me back into Austria. I didn't know whether or not I would be able to keep my super team. It was the only time I felt that there was going to be a big change in my duties.

Arriving in the evening at Padua, we were too late to see anyone at the office, so I told the lads to go off and enjoy themselves and to meet me at the hotel in the morning at 8.30. I was glad to get into my favourite room at the Leone Bianco and to get a good hot bath, change to clean clothes and to have a game of snooker at the Pedrocchi Club.

In the morning, I met the lads and we went round to the office where I saw Captain Peter Reynolds and Philip Manners. We had a chat about all matters relating to the criminal investigations we were pursuing and it was agreed that the unit was doing extremely well, resulting in many convictions. The meeting soon came around to the extraordinary findings to the case of Lieutenant 'Tiger' Llewellyn. The whole office was astounded by the quirk of events which led to the discovery of how the criminals we were after had met their end. The discovery saved us time and money and now I was itching to know what my new assignment would be.

'Ian, have a few days rest if you like, and then we want you to go and find Colonel Bruno Zamboni,' said Captain Reynolds.

'Peter, I thought that we found out he had died of cancer whilst staying with his sister at Merano,' I replied.

'Apparently, Ian, he has been seen again at Bologna, according to our intelligence reports. He goes about with a stick and takes with him, wherever he goes, his dog – which is like a large version of a Jack Russell terrier, part brown and white. Now we know you have done a great deal of work trying to find this man and felt sure that you had the true information about him, but we feel that this latest information is too real to pass over. Go and get him and bring him in. Remember, he was far more cruel than Cerati and those two women. Keep in mind that poor young Flight Sergeant and what he went through. If at the final you have conclusive evidence that the man is not alive, then we shall close the case for good.'

I listened and whilst Peter, was talking, I couldn't stop my mind darting about as to where I should begin.

'Peter, I shall do what I can to find him as you well know but do not expect miracles. I am just as eager to get him as this office is. I'll leave as soon as we get our clean clothing back from the laundry,' I said.

'Good hunting,' said Peter, and Philip gave me the thumbs up sign as I walked out.

I instructed the office clerk to inform the lads that I wanted to see them at my hotel within the hour and I took the office runabout back to the Pedrocchi. I began sorting things out for another long spell away, and was seeing to my laundry when I got a message that George and Floris were in the foyer. I went down and joined them, taking them over to the Pedrocchi Club where we could talk in peace.

'We've had intelligence reports about Bruno Zamboni, that bastard who tormented Flight Sergeant Banks until his death, remember? He is supposed to have been seen at Bologna. Now we have got to find this man and if it is really true that he is still alive, to bring him in,' I told them.

'Perhaps it may be a good idea if we go up to Merano and verify that he has a sister there and find out how the police misled us.'

Floris's suggestion sounded well.

'When can you fellows be ready to move for a long stay away? I think it quite likely that we shall have to be away for quite a while on this one,' I told them.

'Captain, we can be ready by tomorrow,' they said. 'George, you had better check that you have the snow chains with you, for we will have to go up to the mountains again. You can imagine what the Alps are like this time of the year,' I said.

'It's okay, Captain. I've checked. They're on board!' was the cheerful reply.

Chapter Fourteen

The following morning, we were off having left nice and early to get away from the build-up of traffic and the cyclists. They were the worst for they couldn't care about the motorist. It was after one young Italian had been knocked down by a British army vehicle that the short-lived riots, which were fairly ugly at the time, took place. The hotheads hated the British Army of Occupation at Padua, for to them, it was a continuation of foreign authority.

'George, when we get to Vicenza, take the road to Schio. That will save us a long way round,' I suggested.

'Captain, you'll probably have some fun on the pass between there and Rovereto, for I have seen on the map that it looks pretty high and very tricky,' he replied.

Floris was all for a little bit of fun and goaded George on, and said, 'You can do it, George! The jeep has four-wheel drive, hasn't it?'

'If we go that way, George, we can easily make Merano before dark, taking in our lunch break as well,' I put in.

George was willing as ever. That is what I admired with George. He never grumbled and was always ready to tackle anything.

We found the easiest hotel to get to from our entry into Merano, which was the Kurhotel Mirabella. It wasn't very far from the *Questura* which was just the other side of the bridge spanning the river. The jeep, trailer and ourselves were well accommodated for the night, so we went off to have our evening meal. Afterwards, we had a good walkabout, even though it was snowing, but the local council were doing a splendid job keeping the roads and footpaths fairly clear. We wondered what the beautiful place would look like in the better times.

The following morning, George had the jeep round at the hotel and we went off to the *Questura* to make our enquiries about Zamboni. Floris and I walked in and approached the enquiry desk. My uniform surprised them somewhat, and at first made the police very cagey. In perfect English, a policeman asked me what I wanted. We were shepherded into a room sparsely furnished, but adequate and at least warm, and made to feel at ease. I showed the policeman my ID booklet and noted his more serious response and willingness to listen to our enquiries.

'May we have your name, please,' he asked.

'I am Captain Bell and my official interpreter here is Signor Dotto Floris,' I replied.

He then told us his name was Julio Volpe, Commander of the Police Force for the Merano district. He said immediately that he had recently taken over as Commander and was ready to help us in any way he could.

'We are trying to trace a man by the name of Zamboni Bruno, who used to live at Bologna, in 1943 and '44. A few months ago, we were informed that he had left Bologna for good and came to stay with his sister here in Merano,' I explained. 'Do you have an address of his sister, Captain?' the Commander asked.

'No, I would hope you could supply us with that, if we can establish that Zamboni did in fact come here. He walks with a stick and usually has his dog with him, which is a Jack Russell-type terrier, brown and white in colour. Perhaps you have seen somebody strange in town who resembles that description?' I asked.

The Commander suggested that his staff would make some enquiries and if we would come and see him tomorrow, at about four o'clock, he should have some information for us. It was probably better to get their office working on this case, as they would be able to pry into the post office or the local Health Service or the Social Services. The Pension Office would be useful and they could get access to that, whereas we would not be able to.

Once we were again on our own, I said to the lads that we would make our own enquiries about the bus terminal, the barber's, and even one or two of the bars. George stayed with me, whilst Floris called at the bus terminal and went seeking the barber's. I asked at the *giornalaio* and lastly, the hospital.

'Captain, don't you think it strange that no one has seen a man going about, crippled, and with a brown and white dog?' asked George. He was beginning to doubt that Zamboni had a sister in Merano and I said to him that I was beginning to have uneasy doubts too. We met up with Floris who had found out where the sister of Zamboni lives. He was superb at getting information we required. Apparently, he used a ploy at the post office and unwittingly, the clerk gave him the address. Of course he was elated and so were we, so we had a good stiff drink at the nearest bar to warm ourselves up.

We agreed not to let the Commander know that we knew the address, and to hear what he had come up with when we meet him at four o'clock.

'Captain, she lives at Via Dante, it is a small villa, standing on its own, said Floris.

We couldn't get to the jeep quick enough and drove out to look the place over. Sure enough, the villa stood on its own and was very small in comparison to the majority of houses in the town.

As we drew near, we noticed an elderly woman brushing the snow away from her path, so we pulled up and Floris got out and approached her. With his boyish charm, he inveigled his way into her house and as I got no signal from Floris, I left him on his own. Apart from which, I didn't want the old lady to get frightened at seeing my uniform.

We waited long enough for the warmth of the jeep to disappear and to begin feeling damn cold. Finally, Floris appeared at the door, and judging by the smiles and the affable conversation, he seemed to have scored again! He ran to join us, as the door to the villa closed.

'Captain! The old lady's name is Francesca Anastasi. She has a twin sister called Ruona, who lives with her husband Pietro and family, at Aprilia. They are called Vespucchi and have a stonemason's business, quite a profitable one from all accounts.'

'Where the hell is Aprilia, mate?' asked George.

'It is a small village way down south near Anzio. Captain, this man is younger than his sisters. Here, this is his photo taken when he was in the *Brigata Nera,*' replied Floris. He couldn't get it out of his pocket quick enough in his eagerness to show us his prize.

'That's terrific, Floris. What a man you are getting hold of this. Well done!' I said. I was delighted, and the three of us kept passing it from one to the other, in order for us to get his image firmly in our minds. 'Tell us more, lad, you're doing fine so far,' I urged.

'It appears that Bruno shares his existence between his two sisters, taking turn and turn about, usually for about three months at a time. That dog of his... it died of old age last year. The old lady is a widow and lives on her own. They had no family. She hadn't a clue what it was that I was after, so I just said that I was a *giornalista*, writing a story about the *Brigata Nera.*'

'Didn't she seem surprised when you mentioned that?' I asked.

'No, she really seemed too old or uninterested to bother about that. For instance, when I asked her if she had any photographs of her brother, she got out a few and showed me. When I saw this one, I asked her if I could keep it and she willingly said yes.'

Floris went on to tell us more.

'By all accounts, Pietro Vespucchi is a *scalpellino*, a stone carver as well as a stonemason. His business is fairly prosperous,' Floris said, and his tone seemed to portray his conviction on that fact.

'We'll have to judge that when we get down there. Now let's go and see the Commander,' I replied.

We motored back into the town and across the river to the police headquarters. Unfortunately, the Commander had gone to Bolzano, so we saw his No. 2 instead, thanking them for their help and said that we had been called away and couldn't make the appointment for the following day at four o'clock.

'George,' I said, 'let's get the hell out of here and make the quickest way south. We ought to be able to make Verona for tonight. What do you think, George?'

The lad swallowed loudly, giving the thumbs up sign, and added, 'Captain, if you want to get there for tonight, so be it – but you had better hold on tight!'

We passed through Trento in good time and then we stopped for a changeover. I took the driving seat for the rest of the way and it had already been dark twelve miles out, but coming into the city, we passed over the Ponte d'Vittoria and along a street which circled the ancient Arena. It was the sharp eyes of Floris that saw a hotel, but just a little too late to go back, so I drove round the Arena and came to the street where Floris saw the hotel. It was the Colomba d'Oro. To do any distance in reverse with the trailer was never a good idea as we had learnt on many occasion. Dark as it was, I found the garage entrance and drove in. The lads helped to unhitch the trailer so that we could park both units safely.

After we settled into our rooms, we met down in the lobby and strolled off into the centre to seek a good eating house. We found one not very far away and managed to get a suitable table where we could chat in peace and at the same time, view the old Arena from a different angle.

The à la carte was never-ending but each chose the dish of their own taste and would not be persuaded to try something different. I was all for experimenting and chose the more rarer dishes, which turned out to be fantastic.

During the meal, I asked each one to give me their idea as to how best we should operate in catching our Bruno. George said that we should find out if he is at home and then nab him. Floris thought it better to get the local *Carabinieri* to join us and to pick him up in the early hours of the morning. I suggested that perhaps it would be better if we watched the place for a day or two or more if necessary, to obtain the habits of Zamboni. For instance: did he go for a stroll in the morning or in the afternoons. Did he have a favourite bar which he goes to, to join his friends for a game of dominoes? We would first have to see what sort of a place Aprilia was. Did it have shops, a trattoria, a *giornalaio* for instance.

'I know what you are after, Captain. You want to get him out in the open!' said Floris. He was right.

'Yes, fellows,' I said. I want to get him away from the house or business. I want *us* to get him and the moment we have him, we will drive like hell to Rome and put him behind bars until the next day, when we are ready to take him up to Padua. Nobody knows we are here or will be there, so we can use the element of surprise, if we can do what we wish, unobserved.'

Both the lads gave the thumbs up sign and in unison, gave their verbal approval.

'Captain, how far is Aprilia from here?' George asked.

'At a guess George, it is about 325 miles to Rome via Bologna and then add another, say, thirty miles to Aprilia,' I replied.

'What shall we do with the trailer, Captain?' asked Floris.

'I think it would be a good idea if we made our base in Rome. You lads are well looked after there and I can stay at the hotel. George, you can stow the trailer away safely at the barracks. After the initial recce, we will know more about how to do things and what to dress in,' I told them.

After our meal, we had another stroll about the city and wished that it was summertime, for the air was bitterly cold. It was a sheer delight to see some of the wonderfully old buildings and to imagine what the city must have been like in the days of its glory.

The following day, we were on the road south at an early hour, in order to put as many miles behind us as we could in the day. We reckoned the journey would take us about fourteen to fifteen hours, which would get us into Rome at about nine. I know the lads baulked a little having to get up so early but they realised that it was the best thing to do. I had arranged with the hotel to supply us with an early morning hot drink. Food of any description was out of the question – which really we were not bothered about, as we could always get some food on the way at a bar or trattoria.

As we passed through Florence, we affectionately remembered our days spent in that lovely city. Both George and Floris rated the Grand Hotel as their No. 1 on their list of establishments. As it was an hotel for service personnel for Americans, our connections through the CIC, gave us the pass to stay there.

Whenever we had a stop for drinks, like coffee and a toasted cheese sandwich apiece, I would change over with George, to give him a break from driving. It was nine fifteen that night when we pulled up outside the Continentale Hotel in Via Nationale. We were amazed at how busy the city was, then Floris reminded us that the Romans liked to eat out late and go dancing at nightclubs. I retrieved my grips and then I phoned the barracks in order to make sure that the lads had good accommodation and that the NAAFI would be open.

The following morning, as arrangements had been made for the lads to pick me up at the hotel at eight thirty, we drove off, passing the massive and most beautiful remains of the Baths of Caracalla. I always had the urge to stop and go sightseeing whenever I saw such incredible antiquity. Floris was also like myself, whereas George preferred the scenic views. I remember once when we were up in the Dolomites, when he saw the scenery with the snow-capped mountains in the background, towering up above the lush green vegetation below.

He said to me then, 'Captain, 'I wish I could paint!'

I knew at the time how he felt.

About three and a half kilometres out of Aprilia, we had to slow down on account of the road being in great disrepair. The evidence of the terrible battles which raged around the Anzio area was still as it was when it happened. Shell holes had not been filled in. Peasants' houses were still in ruins. The church walls were pitted by shrapnel. The village of Aprilia seemed to be half the size it had once been. We spotted the business and home of the Vespucchis, and even though we had to drive very slowly, George couldn't take his eyes off the road for fear of banging into some huge boulders which had been blown on to the road by the shelling.

We parked the jeep on the far side of the village and walked across the fields towards a farmhouse, neat, to the stonemason's premises.

'Captain, it's no wonder the man has made some money. There must have been thousands and thousands of gravestones to cut,' said Floris.

'Floris, you come with me, and you George, you'd better stay outside and keep an eye open for anybody who seems curious as to what we are doing. We'll go and have a talk with these poor people in this house,' I said.

We both thought it strange that there was no noise of any animal, so we knocked on the door. A couple in their middle fifties came to the door.

'*Buon giorno, Signori*! said Floris in a pleasant greeting, and hoped to have had a similar reply, but there was silence.

I quickly slipped my red booklet into Floris's hand without either of them noticing, before the two opened the door a little wider to allow the lad to enter. I was not invited in, as the door was closed immediately the three were over the threshold. I wasn't worried, for I knew Floris could take care of himself. I stood around on my own outside for quite a while. George was nowhere to be seen. Suddenly, the door opened and I was asked to go inside the house.

It was a typical small peasant farmhouse but one which had apparently fallen on harder times than most, as a result of the War. The couple seemed small in height to me and when they realised that I was in uniform, they became overawed, poor people. Floris introduced me to them.

'Signor and Signora Castellani have lived in this house for twenty-five years and had quite a large farm. When the Germans arrived, they occupied the farm and killed off all the animals. They had to work producing vegetables, then they had to have their home turned into a Signals and Observation Post for part of the Anzio defence line. The couple were forced to live in one room upstairs. They had to serve the SS Panzer officers, and as you can imagine, they had a very rough time,' he explained.

The couple sat huddled together near their kitchen range, keeping warm, for that was their only means of heating their farmhouse.

I was very touched by their abject misery and felt that in some way, I had to help them.

'Floris, will you ask them to tell us something about their neighbours – the Vespucchi family?' I asked.

My gifted interpreter began carefully and slowly to ask questions. I listened but didn't interfere, as Floris was gradually drawing the couple out of their state of shyness. I was happy to notice their acceptable responses and to see them becoming less scared of our visit.

As the questioning was progressing, I noticed a grimace on Castellani's face whenever the name of Vespucchi was mentioned. Floris had seen this too and worded his questioning in order to find out why. He then asked the couple if they wouldn't mind if we could come back after lunch, to chat to them further and they welcomed the idea. Floris also asked the couple not to let anyone know why we were visiting them. We assured them again, that they had nothing to fear from the Vespucchi's, as we would take the matter up with the Consiglio a Roma.

Floris made our departure cordially polite, which gratified the couple, making them feel that they were somebody and not just nobodies, as they had been treated for many years.

'You didn't give a time when we would be back, did you,' I asked.

'No, Captain, they will be pleased for us to return and they will help us in any way they can.'

I had a feeling that they just wanted to be treated as humans, and perhaps they had found in us the very people to do just that.

We walked quite a way to get to George, as he had hidden the jeep well out of sight of the stonemason's premises.

'George, can you find your way out on to the road to Latina, where we will stand a better chance of finding a decent place to eat? Then we can buy some food for our hopeful friends, the Castellanis I said.

'Captain, the turn is just down here a few more hundred yards, and then off to the left to Latina. It is only about thirteen miles away,' he replied.

We bumped and banged until we reached the better made road to the town, and I remarked, 'You know, lads, I feel very conspicuous in my uniform and I am sure you do too George, so we will return today as we are, but tomorrow we will come back here in civvies.'

Floris thought the idea was better too, to be in *mufti*.

Latina itself had also been war-torn but the council had made great progress in clearing up the debris as well as repairing some buildings. We found a reasonable trattoria, with enough good food to satisfy us, and then we went off to look for a store to buy some food and fuel for the Castellanis' kitchen range. It was with my own money that I bought flour, sugar, real coffee beans, butter and biscuits. I felt like buying up the whole store for the poor couple, as they literally hardly had anything in their larder. The matter of finding fuel was proving more difficult, but eventually we found a log merchant and arranged for him to deliver a month's supply of wood and that I would pay him on the site when he made the delivery. That way, I wanted to make sure that the Castellanis got the amount which I had ordered.

So far, our presence had not caused any alarm in the village of Aprilia, so we just tried to remain as inconspicuous as possible. On arriving back from Latina, we waited outside ready to be invited into the house again. As we were well received, we took inside all the goodies that we had bought. The two timid peasant folk were rather bewildered at what they were seeing, as we plonked everything on the kitchen table. It was a joy to be able to give them some help. I owed my life to the Italians and I would never forget it.

Signora Castellani immediately made some coffee for us all, including George, as he had now come to join us. We asked the couple if they would have us back again in the morning, in order to watch the movements of Bruno Zamboni, Signora Vespucchi's brother.

'Oh! *Che brutto uomo!*' exclaimed the woman.

Floris asked her why she thought that. Our two hosts sat at the table next to each other and held each other's hands.

They then told us how over the years, especially when the Nazis came, that the Vespucchis had gradually and cunningly encroached on their land to develop his business. When they had protested, they were threatened by the brother, Zamboni, who was a member of the *Brigata Nera*, and told to shut up or their whole property would be taken over by the Nazis.

'*Signori! Noi non sappiamo cosa fare. Siamo povere gente!*' they said.

George, Floris and I looked at each other, realising what that threat entailed.

We told the couple the whole story about Bruno Zamboni, until they realised the reasons for us being down here. They seemed transformed with relief and offered to help us in any way they could, for us to arrest the brute. Floris told them about the load of wood which should be delivered sometime tomorrow. We would be here to see that they were not cheated and that I would be paying for the wood on the spot. The two couldn't believe what they were hearing and cried with emotion.

Floris asked the couple again if they were agreeable for us to come back in the morning and stay at the house for the best part of the day. Everything was fine and with a last word of advice to them, that they must not be intimidated any more by anyone, we left to go back to Rome.

The lads dropped me off at the hotel and as we arranged to meet in the morning at eight at the hotel, the lads left for their free time. The moment I reached my room, I phoned the Dutch Embassy and spoke to Kitty first, then she put me over to Andrée. It was arranged to meet again for another enjoyable evening of dancing at the Eden Hotel Kitty said that she would get Jan to pick each one of us up in his car at seven thirty.

The following morning, I was reflecting on the super night I had spent in the company of the two Dutch ladies and Jan, while I was shaving. It was so refreshing to be in a young pleasant group, dressed in one's best uniform for a change. The ladies always looked stunning in their evening dresses, of which they appeared to have several to choose from. We had made arrangements for another meeting, but to go to the Opera to see *La Bohème*, for a change. I asked if I could get the tickets but Andrée said that the Embassy would do that for us.

The lads met me on time and we drove out again back to Aprilia. We hid the jeep away and as we were in civvies, we were less conspicuous this time. That morning, we watched the Vespucchi house very carefully and noted the movements of the Vespucchis but never saw anything of Zamboni. As we had our sandwiches of salami, cheese and bread rolls, we didn't leave our positions of watch, so that we wouldn't miss our man should he decide to go out. It was about two o'clock when we saw him come out of the house and take a walk down the road in the Anzio direction.

Floris went after him but at a very safe distance so that he would not give himself away. Just over an hour later, Floris came back from a completely different direction, but arriving almost the same time as Zamboni arrived at the Vespucchi house.

Floris discovered that Zamboni walked to a trattoria or, in his own words, a dump of a place, on the Anzio road. He had a game of dominoes and then walked back.

'How far is the trattoria from here?' I asked.

'It is about one and a half kilometres, not very far.'

'Right, we will see what he does tomorrow, so let's go into the house and tell the Castellanis that we will be back again tomorrow,' I said.

Just as we were about to leave, the truck carrying the wood arrived. I suggested to the couple to have the wood dumped at the side of the house away from the Vespucchis' view. This was done and I paid the man, giving the receipt to the couple. They were beside themselves with gratitude, poor things.

Back in The Eternal City, having made arrangements for the following morning, we went our ways. The lads assured me that they always had a good time, so I was happy to know that they were well looked after to enjoy their free evenings.

Jan picked us all up in his car and we spent a wonderful evening at the Royal Opera House. The building is tremendous. The staff were in black and red livery and the whole interior décor was plush red and gold fittings. The boxes were curtained with heavy red velvet and the walls covered with embossed red velvet paper. The lights were crystal chandeliers of all shapes and sizes throughout the auditorium. It was an experience to just see the inside of that magnificent building. The performance of the opera was superb and the enthusiasm of the audience brought ovation after ovation at the final curtain.

The following morning, dressed in our *mufti*, we drove off back to the farmhouse. Taking up our usual positions of observation, we patiently waited for the first signs of Bruno Zamboni leaving the house. As the stonemason employed two youngsters to help him in his work, we were very careful not to expose our positions to them, for young people are usually much more observant to anything strange happening around them.

It was a dull morning but with no rain, thank goodness. We had arranged a signal between us that if there was an opportune moment to nab the brute, we would give that signal for George to bring up the jeep as quickly as possible, in order to whisk the captive away before anyone realised what has happened.

The morning passed with again, no sign of the man. Sandwiches were distributed as before, and we just had to sit it out until the moment arrived in our favour. At 2.20 the Vespucchi's door opened and Zamboni came out, hobbling with his stick. He saluted the lads in the stoneyard and walked through the side gate on to the main road leading to Anzio. Floris was watching carefully. I mentioned to the Castellanis that if we should suddenly disappear without saying anything to them, they must never worry and think that we had just gone and deserted them. We would be back and say our farewells in a proper manner. They both indicated that they would know the reason for our sudden departure, and wished us well.

All three of us were watching Zamboni walking along the road, and as Floris's position was several hundred yards away from mine, he could see further down the road than I, but he was still in sight of myself and George. Suddenly, Floris gave a sign and I relayed it to George. It seemed only seconds before the jeep arrived to pick me up and to move down the road. Floris had ran along a vine ditch to bring himself in front of the man and we converged, pulling up just behind the cripple.

I jumped out and faced the man as he heard the jeep coming close to him. Although I was shaking with internal excitement, I was able to tell him to stand still, in his own language. Floris came up from behind and surprised me even, as he had his Beretta pointing at Zamboni. George leaped out of the jeep with the handcuffs but unfortunately was too late to slip them on our captive before he raised his stick in his defence. It came crashing down, missing me by inches, and hit the hard road surface, when it broke. With almost a growl, the man tried to struggle away from George's grip but Floris yelled his orders in Italian, making the old man see sense not to struggle any further. Whipping round, he saw the Beretta levelled at him. Once George had the handcuffs firmly placed on both the prisoner's wrists, we bundled him into the jeep and then told him that we were British Judiciary, arresting him for the war crimes against our Flight Sergeant Arthur Banks of the Royal Air Force. The full title made it sound most impressive to him. He glared in astonishment and shook like a blade of marram grass in the breeze.

We refreshed his memory about the prisons at Adria and Ariano nel Polesine and lastly, the infamous one at Rovigo. We also refreshed his memory about Lieutenant Emilio Cerati of the *Brigata Nera*. At the mention of that name, he proudly stuck his chin out, like Mussolini used to do, and adopted a 'bull elephant' manner. George was now on to the road leading to Rome, which made our captive bawl and shout for help. Floris stuck his handkerchief into his mouth to shut him up.

He began to wriggle and heave his frame about the car, so Floris told him that if he didn't behave we would have to do something serious to him. He replied with abusive language, so when George found a quiet spot off the road, we stopped out of sight of anyone and got Zamboni out.

We blindfolded him and pushed him against a tree, fastening his handcuffs so that he couldn't bring his hands forward. Then Floris fired a few rounds of his automatic. If I had fired my service revolver, I would have awakened the dead, as they were not as silent as one would have liked on these occasions.

Having frightened the man into complete submission, we unfastened his short chain on the handcuffs and still with his hands behind him well secured, we pushed him into the back of the jeep and turned the vehicle round, getting back on to the main road. Every now and again, pathetic words of pleading would issue forth from the foul mouth, on to deaf ears. We asked him what he was doing in 1943–44. He admitted that he was promoted to the rank of colonel in 1943. He also admitted that he was made Commander of the *Brigata Nera* of 'V' Zone. That was the first time we had heard of the 'V' Zone. We showed him the photograph of himself with his sister at Merano. He knew then that we had done our work in tracking him down.

It was dark when we arrived at the Regina Coeli Prison in the old part of the city, and on our sounding the twin-tone horns of the car, the big doors opened to accept our prize.

Floris went to the Reception Room and presented my ID booklet and told the night staff that we had a prisoner whom we wished to have locked up for a few nights. The *Capo* sounded a few bells and using an internal phone, gave instructions to the person on the other end.

George said to me, while we were waiting for Floris to rejoin us, 'What a shock the Vespucchis will get when Zamboni doesn't return after his walk!'

'Floris is now attending to that, as he is getting the person in charge in that office to ring through to the *Carabinieri* at Anzio to inform them as to what has happened, and to inform the Vespucchis,' I said.

I was in no mood to be sentimental over this issue. As far as I was feeling towards this brute, I could have easily carried out a summary execution when we turned off the road earlier on. The more I saw of this man, the more I hated him, even though he was disabled. Two warders came to accept our prisoner into their custody and walked him away to be put into a cell on his own.

I was asked to wait until he was safely inside, then I was requested to make a formal statement of indictment for the prison's records. This was done in the cell in front of the prisoner and the officer in charge.

Once outside the Reception Room, the three of us placed our right arms out and took each of the other's hands and shook them, in triumph at our success. Thanking the men in that office, we jumped into the jeep and made our way up to the Hotel Continentale. Having dropped me off and after arranging to meet in the morning at the usual hour, the lads went off to their customary haunt.

Even before I had taken my keys to my room, I phoned the Embassy from the porter's desk. The operator must have recognised my voice, for she put me straight through to Andrée. The usual greetings were made, but before I was able to ask her if we could go out dancing again, she said that we must meet somewhere together in order to discuss how we could get Kitty and Jan together, as they apparently were in love but neither of them would say so. Andrée wanted me to find a way of bringing the two into line! I suggested that we should meet at the Mille Luce nightclub in Via Nationale. She would be able to be dropped off there by the Embassy car and I would be able to walk across from my hotel. The meeting was arranged for five o'clock.

I wallowed in a good hot bath in my room and shaved then dressed in my best uniform. Feeling on top of the world, I walked over to the nightclub, where the young lady met me on time. We chose a small table at the side of the little dance floor and ordered drinks. In one of the far corners of the dimly lit room, was a small rhythm group softly playing a tune.

Andrée began to tell me that she was absolutely certain that Kitty was in love with Jan and that there was no doubt at all that Jan was in love with Kitty. Unfortunately for Andrée, who had to work alongside Kitty all day, she was getting anxious that neither of them would say that they were in love.

I asked Andrée what she knew about Kitty. She told me that she is the daughter of the Dutch Consul in Rome and that their family were great friends of the Ambassador and his wife.

She went on to tell me that she and Kitty had been friends since the liberation of Rome by the Allies, where they met up at the Dutch Embassy on its reopening. Andrée then asked me what I knew of Jan, mainly about his character, as I knew him more than Andrée did, having met him firstly in Austria.

While we were swapping stories about Kitty and then Jan and forming our own opinions about how couples should be together, I suddenly thought to myself, 'What a delightful lady you are. What wonderful sentiments you have about life and marriage.'

So, on impulse I said to her, 'I'm going to ask you something now. You'll probably think it crazy, but—' I was interrupted by her saying, 'Well go on, do!'

'Will you marry me?' I asked.

In a flash she replied, 'What? You *are* crazy – but I will!'

I leant over the table, nearly spilling my glass of wine, and gave her a kiss; then I said to please stay put as I wanted to find out what tune the group was playing.

I dashed across the dance floor and asked the leader. It was called 'Appassionatamente'. It was a delightful tune and I called out to Andrée that I was just going to the music shop down the street, to buy the record. I did just that and gave it to her. Coincidentally, it was called 'Passionately', which I shall never forget.

After having spent the best part of the previous night celebrating our engagement with our Dutch friends at the Eden Hotel, work had to be carried on and to my surprise when the lads met me at the Hotel in the morning, Floris presented his brother to me, who had travelled down from his school in Monte San Savino to spend a few days with him.

As he was only a slight lad, he was no encumbrance to us in the jeep, so we took him with us, to his delight. I don't know how much younger the lad Milton was but he quickly adapted himself to our strange life of dashing about the countryside. Obviously, Floris had told his family how he was faring, from time to time, which must have fired the adventurist spirit in the youth.

'Floris, firstly, I want to go to the Ministry of the Interior, to find out what I can do about the Castellanis' property,' I said.

'Captain, if you will allow me to make a suggestion.'

'Please, Floris, I am glad you want to say something,' I replied.

'Milton and I can stay here in the city and make all the necessary enquiries on behalf of the *contadini*, whilst you go to Aprilia. It would be a waste of time to have me along with you, and as you can now cope very well with the language, you don't really need me,' he said.

'What do you think of that, George?' I asked, catching him unawares as he was sitting behind the wheel.

'Sounds good to me, Captain.'

'Okay. Get through to the right people and tell them that I am coming to see them. Make an appointment for me and we will meet here tonight at about five o'clock,' I said.

We left the two brothers walking away down Via Nationale towards the Piazza Venezia. George and I went off to Aprilia and to make sure that the Vespucchi family did not interfere again in the lives of the Castellanis. Stopping firstly at the *Carabinieri* at Anzio, we took the *Maresciallo* with us, after explaining exactly why we were in the area, to Aprilia. As he was the Chief Officer in the area, we had to take his sidekick with us – and he was big enough to fill the whole jeep on his own!

The whole business of the Vespucchi family encroaching on the land belonging to the Castellanis; was completely new to the police; however, they were on our side and thank goodness, they stopped their antics right away, threatening them with prosecution if they moved one metre more. I told them that they would be served with a writ from one of the top lawyers in Rome and that the Council at Anzio, would be making out a compulsory purchase order to acquire their business, as it had been created falsely, by theft. That really scared them, which was exactly what I wanted. I then told them about their Bruno. There was a tear and a wail but I was not the least bit worried. I told them that they would not see their Bruno at their home again.

The *Maresciallo* reiterated what I had said but mentioned that they would be able to visit him at the prison in Rome. I didn't tell the *Maresciallo* that I would be taking the brute up to Padua. Then, leaving the Vespucchis in no doubt as to what the position was with their brother Bruno Zamboni, we left to go over to the farmhouse of the Castellanis.

They became frightened again when they saw the *Maresciallo*, but I soon calmed them down when I told them that we had begun a movement to get their land back and to have their farmhouse rebuilt, with reparations money. I was really sad to leave the two poor souls and only hoped that fortune would come their way to relieve them after their years of torment.

We dropped the *Maresciallo* and his aide off at the police station at Anzio and made our way back to Rome. It was very near to five o'clock when we drew up at the kerbside in front of the hotel and the two brothers came out of the foyer to meet us. Their news was great, as they had all the right departments listed to carry out our intentions regarding the Castellanis. I dismissed the lads, for I knew they were dying to get away for a good night's fun together.

I went up to my room and went through my usual routine of having a bath, shave and getting smartened up in my dress uniform, ready to meet my fiancée. I rang my HQ at Padua and told them that I had arrested Zamboni down at Aprilia near Anzio and that he was in the central prison at Rome. They were overjoyed at the news and instructed me to stay in Rome, to await further instructions. They told me that Zamboni should be kept in solitary confinement until arrangements were made for his transfer to the gaol at Padua. Captain Peter Reynolds pointed out to me that one must never just take things for granted on hearsay.

I welcomed the advice, for I realised that with Zamboni, I had listened and accepted what was told to me by the police on my first visit to Merano, instead of following the investigations through to the final to satisfy myself. Perhaps if I had not accepted what the police told me about Zamboni then, and pursued my enquiries further, we might have found him there at his sister's villa and saved a great deal of time and money. I entered that experience in my mental 'notebook', so that I would not make that mistake again.

I now reflected on what I had done to change the whole pattern of my life, by becoming engaged. Of course I had no regrets, I said to myself. Damn! I should have told my Adjutant the news. I will tell HQ in the morning, first thing. So many such thoughts went through my mind and I found myself giving questions and answers, in order to plan sensibly.

February 1947 was a momentous month. I had safely concluded the tasks that had been given me; to find and apprehend wanted war criminals to be tried for their crimes against Allied service personnel. I had become engaged to be married. I had been given a brand new American army jeep which I had made into a station wagon-type car, and I'd bought a trailer to go with it. I was proud to own something which had caused a precedent. I asked myself, Are you going to stay in the army or get out into civvy street, once you are married? I tussled with the prospects and thought that perhaps I could give my future wife a better life if I were to leave the forces.

I would certainly discuss with my fiancée what she would like me to do. Would she prefer me to stay on in the army to further my career or to opt out and take a job in civvy street?

Plans were made for the wedding to take place in Rome, on Saturday, 29th March, 1947. So much had to be organised by my immediate superiors. The Dutch authorities had to be consulted for security reasons and lastly, the War Office had to sanction the union.

The wedding turned out to be the social highlight of the Roman calendar month, for unknown to me at the time I asked Andrée to marry me, her illustrious grandmother was the Dame Anna Haardt, the *haute couturiste*, whose friends and clientele were the aristocracy of many nations. She had been a great personal friend of the Italian Queen. The Dutch Embassy closed its doors for business, as the entire staff including the Ambassador, his wife and the Consul with his family, attended the Service and the reception, which was held at the Hotel Continentale.

During our long honeymoon in Venice at the Hotel Royal Daniele, I was given the honour of being the Marshal at the Law Court, for the war crimes trial of Field Marshal Albert Kesselring. That was a tremendous experience and one which I would never forget.

In complete harmony with everyone, I received my demobilisation in May at York, after serving for seven and a half years. With a wealth of experience behind me and, thank God, good health too, I was ready to enter civilian life and to take up a fitting career to suit my abilities.